PLAYFAIR
AMERICAN
FOOT[BALL]
ANNU[AL]

Compiled and ed[ited]

C000229855

Futura/Queen Anne Press

A *Queen Anne Press* BOOK

© NFL Properties 1985.
Officially Licensed Product by NFL Properties

First published in Great Britain in 1985 by
Queen Anne Press, a division of
Macdonald & Co (Publishers) Ltd
Maxwell House, Worship Street
London EC2A 2EN
A BPCC plc Company

Cover photograph: Eric Dickerson of L.A. Rams (All-Sport)

British Library Cataloguing in Publication Data
Playfair American Football Annual — 1985
1.Football — Periodicals
796.332'05 GV937
ISBN 0 708 2924 4

Typeset by Visage Typesetting Ltd., London SW19
Reproduced, printed and bound in Great Britain by
Hazell, Watson & Viney Limited,
Member of the BPCC Group,
Aylesbury, Bucks.

CONTENTS

AMERICAN FOOTBALL

What is American Football? It's not all that different from rugby, indeed, that's how it all started in the American Universities round about 1870. Just like rugby, it's a game of gaining territory, moving down the field and somehow getting the ball across the opposing team's goal line.

How does a team move the ball? *The 4-Down system:* The team in possession (the Offense) is allowed four downs (attempts) to gain 10 or more yards' progress towards the opposing goal line. These 10 or more yards may be gained on just one down (attempt) or, if necessary, by using all four downs. The immediate reward for gaining the 10 yards is that the offense retains the possession of the ball and is allowed another series of four downs to gain 10 or more yards, and so on.

Scoring *Touchdown and Conversion:* Of course, the object is to score more points than your opponent. The most valuable score is a Touchdown, rather like a try in rugby. The difference is that, unlike a try, the ball need not be placed down onto the playing surface. Rather, it has simply to be taken over the goal line — into the so-called End Zone. A touchdown, which is worth six points, is immediately followed by a kick from directly in front of the goal posts. This is equivalent to the conversion in rugby and is known as an Extra Point Attempt, Point After Touchdown (PAT for short); a PAT is worth one point. It may not seem much but it is very important as many games are decided by just one point.

Field Goal: This is exactly like a penalty kick at goal in rugby, though in American football a team doesn't need to be awarded a penalty to have a go. In fact, a team can take a field goal kick on any one of its four downs, but they usually wait until the fourth down, and even then, only when they're no more than 40 yards from their opponent's goal line. If the kick is successful, it's worth three points.

Safety: A safety is *given up* by a team when one of its players who has the ball is tackled *inside his own end zone.* In this case, the unlucky team gives up two points to the opposition.

The Playing Field The playing surface can be AstroTurf, Tartan Turf, (both man-made fibre) or grass. The field of play is 120 yards long and 53⅓rd yards wide. The end zones take up 10 yards at each end of the field. In addition to the obvious gridiron markings, there are two lines of marks stretching the length of the field. These are called 'Hashmarks' and define a strip of ground in the middle of the field where all the downs begin.

Starting the Game The captains toss a coin and the winner decides *either* to kick off or to face the kick, *or* the direction in which to play. The action starts when the kicker boots the ball as far as possible down the field. The man who makes the catch runs as far as possible up the field until he is tackled. His team keeps possession of the ball and they set off on their first series of four downs.

The Squads Each 45-man squad has three teams of 11 men plus a few reserves. They are known as the Offense, the Defense and the Special Team. The offense tries to score points, the defense tries to stop the opposition from scoring and the special team comes on when attempting or facing a kick. So there is a great deal of coming and going as the different teams enter and leave the field.

The League System All 28 professional teams form the National Football League but for competition (and historical reasons) they are divided into two 14-team Conferences, the American Football Conference and the National Football Conference. Each Conference is divided into three Divisions, not first, second and third, as in the Football League, but Eastern, Central and Western Divisions. All the divisions are meant to be of the same standard, the object being to group local teams together.

The Road to the Super Bowl There is a 16-week regular season in which the teams play normal league football. At the end of this, the top four teams in each Conference go into a knockout competition to decide the 'World Championship'. One week after the whole season is over the best players in each Conference form teams who play in the Pro Bowl, held in Hawaii. To be selected for the Pro Bowl is a great honour, even though both teams ease off a bit and the tackling isn't quite as tough.

PLAYERS' NUMBERS

All NFL Players are numbered according to their position*
 1-19   Quarterbacks and Kickers
20-49   Running Backs and Defensive Backs
50-59   Centers and Linebackers
60-79   Defensive Linemen and Interior Offensive Linemen
80-89   Wide Receivers and Tight Ends
90-99   Defensive Linemen
*All players who had been in the National Football League prior
to 1972 may use their old numbers.

OFFENSE

Quarterback: he directs the play by 'handing off' to a Running Back
or throwing a forward pass.
Center, Guards and Tackles: The interior line — they pave the way
for the Running Back or protect the Quarterback on passing plays.
Tight End: he has the dual role of blocking like an interior Lineman
or catching medium range passes.
The Wide Receiver: The 'flyer' who catches the full range of passes.
The Half Back*: The lighter more elusive runner.
The Full Back*: The heavyweight power runner.
*Known as the Running Backs who 'rush' with the ball and catch short
passes.

DEFENSE

Tackles and Ends: The defensive line — they tackle the Running Back
or kill the play at source by 'sacking' the Quarterback.
Linebackers: They pursue the Running Back on rushing plays or, on
obvious passing plays, drop back to reinforce the Defensive Backs.
Cornerbacks and Safeties: The Defensive Backs — primarily defend
against the pass, they also advance to assist the Linebackers on
rushing plays.

KEY TO DEPTH CHART

OFFENSE
WR — wide receiver
T — tackle
OLT — offensive left tackle
G — guard
OLG — offensive left guard
C — center
ORG — offensive right guard
ORT — offensive right tackle
TE — tight end
QB — quarterback
H-B — H-back
RB — running back

SPECIAL TEAMS
P — punter
K — kicker
H — holder
PR — punt returner
KR — kick returner
LSN — long snapper

DEFENSE
DE — defensive end
DLE — defensive left end
DT — defensive tackle
DLT — defensive left tackle
NT — nose tackle
MG — middle guard
DRT — defensive right tackle
DRE — defensive right end
LB — linebacker
LOLB — left outside linebacker
LLB — left linebacker
LILB — left inside linebacker
MLB — middle linebacker
RILB — right inside linebacker
RLB — right linebacker
ROLB — right outside linebacker
CB — cornerback
LCB — left cornerback
RCB — right cornerback
S — safety
SS — strong safety
LS — left safety
FS — free safety
RS — right safety

AMERICAN FOOTBALL CONFERENCE

Buffalo Bills
Cincinnati Bengals
Cleveland Browns
Denver Broncos
Houston Oilers
Indianapolis Colts
Kansas City Chiefs
Los Angeles Raiders
Miami Dolphins
New England Patriots
New York Jets
Pittsburgh Steelers
San Diego Chargers
Seattle Seahawks

BUFFALO BILLS
AFC Eastern Division

Address: One Bills Drive, Orchard Park, New York 14127
Telephone: (716) 648-1800

CLUB OFFICIALS
President: Ralph C. Wilson, Jr.
Executive-Vice President: Patrick J. McGroder, Jr.
Vice President, Administration and General Manager:
   Terry Beldsoe
Vice President, Player Personnel: Norm Pollom
Vice President: Richard O. Morrison
Vice President, Public Relations: L. Budd Thalman
Director of Purchasing and Marketing: Bill Munson
Vice President and Head Coach: Kay Stephenson
Assistant Coaches: John Becker, Pete Carroll, Milt Jackson,
   Monte Kiffin, Don Lawrence, Perry Moss, Andy MacDonald,
   Miller McCalmon, Jim Niblack
Assistant Director of Player Personnel: Bob Ferguson
Trainers: Ed Abramoski, Bud Carpenter
Strength and Conditioning Coordinator: Rusty Jones
Equipment Manager: Dave Hojnowski
Assistant Equipment Manager: Randy Ribbeck
Ticket Director: Jim Cipriano
Assistant Ticket Director: Adam Ziccardi
Assistant Director of Public Relations: Dave Senko

Stadium: Rich Stadium (Capacity 80,290)
Playing Surface: AstroTurf
Stadium Address: One Bills Drive, Orchard Park, N.Y. 14127
Colours: Royal Blue, Scarlet Red and White
Summer Training Camp: Fredonia State University College,
   Fredonia, N.Y. 14063

BUFFALO BILLS 1985 SCHEDULE

PRE-SEASON

Aug.	10	at Detroit	8:00
Aug.	17	at Miami	8:00
Aug.	24	CLEVELAND	6:00
Aug.	31	at Chicago	6:00

REGULAR SEASON

Sep.	8	SAN DIEGO	4:00
Sep.	15	at New York Jets	1:00
Sep.	22	NEW ENGLAND	1:00
Sep.	29	MINNESOTA	1:00
Oct.	6	at Indianapolis	12:00
Oct.	13	at New England	1:00
Oct.	20	INDIANAPOLIS	1:00
Oct.	27	at Philadelphia	1:00
Nov.	3	CINCINNATI	1:00
Nov.	10	HOUSTON	1:00
Nov.	17	at Cleveland	1:00
Nov.	24	MIAMI	1:00
Dec.	1	at San Diego	1:00
Dec.	8	NEW YORK JETS	1:00
Dec.	15	at Pittsburgh	1:00
Dec.	22	at Miami	1:00

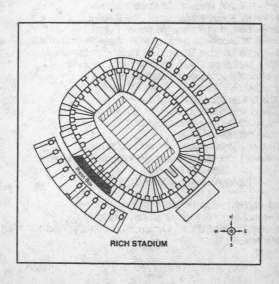

RICH STADIUM

BUFFALO BILLS
END OF SEASON DEPTH CHART

OFFENSE

WR	—	83 Preston Dennard, 89 Julius Dawkins, 27 Craig White
OLT	—	72 Ken Jones, 61 Tom Lynch
OLG	—	51 Jim Ritcher, 65 Tim Vogler
C	—	53 Will Grant, 65 Tim Vogler
ORG	—	73 Jon Borchardt, 65 Tim Vogler
ORT	—	70 Joe Devlin, 61 Tom Lynch
TE	—	87 Tony Hunter, 84 Buster Barnett, 49 Ulysses Norris, 86 Mark Brammer
WR	—	85 Byron Franklin, 81 Mitchell Brookins, 88 Mike Mosley
QB	—	19 Joe Dufek, 12 Joe Ferguson, 10 Matt Kofler
RB	—	34 Booker Moore, 41 Speedy Neal
RB	—	28 Greg Bell, 23 Van Williams, 40 Robb Riddick

DEFENSE

DLE	—	77 Ben Williams, 95 Sean McNanie
NT	—	76 Fred Smerlas, 75 Bill Acker
DRE	—	91 Ken Johnson, 79 Dean Prater
LOLB	—	52 Chris Keating, 59 Stan David, 60 Al Wenglikowski
LILB	—	55 Jim Haslett, 52 Chris Keating
RILB	—	54 Eugene Marve, 50 Joe Azelby
ROLB	—	56 Darryl Talley, 58 Steve Potter
LCB	—	30 Brian Carpenter, 36 Rodney Bellinger
RCB	—	26 Charles Romes, 48 Lawrence Johnson
SS	—	22 Steve Freeman, 43 Martin Bayless
FS	—	42 Rod Kush, 21 Don Wilson

SPECIAL TEAMS

P	—	4 John Kidd
K	—	13 Chuck Nelson
H	—	10 Matt Kofler
PR	—	21 Don Wilson, 81 Mitchell Brookins
KR	—	21 Don Wilson, 23 Van Williams, 28 Greg Bell, 81 Mitchell Brookins
LSN	—	86 Mark Brammer, 52 Chris Keating

ALSO WITH THE BUFFALO BILLS
80 Jerry Butler (WR), 82 Eric Richardson (WR),
63 Justin Cross (T/G), 57 Lucius Sanford (LB), Rod Hill (CB),
38 Jeff Nixon (S)

BUFFALO BILLS

INDIVIDUAL RUSHERS

	Att	Yards	Avg	Long	TD
Bell, Greg	262	1100	4.2	t85	7
Neal, Speedy	49	175	3.6	10	1
Ferguson, Joe	19	102	5.4	20	0
Moore, Booker	24	84	3.5	21	0
Kofler, Matt	10	80	8.0	19	0
Williams, Van	18	51	2.8	7	0
Brookins, Mitchell	2	27	13.5	16	0
Dufek, Joe	9	22	2.4	13	1
Hunter, Tony	1	6	6.0	6	0
Riddick, Robb	3	3	1.0	6	0
Franklin, Byron	1	−7	−7.0	−7	0

INDIVIDUAL PASSING

	Att	Comp	Pct Comp	Yds	Avg Gain	TD	Pct TD	Long	Int	Pct Int	Rating Points
Ferguson, Joe	344	191	55.5	1991	5.79	12	3.5	t68	17	4.9	63.5
Dufek, Joe	150	74	49.3	829	5.53	4	2.7	t64	8	5.3	52.9
Kofler, Matt	93	33	35.5	432	4.65	2	2.2	t70	5	5.4	35.8
Mosley, Mike	1	0	0.0	0	0.00	0	0.0	0	0	0.0	39.6

INDIVIDUAL RECEIVERS

	No	Yards	Avg	Long	TD
Franklin, Byron	69	862	12.5	t64	4
Bell, Greg	34	277	8.1	37	1
Hunter, Tony	33	331	10.0	30	2
Moore, Booker	33	172	5.2	14	0
Dennard, Preston	30	417	13.9	t68	7
Riddick, Robb	23	276	12.0	38	0
Dawkins, Julius	21	295	14.0	t37	2
Brookins, Mitchell	18	318	17.7	t70	1
Neal, Speedy	9	76	8.4	18	0
Barnett, Buster	8	67	8.4	18	0
Brammer, Mark	7	49	7.0	12	0
Williams, Van	5	46	9.2	32	1
Mosley, Mike	4	38	9.5	17	0
White, Craig	4	28	7.0	11	0

INDIVIDUAL INTERCEPTORS

	No	Yards	Avg	Long	TD
Romes, Charles	5	130	26.0	55	0
Freeman, Steve	3	45	15.0	45	0
Carpenter, Brian, Wash.-Buff.	3	11	3.7	11	0
Smerlas, Fred	1	25	25.0	25	0
Kush, Rod	1	15	15.0	15	0
Smith, Lucious	1	7	7.0	7	0

	No	Yards	Avg	Long	TD
Bellinger, Rodney	1	0	0.0	0	0
Talley, Darryl	1	0	0.0	0	0

INDIVIDUAL KICKOFF RETURNERS

	No	Yards	Avg	Long	TD
Williams, Van	39	820	21.0	65	0
Wilson, Don	34	576	16.9	36	0
Bell, Greg	1	15	15.0	15	0
David, Stan	1	6	6.0	6	0
White, Craig	1	5	5.0	5	0

INDIVIDUAL PUNTERS

	No	Yards	Long	Avg	Total Punts	TB	Blk	Opp Ret	Ret Yds	In 20	Net Avg
Kidd, John	88	3696	63	42.0	90	8	2	52	597	16	32.7

INDIVIDUAL PUNT RETURNERS

	No	FC	Yards	Avg	Long	TD
Wilson, Don	33	8	297	9.0	t65	1
Smith, Lucious, Buff.-S.D.	1	0	0	0.0	0	0

INDIVIDUAL SCORERS

KICKERS	XP	XPA	FG	FGA	PTS
Danelo, Joe	17	17	8	16	41
Nelson, Chuck	14	14	3	5	23

NON-KICKERS	TD	TDR	TDP	TDM	PTS
Bell, Greg	8	7	1	0	48
Dennard, Preston	7	0	7	0	42
Franklin, Byron	4	0	4	0	24
Dawkins, Julius	2	0	2	0	12
Hunter, Tony	2	0	2	0	12
Brookins, Mitchell	1	0	1	0	6
David, Stan	1	0	0	1	6
Dufek, Joe	1	1	0	0	6
Keating, Chris	1	0	0	1	6
Neal, Speedy	1	1	0	0	6
Sanford, Lucius	1	0	0	1	6
Williams, Van	1	0	1	0	6
Wilson, Don	1	0	0	1	6

t = Touchdown

CINCINNATI BENGALS
AFC Central Division

Address: 200 Riverfront Stadium, Cincinnati, Ohio 45202
Telephone: (513) 621-3550

CLUB OFFICIALS
President: John Sawyer
General Manager: Paul E. Brown
Head Coach: Sam Wyche
Assistant Coaches: Jim Anderson, Bruce Coslet, Joe Faragalli
   Dick LeBeau, Jim McNally, Dick Selcer, Bill Urbanik,
   Trent Walters, Kim Wood
Assistant General Manager: Michael Brown
Business Manager: Bill Connelly
Consultant: John Murdough
Director of Public Relations: Allan Heim
Director of Player Personnel: Pete Brown
Ticket Manager: Paul Kelly
Trainer: Marv Pollins
Equipment Managers: Tom Gray, Al Davis

Stadium: Riverfront Stadium (Capacity 59,754)
Playing Surface: AstroTurf
Stadium Address: 200 Riverfront Stadium, Cincinnati, Ohio 45202
Colours: Black, Orange and White
Summer Training Camp: Wilmington College, Wilmington,
   Ohio 45177

CINCINNATI BENGALS 1985 SCHEDULE

PRE-SEASON

Aug.	10	KANSAS CITY	7:00
Aug.	17	NEW YORK JETS	7:00
Aug.	24	at Detroit	7:00
Aug.	30	at Indianapolis	7:00

REGULAR SEASON

Sep.	8	SEATTLE	1:00
Sep.	15	at St. Louis	12.00
Sep.	22	SAN DIEGO	1:00
Sep.	30	at Pittsburgh	9:00
Oct.	6	NEW YORK JETS	4:00
Oct.	13	NEW YORK GIANTS	1:00
Oct.	20	at Houston	12:00
Oct.	27	PITTSBURGH	4:00
Nov.	3	at Buffalo	1:00
Nov.	10	CLEVELAND	1:00
Nov.	17	at Los Angeles Raiders	1:00
Nov.	24	at Cleveland	1:00
Dec.	1	HOUSTON	1:00
Dec.	8	DALLAS	1:00
Dec.	15	at Washington	1:00
Dec.	22	at New England	1:00

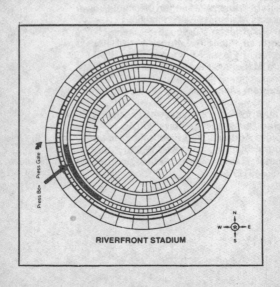

RIVERFRONT STADIUM

CINCINNATI BENGALS
END OF SEASON DEPTH CHART

OFFENSE

WR — 80 Cris Collinsworth, 86 Steve Kreider, 84 Gary Williams
OLT — 78 Anthony Munoz, 75 Bruce Reimers
OLG — 74 Brian Blados, 62 Gary Smith
C — 52 Dave Rimington, 64 Bruce Kozerski
ORG — 65 Max Montoya, 64 Bruce Kozerski, 62 Gary Smith
ORT — 77 Mike Wilson, 64 Bruce Kozerski, 74 Brian Blados
TE — 83 M.L. Harris, 82 Rodney Holman, 89 Don Kern
WR — 85 Isaac Curtis, 88 Mike Martin, 81 David Verser
QB — 14 Ken Anderson, 7 Boomer Esiason, Bryan Clark
RB — 21 James Brooks, 36 Stanford Jennings, 33 John Farley
RB — 28 Larry Kinnebrew, 40 Charles Alexander

DEFENSE

DLE — 73 Eddie Edwards, 71 Pete Koch
NT — 69 Tim Krumrie, 61 Jerry Boyarsky
DRE — 79 Ross Browner, 76 Glen Collins
LOLB — 59 Jeff Schuh, 58 Guy Frazier
LILB — 56 Ron Simpkins, 51 Rick Razzano
RILB — 50 Glenn Cameron, 55 Steve Maidlow
ROLB — 57 Reggie Williams, 53 Leo Barker
LCB — 34 Louis Breeden, 44 Ray Griffin
RCB — 20 Ray Horton, 25 John Simmons
SS — 26 Bobby Kemp, 35 Jimmy Turner
FS — 37 Robert Jackson, 22 James Griffin

SPECIAL TEAMS

P — 87 Pat McInally, 3 Jim Breech
K — 3 Jim Breech, 82 Rodney Holman
H — 86 Steve Kreider
PR — 88 Mike Martin, 25 John Simmons
KR — 88 Mike Martin, 36 Stanford Jennings
LSN — 64 Bruce Kozerski, 52 Dave Rimington

ALSO WITH THE CINCINNATI BENGALS

68 Mike Obrovac (G), 15 Turk Schonert (QB),
32 Stanley Wilson (RB), 97 Brian Pillman (LB), 27 Bryan Hicks (S)

CINCINNATI BENGALS

INDIVIDUAL RUSHERS

	Att	Yards	Avg	Long	TD
Kinnebrew, Larry	154	623	4.0	23	9
Alexander, Charles	132	479	3.6	22	2
Brooks, James	103	396	3.8	33	2
Jennings, Stanford	79	379	4.8	t20	2
Schonert, Turk	13	77	5.9	17	1
Wilson, Stanley	17	74	4.4	9	0
Anderson, Ken	11	64	5.8	14	0
Esiason, Boomer	19	63	3.3	9	2
Farley, John	7	11	1.6	5	0
Collinsworth, Cris	1	7	7.0	7	0
Verser, David	2	5	2.5	3	0
Martin, Mike	1	3	3.0	3	0
Harris, M.L.	1	-2	-2.0	-2	0

INDIVIDUAL PASSING

	Att	Comp	Pct Comp	Yds	Avg Gain	TD	Pct TD	Long	Int	Pct Int	Rating Points
Anderson, Ken	275	175	63.6	2107	7.66	10	3.6	t80	12	4.4	81.0
Schonert, Turk	117	78	66.7	945	8.08	4	3.4	t57	7	6.0	77.8
Esiason, Boomer	102	51	50.0	530	5.20	3	2.9	36	3	2.9	62.9
McInally, Pat	2	2	100.0	77	38.50	0	0.0	43	0	0.0	118.8

INDIVIDUAL RECEIVERS

	No	Yards	Avg	Long	TD
Collinsworth, Cris	64	989	15.5	t57	6
Harris, M. L.	48	759	15.8	t80	2
Jennings, Stanford	35	346	9.9	43	3
Brooks, James	34	268	7.9	t27	2
Alexander, Charles	29	203	7.0	22	0
Holman, Rodney	21	239	11.4	27	1
Kreider, Steve	20	243	12.2	27	1
Kinnebrew, Larry	19	159	8.4	22	1
Curtis, Issac	12	135	11.3	22	0
Martin, Mike	11	164	14.9	42	0
Verser, David	6	113	18.8	28	0
Wilson, Stanley	2	15	7.5	11	0
Kern, Don	2	14	7.0	9	0
Farley, John	2	11	5.5	10	0
Munoz, Anthony	1	1	1.0	t1	1

INDIVIDUAL INTERCEPTORS

	No	Yards	Avg	Long	TD
Breeden, Louis	4	96	24.0	70	0
Jackson, Robert	4	32	8.0	t28	1
Kemp, Bobby	4	27	6.8	14	0
Horton, Ray	3	48	16.0	t48	1
Simmons, John	2	43	21.5	t43	1
Williams, Reggie	2	33	16.5	33	0

	No	Yards	Avg	Long	TD
Griffin, Ray	2	13	6.5	13	0
Griffin, James	1	57	57.0	t57	1
Cameron, Glenn	1	15	15.0	15	0
Turner, Jim	1	4	4.0	4	0
Schuh, Jeff	1	0	0.0	0	0

INDIVIDUAL KICKOFF RETURNERS

	No	Yards	Avg	Long	TD
Jennings, Stanford	22	452	20.5	46	0
Martin, Mike	19	386	20.3	44	0
Brooks, James	7	144	20.6	37	0
Farley, John	6	93	15.5	32	0
Verser, David	3	46	15.3	23	0
Simmons, John	1	15	15.0	15	0
Harris, M.L.	1	12	12.0	12	0
Kinnebrew, Larry	1	7	7.0	7	0
Williams, Gary	1	0	0.0	0	0

INDIVIDUAL PUNTERS

	No	Yards	Long	Avg	Total Punts	TB	Blk	Opp Ret	Ret Yds	In 20	Net Avg
McInally, Pat	67	2832	61	42.3	67	8	0	38	310	19	35.3

INDIVIDUAL PUNT RETURNERS

	No	FC	Yards	Avg	Long	TD
Martin, Mike	24	5	376	15.7	55	0
Simmons, John	12	6	98	8.2	30	0
Horton, Ray	2	0	-1	-0.5	1	0

INDIVIDUAL SCORERS

KICKERS

	XP	XPA	FG	FGA	PTS
Breech, Jim	37	37	22	31	103

NON-KICKERS

	TD	TDR	TDP	TDM	PTS
Kinnebrew, Larry	10	9	1	0	60
Collinsworth, Cris	6	0	6	0	36
Jennings, Stanford	5	2	3	0	30
Brooks, James	4	2	2	0	24
Alexander, Charles	2	2	0	0	12
Esiason, Boomer	2	2	0	0	12
Harris, M.L.	2	0	2	0	12
Griffin, James	1	0	0	1	6
Holman, Rodney	1	0	1	0	6
Horton, Ray	1	0	0	1	6
Jackson, Robert	1	0	0	1	6
Kreider, Steve	1	0	1	0	6
Munoz, Anthony	1	0	1	0	6
Schonert, Turk, Cin.	1	1	0	0	6
Simmons, John, Cin.	1	0	0	1	6

CLEVELAND BROWNS
AFC Central Division

Address: Tower B, Cleveland Stadium, Cleveland, Ohio 44114
Telephone: (216) 696-5555

CLUB OFFICIALS
President: Arthur B. Modell
Executive Vice President-Legal and Administrative: Jim Bailey
Assistant to the President: Ernie Accorsi
Vice President, Finance: Mike Poplar
Director of Operations: Denny Lynch
Director of Public Relations: Kevin Byrne
Head Coach: Marty Schottenheimer
Assistant Coaches: Dave Adolph, Joe Daniels, Jim Garrett,
   Howard Mudd, John Petercuskie, Tom Pratt, Dave Redding,
   Joe Scannella, Darvin Wallis
Director of Player Personnel: Bill Davis
Area Scouts: Dom Anile, Dave Beckman, Tom Heckert,
   Tom Miner, Mike Santiago
Film Coordinator: Ed Ulinski
Ticket Director: Bill Breit
Head Trainer: Bill Tessendorf
Equipment Manager: Charley Cusick

Stadium: Cleveland Stadium (Capacity 80,098)
Playing Surface: Grass
Stadium Address: West 3rd Street, Cleveland, Ohio 44114
Colours: Seal Brown, Orange and White
Summer Training Camp: Lakeland Community College, Mentor,
   Ohio 44094

CLEVELAND BROWNS 1985 SCHEDULE

PRE-SEASON

Aug.	10	at San Diego	6:00
Aug.	17	PHILADELPHIA	7:30
Aug.	24	at Buffalo	6:00
Aug.	31	LOS ANGELES RAIDERS	7:30

REGULAR SEASON

Sep.	8	ST. LOUIS	1:00
Sep.	16	PITTSBURGH	9:00
Sep.	22	at Dallas	12:00
Sep.	29	at San Diego	1:00
Oct.	6	NEW ENGLAND	1:00
Oct.	13	at Houston	12:00
Oct.	20	LOS ANGELES RAIDERS	1:00
Oct.	27	WASHINGTON	1:00
Nov.	3	at Pittsburgh	1:00
Nov.	10	at Cincinnati	1:00
Nov.	17	BUFFALO	1:00
Nov.	24	CINCINNATI	1:00
Dec.	1	at New York Giants	1:00
Dec.	8	at Seattle	1:00
Dec.	15	HOUSTON	1:00
Dec.	22	at New York Jets	1:00

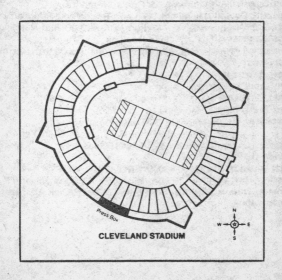

Press Box

CLEVELAND STADIUM

CLEVELAND BROWNS
END OF SEASON DEPTH CHART

OFFENSE
WR   — 86 Brian Brennan, 89 Dwight Walker
OLT   — 73 Doug Dieken, 74 Paul Farren, 62 George Lilja
OLG   — 68 Robert E. Jackson, 54 Tom DeLeone
C   — 61 Mike Baab, 54 Tom DeLeone
ORG   — 64 Joe DeLamielleure, 54 Tom DeLeone
ORT   — 74 Paul Farren, 62 George Lilja, Robert Sikora
TE   — 82 Ozzie Newsome, 80 Willis Adams, 81 Harry Holt, 87 Darryl Lewis
WR   — 85 Bruce Davis, 83 Ricky Feacher, 84 Glen Young
QB   — 16 Paul McDonald, 10 Tom Flick, 7 Terry Nugent
RB   — 30 Boyce Green, 43 Mike Pruitt
RB   — 44 Earnest Byner, 38 Johnny Davis

DEFENSE
DLE   — 96 Reggie Camp, 94 Elvis Franks
NT   — 79 Bob Golic, 72 Dave Puzzuoli
DRE   — 99 Keith Baldwin, 78 Carl Hairston
LOLB — 56 Chip Banks, 55 Curtis Weathers
LILB   — 51 Eddie Johnson, 58 Scott Nicolas, 59 David Marshall
RILB   — 50 Tom Cousineau, 58 Scott Nicolas, 53 Stuart Anderson
ROLB — 57 Clay Matthews, 55 Curtis Weathers
LCB   — 31 Frank Minnifield, 47 Larry Braziel, 40 Rod Perry
RCB   — 29 Hanford Dixon, 47 Larry Braziel, 40 Rod Perry
SS   — 27 Al Gross, 37 Chris Rockins, 24 Greg Best
FS   — 20 Don Rogers, 37 Chris Rockins, 49 Clinton Burrell

SPECIAL TEAMS
P   — 15 Steve Cox
K   — 9 Matt Bahr, 15 Steve Cox
H   — 16 Paul McDonald, 10 Tom Flick
PR   — 86 Brian Brennan, 89 Dwight Walker
KR   — 85 Bruce Davis, 44 Earnest Byner, 84 Glen Young
LSN   — 54 Tom DeLeone, 58 Scott Nicolas

ALSO WITH THE CLEVELAND BROWNS
88 Rickey Bolden (TE), Tim Stracka (TE), 63 Cody Risien (T),
25 Charles White (RB), 75 Bill Contz (T/G), 52 Dick Ambrose (LB),
21 Mike Whitwell (S)

CLEVELAND BROWNS

INDIVIDUAL RUSHERS

	Att	Yards	Avg	Long	TD
Green, Boyce	202	673	3.3	29	0
Pruitt, Mike	163	506	3.1	14	6
Byner, Earnest	72	426	5.9	54	2
White, Charles	24	62	2.6	8	0
Davis, Johnny	3	15	5.0	8	1
Holt, Harry	1	12	12.0	12	0
Davis, Bruce	1	6	6.0	6	0
McDonald, Paul	22	4	0.2	10	1
Walker, Dwight	1	−8	−8.0	−8	0

INDIVIDUAL PASSING

	Att	Comp	Pct Comp	Yds	Avg Gain	TD	Pct TD	Long	Int	Pct Int	Rating Points
McDonald, Paul	493	271	55.0	3472	7.04	14	2.8	64	23	4.7	67.3
Cox, Steve	1	1	100.0	16	16.00	0	0.0	16	0	0.0	118.8
Flick, Tom	1	1	100.0	2	2.00	0	0.0	2	0	0.0	79.2

INDIVIDUAL RECEIVERS

	No	Yards	Avg	Long	TD
Newsome, Ozzie	89	1001	11.2	52	5
Brennan, Brian	35	455	13.0	52	3
Feacher, Ricky	22	382	17.4	64	1
Adams, Willis	21	261	12.4	24	0
Holt, Harry	20	261	13.1	36	0
Green, Boyce	12	124	10.3	t44	1
Byner, Earnest	11	118	10.7	26	0
Walker, Dwight	10	122	12.2	25	0
Davis, Bruce	7	119	17.0	t43	2
Pruitt, Mike	5	29	5.8	9	0
White, Charles	5	29	5.8	17	0
Young, Glen	1	47	47.0	47	0
Bolden, Rickey	1	19	19.0	19	0
Stracka, Tim	1	15	15.0	15	0
McDonald, Paul	1	−4	−4.0	−4	0

INDIVIDUAL INTERCEPTORS

	No	Yards	Avg	Long	TD
Gross, Al	5	103	20.6	47	0
Dixon, Hanford	5	31	6.2	18	0
Cousineau, Tom	2	9	4.5	9	0
Johnson, Eddie	2	3	1.5	3	0
Rogers, Don	1	39	39.0	39	0
Minnifield, Frank	1	26	26.0	26	0
Perry, Rod	1	17	17.0	17	0
Banks, Chip	1	8	8.0	8	0

	No	Yards	Avg	Long	TD
Johnson, Lawrence	1	0	0.0	0	0
Rockins, Chris	1	0	0.0	0	0

INDIVIDUAL KICKOFF RETURNERS

	No	Yards	Avg	Long	TD
Byner, Earnest	22	415	18.9	28	0
Davis, Bruce	18	369	20.5	40	0
Brown, Preston	8	136	17.0	27	0
Young, Glen	5	134	26.8	36	0
White, Charles	5	80	16.0	23	0
Nicolas, Scott	1	12	12.0	12	0
Contz, Bill	1	10	10.0	10	0
Holt, Harry	1	1	1.0	1	0

INDIVIDUAL PUNTERS

	No	Yards	Long	Avg	Total Punts	TB	Blk	Opp Ret	Ret Yds	In 20	Net Avg
Cox, Steve	74	3213	69	43.4	76	8	2	43	489	16	33.7

INDIVIDUAL PUNT RETURNERS

	No	FC	Yards	Avg	Long	TD
Brennan, Brian	25	10	199	8.0	19	0
Walker, Dwight	6	3	50	8.3	13	0

INDIVIDUAL SCORERS

KICKERS	XP	XPA	FG	FGA	PTS
Bahr, Matt	25	25	24	32	97
Cox, Steve	0	0	1	3	3

NON-KICKERS	TD	TDR	TDP	TDM	PTS
Pruitt, Mike	6	6	0	0	36
Newsome, Ozzie	5	0	5	0	30
Brennan, Brian	3	0	3	0	18
Byner, Earnest	3	2	0	1	18
Davis, Bruce	2	0	2	0	12
Davis, Johnny	1	1	0	0	6
Feacher, Ricky	1	0	1	0	6
Green, Boyce	1	0	1	0	6
McDonald, Paul	1	1	0	0	6

DENVER BRONCOS
AFC Western Division

Address: 5700 Logan Street, Denver, Colorado 80216
Telephone: (303) 296-1982

CLUB OFFICIALS
President, Chief Executive Officer: Patrick D. Bowlen
Assistant General Manager: John Beake
Director of Administration: Sandy Waters
Coordinator of College Scouting: Reed Johnson
Coordinator of Combine Scouting: Carroll Hardy
Head Coach: Dan Reeves
Assistant Coaches: Marvin Bass, Joe Collier, Alex Gibbs,
 Stan Jones, Myrel Moore, Nick Nicolau, Fran Polsfoot,
 Mike Shanahan, Charlie West
Director of Public Relations: Charlie Lee
Publicity Director: Jim Saccomano
Treasurer: Robert M. Hurley
Ticket Manager: Gail Stuckey
Equipment Manager: Bill Harpole
Trainer: Steve Antonopulos

Stadium: Denver Mile High Stadium (Capacity 75,100)
Playing Surface: Grass (PAT)
Stadium Address: 1900 West Eliot, Denver, Colorado 80204
Colours: Orange, Royal Blue and White
Summer Training Camp: University of Northern Colorado,
 Greeley, Colorado 80521

DENVER BRONCOS 1985 SCHEDULE

PRE-SEASON

Aug.	10	NEW YORK GIANTS	7:00
Aug.	19	at San Francisco	6:00
Aug.	24	INDIANAPOLIS	7:00
Aug.	30	MINNESOTA	7:00

REGULAR SEASON

Sep.	8	at Los Angeles Rams	1:00
Sep.	15	NEW ORLEANS	2:00
Sep.	22	at Atlanta	1:00
Sep.	29	MIAMI	2:00
Oct.	6	HOUSTON	2:00
Oct.	13	at Indianapolis	12:00
Oct.	20	SEATTLE	2:00
Oct.	27	at Kansas City	12:00
Nov.	3	at San Diego	1:00
Nov.	11	SAN FRANCISCO	7:00
Nov.	17	SAN DIEGO	2:00
Nov.	24	at Los Angeles Raiders	1:00
Dec.	1	at Pittsburgh	1:00
Dec.	8	LOS ANGELES RAIDERS	2:00
Dec.	14	KANSAS CITY	2:00
Dec.	20	at Seattle	5:00

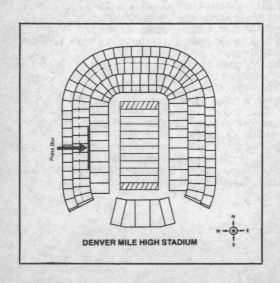

DENVER MILE HIGH STADIUM

DENVER BRONCOS
END OF SEASON DEPTH CHART

OFFENSE
WR   — 86 Butch Johnson, 84 Clinton Sampson
OLT   — 70 Dave Studdard, 72 Marsharne Graves
OLG   — 54 Keith Bishop, 62 Mike Freeman
C   — 64 Bill Bryan, 62 Mike Freeman
ORG   — 60 Paul Howard, Glenn Hyde
ORT   — 76 Ken Lanier, 74 Winford Hood
TE   — 88 Clarence Kay, 87 Jim Wright
WR   — 81 Steve Watson, 80 Ray Alexander
QB   — 7 John Elway, 8 Gary Kubiak
RB   — 23 Sammy Winder, 47 Gerald Willhite, 24 Rick Parros,
         39 Jesse Myles, 33 Gene Lang, 26 Chris Brewer
H-B   — 87 Jim Wright, 85 Don Summers

DEFENSE
DLE   — 79 Barney Chavous, 65 Walt Bowyer, 69 Brison Manor
NT   — 68 Rubin Carter, 66 Scott Garnett
DRE   — 75 Rulon Jones, 61 Andre Townsend
LOLB — 50 Jim Ryan, 52 Ken Woodard
LILB — 55 Rick Dennison, 77 Karl Mecklenburg
RILB — 58 Steve Busick, 59 Darren Comeaux, 98 Ricky Hunley
ROLB — 57 Tom Jackson, 52 Ken Woodard
LCB   — 20 Louis Wright, 45 Steve Wilson
RCB   — 31 Mike Harden, 45 Steve Wilson
SS   — 49 Dennis Smith, 48 Randy Robbins
FS   — 43 Steve Foley, 28 Roger Jackson, 22 Tony Lilly

SPECIAL TEAMS
P   — 1 Chris Norman
K   — 3 Rich Karlis
H   — 1 Chris Norman, 8 Gary Kubiak
PR   — 47 Gerald Willhite, 31 Mike Harden
KR   — 47 Gerald Willhite, 33 Gene Lang
LSN   — 54 Keith Bishop, 64 Bill Bryan

ALSO WITH THE DENVER BRONCOS
83 John Sawyer (TE), 12 Scott Brunner (QB),
63 Mark Cooper (G), 56 Aaron Smith (LB), 51 Bob Swenson (LB),
29 Wilbur Myers (S)

DENVER BRONCOS

INDIVIDUAL RUSHERS

	Att	Yards	Avg	Long	TD
Winder, Sammy	296	1153	3.9	24	4
Willhite, Gerald	77	371	4.8	52	2
Elway, John	56	237	4.2	21	1
Parros, Rick	46	208	4.5	25	2
Lang, Gene	8	42	5.3	15	2
Brewer, Chris	10	28	2.8	8	0
Kubiak, Gary	9	27	3.0	17	1
Myles, Jesse	5	7	1.4	2	0
Johnson, Butch	1	3	3.0	3	0

INDIVIDUAL PASSING

	Att	Comp	Pct Comp	Yds	Avg Gain	TD	Pct TD	Long	Int	Pct Int	Rating Points
Elway, John	380	214	56.3	2598	6.84	18	4.7	73	15	3.9	76.8
Kubiak, Gary	75	44	58.7	440	5.87	4	5.3	41	1	1.3	87.6
Stankavage, Scott	18	4	22.2	58	3.22	0	0.0	16	1	5.6	17.4
Willhite, Gerald	2	1	50.0	20	10.00	0	0.0	20	0	0.0	85.4

INDIVIDUAL RECEIVERS

	No	Yards	Avg	Long	TD
Watson, Steve	69	1170	17.0	73	7
Winder, Sammy	44	288	6.5	21	2
Johnson, Butch	42	587	14.0	49	6
Willhite, Gerald	27	298	11.0	63	0
Sawyer, John	17	122	7.2	25	0
Kay, Clarence	16	136	8.5	21	3
Wright, James	11	118	10.7	21	1
Sampson, Clinton	9	123	13.7	25	1
Alexander, Ray	8	132	16.5	41	1
Parros, Rick	6	25	4.2	9	0
Lang, Gene	4	24	6.0	t9	1
Summers, Don	3	32	10.7	16	0
Myles, Jesse	2	22	11.0	12	0
Brewer, Chris	2	20	10.0	16	0
Kubiak, Gary	1	20	20.0	20	0
Logan, Dave	1	3	3.0	3	0
Studdard, Dave	1	−4	−4.0	−4	0

INDIVIDUAL INTERCEPTORS

	No	Yards	Avg	Long	TD
Foley, Steve	6	97	16.2	t40	1
Harden, Mike	6	79	13.2	t45	1
Wilson, Steve	4	59	14.8	22	0
Smith, Dennis	3	13	4.3	10	0
Mecklenburg, Karl	2	105	52.5	63	0
Robbins, Randy	2	62	31.0	t62	1
Busick, Steve	2	21	10.5	16	0

	No	Yards	Avg	Long	TD
Woodard, Ken	1	27	27.0	t27	1
Jackson, Roger	1	23	23.0	23	0
Ryan, Jim	1	13	13.0	13	0
Comeaux, Darren	1	5	5.0	5	0
Lilly, Tony	1	5	5.0	5	0
Wright, Louis	1	1	1.0	1	0

INDIVIDUAL KICKOFF RETURNERS

	No	Yards	Avg	Long	TD
Lang, Gene	19	404	21.3	38	0
Willhite, Gerald	4	109	27.3	40	0
Dennison, Rick	2	27	13.5	16	0
Harden, Mike	1	4	4.0	4	0
Smith, Aaron	1	2	2.0	2	0

INDIVIDUAL PUNTERS

	No	Yards	Long	Avg	Total Punts	TB	Blk	Opp Ret	Ret Yds	In 20	Net Avg
Norman, Chris	96	3850	83	40.1	96	6	0	44	335	16	35.4

INDIVIDUAL PUNT RETURNERS

	No	FC	Yards	Avg	Long	TD
Willhite, Gerald	20	9	200	10.0	35	0
Wilson, Steve	1	0	0	0.0	0	0

INDIVIDUAL SCORERS

KICKERS

	XP	XPA	FG	FGA	PTS
Karlis, Rich	38	41	21	28	101

NON-KICKERS

	TD	TDR	TDP	TDM	PTS
Watson, Steve	7	0	7	0	42
Johnson, Butch	6	0	6	0	36
Winder, Sammy	6	4	2	0	36
Kay, Clarence	3	0	3	0	18
Lang, Gene	3	2	1	0	18
Foley, Steve	2	0	0	2	12
Parros, Rick	2	2	0	0	12
Willhite, Gerald	2	2	0	0	12
Alexander, Ray	1	0	1	0	6
Elway, John	1	1	0	0	6
Harden, Mike	1	0	0	1	6
Jones, Rulon	1	0	0	1	6
Kubiak, Gary	1	1	0	0	6
Robbins, Randy	1	0	0	1	6
Sampson, Clinton	1	0	1	0	6
Smith, Dennis	1	0	0	1	6
Woodard, Ken	1	0	0	1	6
Wright, James	1	0	1	0	6
Wright, Louis	1	0	0	1	6

HOUSTON OILERS
AFC Central Division

Address: Box 1516, Houston, Texas 77001
Telephone: (713) 797-9111

CLUB OFFICIALS
President: K.S. 'Bud' Adams, Jr.
Executive Vice President/General Manager: Ladd K. Herzeg
Vice President/Player Personnel: Mike Holovak
Director of Administration: Rick Nichols
Media Relations Director: Bob Hyde
Marketing/Media Relations Assistant: Gregg Stengel
Ticket Manager: David Fuqua
Head Coach: Hugh Campbell
Assistant Coaches: Bill Allerheiligen, O. Kay Dalton, John Devlin,
  Gene Gaines, Jerry Glanville, Ken Houston, Bruce Lemmerman,
  Bob Padilla, Al Roberts, Bill Walsh
Scouts: Bill Bell, C.O. Brocato, Dub Fesperman, Bill Young
Coordinator/Pro Scouting: Walt Schlinkman
Strength and Conditioning: Bill Allerheiligen
Head Trainer: Jerry Meins
Assistant Trainer: Joel Krekelberg
Equipment Manager: Gordon Batty
Equipment Assistant: Bill Lackey

Stadium: Astrodome (Capacity 50,496)
Playing Surface: AstroTurf
Stadium Address: Loop 610, Kirby and Fannin Streets, Houston,
  Texas 77054
Colours: Columbia Blue, Scarlet and White
Summer Training Camp: Angelo State University, San Angelo,
  Texas 76901

HOUSTON OILERS 1985 SCHEDULE

PRE-SEASON

Aug.	3	vs. N.Y. Giants (Hall of Fame Game)	2:30
Aug.	10	at Los Angeles Rams	7:00
Aug.	17	at New Orleans	8:00
Aug.	24	KANSAS CITY	8:00
Aug.	31	at Dallas	8:00

REGULAR SEASON

Sep.	8	MIAMI	12:00
Sep.	15	at Washington	1:00
Sep.	22	at Pittsburgh	1:00
Sep.	29	DALLAS	12:00
Oct.	6	at Denver	2:00
Oct.	13	CLEVELAND	12:00
Oct.	20	CINCINNATI	12:00
Oct.	27	at St. Louis	12:00
Nov.	3	KANSAS CITY	12:00
Nov.	10	at Buffalo	1:00
Nov.	17	PITTSBURGH	12:00
Nov.	24	SAN DIEGO	12:00
Dec.	1	at Cincinnati	1:00
Dec.	8	NEW YORK GIANTS	3:00
Dec.	15	at Cleveland	1:00
Dec.	22	at Indianapolis	4:00

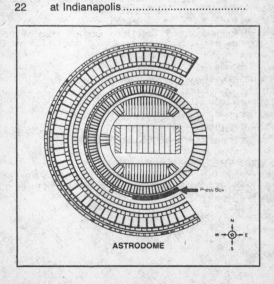

Press Box

ASTRODOME

N
W E
S

HOUSTON OILERS
END OF SEASON DEPTH CHART

OFFENSE
WR — 83 Tim Smith, 84 Mike Holston, 85 Carl Roaches
OLT — 73 Harvey Salem, 76 Eric Moran
OLG — 63 Mike Munchak, 62 John Schuhmacher
C — 55 Jim Romano, 74 Bruce Matthews
ORG — 62 John Schuhmacher, 66 Pat Howell
ORT — 74 Bruce Matthews, 76 Eric Moran
TE — 87 Jamie Williams, 89 Mike McCloskey
WR — 82 Herkie Walls, 81 Steve Bryant, 80 Eric Mullins
QB — 1 Warren Moon, 10 Oliver Luck, 12 Brian Ransom
RB — 30 Larry Moriarty, 32 Stan Edwards, 38 Willie Joyner, 35 Richard Williams
H-B — 88 Chris Dressel, 87 Jamie Williams

DEFENSE
DLE — 90 Bob Hamm, 78 Jerome Foster
MG — 67 Mike Stensrud, 72 Brian Sochia
DRE — 75 Jesse Baker, 97 Mike Johnson
LOLB — 53 Avon Riley, 51 Ted Thompson, 91 Johnny Meads
LILB — 54 Gregg Bingham, 59 John Grimsley, 50 Daryl Hunt
RILB — 56 Robert Abraham, 59 John Grimsley, 50 Daryl Hunt
ROLB — 52 Robert Brazile, 57 Tim Joiner, 91 Johnny Meads
LCB — 24 Steve Brown, 29 Patrick Allen
RCB — 20 Willie Tullis, 29 Patrick Allen
SS — 25 Keith Bostic, 31 Jeff Donaldson, 27 Mike Kennedy
FS — 21 Bo Eason, 26 Darryl Meadows

SPECIAL TEAMS
P — 6 John James, 83 Tim Smith
K — 8 Joe Cooper, 51 Ted Thompson
H — 6 John James, 10 Oliver Luck
PR — 85 Carl Roaches, 82 Herkie Walls
KR — 85 Carl Roaches, 82 Herkie Walls
LSN — 74 Bruce Matthews, 55 Jim Romano

ALSO WITH THE HOUSTON OILERS
4 Florian Kempf (K), 77 Doug France (T), 70 Dean Steinkuhler (T), 28 Allen Lyday (S), 36 Carter Hartwig (S), 93 Robert Lyles (LB), 98 Mark Studaway (DE)

HOUSTON OILERS

INDIVIDUAL RUSHERS

	Att	Yards	Avg	Long	TD
Moriarty, Larry	189	785	4.2	t51	6
Edwards, Stan	60	267	4.5	20	1
Moon, Warren	58	211	3.6	31	1
Luck, Oliver	10	75	7.5	18	1
Joyner, Willie	14	22	1.6	9	0
Walls, Herkie	4	20	5.0	20	0
Mullins, Eric	1	0	0.0	0	0
Cooper, Joe	1	−2	−2.0	−2	0

INDIVIDUAL PASSING

	Att	Comp	Pct Comp	Yds	Avg Gain	TD	Pct TD	Long	Int	Pct Int	Rating Points
Moon, Warren	450	259	57.6	3338	7.42	12	2.7	76	14	3.1	76.9
Luck, Oliver	36	22	61.1	256	7.11	2	5.6	37	1	2.8	89.6
Moriarty, Larry	1	1	100.0	16	16.00	0	0.0	16	0	0.0	118.8

INDIVIDUAL RECEIVERS

	No	Yards	Avg	Long	TD
Smith, Tim	69	1141	16.5	t75	4
Williams, Jamie	41	545	13.3	32	3
Dressel, Chris	40	378	9.5	42	2
Moriarty, Larry	31	206	6.6	24	1
Holston, Michael	22	287	13.0	28	1
Edwards, Stan	20	151	7.6	20	0
Bryant, Steve	19	278	14.6	28	0
Walls, Herkie	18	291	16.2	76	1
McCloskey, Mike	9	152	16.9	51	1
Mullins, Eric	6	85	14.2	25	1
Roaches, Carl	4	69	17.3	24	0

INDIVIDUAL INTERCEPTORS

	No	Yards	Avg	Long	TD
Tullis, Willie	4	48	12.0	22	0
Hartwig, Carter	3	23	7.7	19	0
Brown, Steve	1	26	26.0	26	0
Eason, Bo	1	20	20.0	20	0
Lyday, Allen	1	12	12.0	12	0
Allen, Patrick	1	2	2.0	2	0
Brazile, Robert	1	2	2.0	2	0
Abraham, Robert	1	1	1.0	1	0
Thompson, Ted	0	5	—	5	0

INDIVIDUAL KICKOFF RETURNERS

	No	Yards	Avg	Long	TD
Roaches, Carl	30	679	22.6	49	0
Walls, Herkie	15	289	19.3	29	0
Allen, Patrick	11	210	19.1	23	0
Williams, Richard, Atl.-Hou.	5	84	16.8	21	0
Joyner, Willie	3	57	19.0	24	0
Brown, Steve	3	17	5.7	17	0
Thompson, Ted	1	16	16.0	16	0
Williams, Jamie	1	0	0.0	0	0

INDIVIDUAL PUNTERS

	No	Yards	Long	Avg	Total Punts	TB	Blk	Opp Ret	Ret Yds	In 20	Net Avg
James, John	88	3482	55	39.6	88	5	0	60	618	20	31.4

INDIVIDUAL PUNT RETURNERS

	No	FC	Yards	Avg	Long	TD
Roaches, Carl	26	8	152	5.8	18	0

INDIVIDUAL SCORERS

KICKERS	XP	XPA	FG	FGA	PTS
Cooper, Joe	13	13	11	13	46
Kempf, Florian	14	14	4	6	26

NON-KICKERS	TD	TDR	TDP	TDM	PTS
Moriarty, Larry	7	6	1	0	42
Smith, Tim	4	0	4	0	24
Williams, Jamie	3	0	3	0	18
Dressel, Chris	2	0	2	0	12
Bostic, Keith	1	0	0	1	6
Edwards, Stan	1	1	0	0	6
Holston, Michael	1	0	1	0	6
Luck, Oliver	1	1	0	0	6
McCloskey, Mike	1	0	1	0	6
Moon, Warren	1	1	0	0	6
Mullins, Eric	1	0	1	0	6
Walls, Herkie	1	0	1	0	6

INDIANAPOLIS COLTS
AFC Eastern Division

Address: PO Box 54000, Indianapolis, Indiana 46254
Telephone: (317) 252-2658

CLUB OFFICIALS
President-Treasurer: Robert Irsay
Vice President-General Manager: James Irsay
Vice President-General Counsel: Michael G. Chernoff
Assistant General Manager: Bob Terpening
Director of Player Personnel: Jack Bushofsky
Director of College Scouting: Clyde Powers
Controller: Kurt Humphrey
Director of Operations: Pete Ward
Director of Public Relations: Bob Eller
Assistant Director of Public Relations: Craig Kelley
Purchasing Administrator: David Filer
Head Coach: Rod Dowhower
Assistant Coaches: Zeke Bratkowski, George Catavolos,
    Gunther Cunningham, Hal Hunter, Richard Mann,
    Roger Theder, Rick Venturi, Mike Westhoff
Equipment Manager: Jon Scott
Assistant Equipment Manager: John Starliper
Cheerleader Director: Meg Irsay

Stadium: Hoosier Dome (Capacity 60,127)
Playing Surface: AstroTurf
Stadium Address: 100 South Capitol Avenue, Indianapolis,
    Indiana 46225
Colours: Royal Blue, White and Silver
Summer Training Camp: Anderson College, Anderson,
    Indiana 46011

INDIANAPOLIS COLTS 1985 SCHEDULE

PRE-SEASON

Aug.	10	SEATTLE	7:30
Aug.	17	at Chicago	6:00
Aug.	24	at Denver	7:00
Aug.	30	CINCINNATI	7:30

REGULAR SEASON

Sep.	8	at Pittsburgh	1:00
Sep.	15	at Miami	1:00
Sep.	22	DETROIT	12:00
Sep.	29	at New York Jets	4:00
Oct.	6	BUFFALO	12:00
Oct.	13	DENVER	12:00
Oct.	20	at Buffalo	1:00
Oct.	27	GREEN BAY	1:00
Nov.	3	NEW YORK JETS	4:00
Nov.	10	at New England	1:00
Nov.	17	MIAMI	1:00
Nov.	24	at Kansas City	3:00
Dec.	1	NEW ENGLAND	1:00
Dec.	8	at Chicago	12:00
Dec.	15	at Tampa Bay	1:00
Dec.	22	HOUSTON	4:00

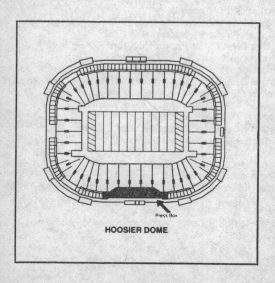

Press Box

HOOSIER DOME

INDIANAPOLIS COLTS
END OF SEASON DEPTH CHART

OFFENSE

WR — 80 Raymond Butler, 88 Bernard Henry
OLT — 71 Ted Petersen, 73 Steve Wright
OLG — 64 Ben Utt, 63 Mark Kirchner
C — 53 Ray Donaldson, 61 Don Bailey
ORG — 66 Ron Solt, 63 Mark Kirchner
ORT — 76 Jim Mills, 72 Kevin Call
TE — 83 Tim Sherwin, 81 Dave Young, 48 Mark Bell
WR — 87 Tracy Porter, 85 Matt Bouza, 86 Phil Smith
QB — 10 Art Schlichter, 18 Mike Pagel, 9 Mark Herrmann
RB — 43 Frank Middleton, 23 Alvin Moore
RB — 32 Randy McMillan, 34 George Wonsley

DEFENSE

DLE — 99 Donnell Thompson, 91 Byron Smith
NT — 92 Brad White, 95 Chris Scott
DRE — 96 Blaise Winter, 95 Chris Scott, Scott Virkus
LOLB — 98 Johnie Cooks, 52 Greg Bracelin
LILB — 93 Cliff Odom, 57 Mike Humiston, 90 Gary Padjen
RILB — 55 Barry Krauss, 57 Mike Humiston, 90 Gary Padjen
ROLB — 56 Vernon Maxwell, 52 Greg Bracelin
LCB — 38 Eugene Daniel, 35 Tate Randle, Isaac Metcalf
RCB — 27 Preston Davis, 35 Tate Randle, Isaac Metcalf
SS — 29 Mark Kafentzis, 30 Larry Anderson,
        40 Vaughn Williams
FS — 25 Nesby Glasgow, 21 George Radachowsky

SPECIAL TEAMS

P — 3 Rohn Stark, 18 Mike Pagel
K — 2 Raul Allegre, 5 Dean Biasucci
H — 3 Rohn Stark
PR — 30 Larry Anderson, 25 Nesby Glasgow
KR — 86 Phil Smith, 30 Larry Anderson, 29 Mark Kafentzis
LSN — 61 Don Bailey, 53 Ray Donaldson

ALSO WITH THE INDIANAPOLIS COLTS

39 Newton Williams (RB), 33 Curtis Dickey (RB), Pat Beach (TE),
84 Victor Oatis (WR), 75 Chris Hinton (G/T) 79 Andy Ekern (T),
65 Ellis Gardner (T), 69 Leo Wisniewski (NT),
45 James Burroughs (CB), 51 Ricky Jones (LB),
58 Steve Hathaway (LB)

INDIANAPOLIS COLTS

INDIVIDUAL RUSHERS

	Att	Yards	Avg	Long	TD
McMillan, Randy	163	705	4.3	t31	5
Dickey, Curtis	131	523	4.0	30	3
Middleton, Frank	92	275	3.0	20	1
Pagel, Mike	26	149	5.7	23	1
Schlichter, Art	19	145	7.6	22	1
Moore, Alvin	38	127	3.3	18	2
Wonsley, George	37	111	3.0	13	0
Stark, Rohn	2	0	0.0	0	0
Smith, Phil	2	−10	−5.0	−3	0

INDIVIDUAL PASSING

	Att	Comp	Pct Comp	Yds	Avg Gain	TD	Pct TD	Long	Int	Pct Int	Rating Points
Pagel, Mike	212	114	53.8	1426	6.73	8	3.8	t54	8	3.8	71.8
Schlichter, Art	140	62	44.3	702	5.01	3	2.1	54	7	5.0	46.2
Herrmann, Mark	56	29	51.8	352	6.29	1	1.8	t74	6	10.7	37.8
Dickey, Curtis	1	1	100.0	63	63.00	1	100.0	t63	0	0.0	158.3
Moore, Alvin	1	0	0.0	0	0.00	0	0.0	0	0	0.0	39.6
Stark, Rohn	1	0	0.0	0	0.00	0	0.0	0	1	100.0	0.0

INDIVIDUAL RECEIVERS

	No	Yards	Avg	Long	TD
Butler, Raymond	43	664	15.4	t74	6
Porter, Tracy	39	590	15.1	t63	2
Bouza, Matt	22	270	12.3	22	0
McMillan, Randy	19	201	10.6	44	0
Middleton, Frank	15	112	7.5	16	1
Young, Dave	14	164	11.7	28	2
Dickey, Curtis	14	135	9.6	33	0
Sherwin, Tim	11	169	15.4	26	0
Henry, Bernard	11	139	12.6	t19	2
Moore, Alvin	9	52	5.8	12	0
Wonsley, George	9	47	5.2	17	0

INDIVIDUAL INTERCEPTORS

	No	Yards	Avg	Long	TD
Daniel, Eugene	6	25	4.2	18	0
Randle, Tate	3	66	22.0	54	0
Krauss, Barry	3	20	6.7	18	0
Burroughs, Jim	3	9	3.0	6	0
Kafentzis, Mark	1	59	59.0	t59	1
Glasgow, Nesby	1	8	8.0	8	0
Davis, Preston	1	3	3.0	3	0

INDIVIDUAL KICKOFF RETURNERS

	No	Yards	Avg	Long	TD
Anderson, Larry	22	525	23.9	69	0
Smith, Phil	32	651	20.3	t96	1
Kafentzis, Mark	5	69	13.8	22	0
Wonsley, George	4	52	13.0	20	0
Moore, Alvin	2	19	9.5	10	0
Middleton, Frank	1	11	11.0	11	0
Hathaway, Steve	1	2	2.0	2	0
Sherwin, Tim	1	2	2.0	2	0
Radachowsky, George	1	0	0.0	0	0

INDIVIDUAL PUNTERS

	No	Yards	Long	Avg	Total Punts	TB	Blk	Opp Ret	Ret Yds	In 20	Net Avg
Stark, Rohn	98	4383	72	44.7	98	7	0	62	600	21	37.2

INDIVIDUAL PUNT RETURNERS

	No	FC	Yards	Avg	Long	TD
Anderson, Larry	27	7	182	6.7	19	0
Glasgow, Nesby	7	2	79	11.3	35	0
Bouza, Matt	3	3	17	5.7	11	0
Padjen, Gary	1	0	0	0.0	0	0

INDIVIDUAL SCORERS

KICKERS

	XP	XPA	FG	FGA	PTS
Allegre, Raul	14	14	11	18	47
Biasucci, Dean	13	14	3	5	22

NON-KICKERS

	TD	TDR	TDP	TDM	PTS
Butler, Raymond	6	0	6	0	36
McMillan, Randy	5	5	0	0	30
Dickey, Curtis	3	3	0	0	18
Henry, Bernard	2	0	2	0	12
Middleton, Frank	2	1	1	0	12
Moore, Alvin	2	2	0	0	12
Porter, Tracy	2	0	2	0	12
Young, Dave	2	0	2	0	12
Kafentzis, Mark	1	0	0	1	6
Pagel, Mike	1	1	0	0	6
Schlichter, Art	1	1	0	0	6
Smith, Phil	1	0	0	1	6
Humiston, Mike	0	0	0	0	2

KANSAS CITY CHIEFS
AFC Western Division

Address: One Arrowhead Drive, Kansas City, Missouri 64129
Telephone: (816) 924-9300

CLUB OFFICIALS
Owner: Lamar Hunt
President: Jack Steadman
Vice President and General Manager: Jim Schaaf
Head Coach: John Mackovic
Assistant Coaches: Bud Carson, Walt Corey, Dan Daniel,
  Doug Graber, J.D. Helm, C.T. Hewgley, Rod Humenuik,
  Pete McCulley, Willie Peete, Jim Vechiarella,
  Richard Williamson
Director of Player Personnel: Les Miller
Director of Research and Development: Ron Waller
Treasurer: Randy Cooper
Secretary: Jim Seigfried
Manager of Administration: Don Steadman
Stadium Manager: Bob Wachter
Ticket Manager: Joe Mazza
Public Relations Director: Bob Sprenger
Assistant Director of Public Relations: Gary Heise
Promotions Director: Mitch Wheeler
Director of Arrowhead Stadium: David Smith
Trainer: Dave Kendall
Equipment Coordinator: Jon Phillips

Stadium: Arrowhead Stadium (Capacity: 78,067)
Playing Surface: AstroTurf-8
Stadium Address: One Arrowhead Drive, Kansas City,
  Missouri 64129
Colours: Red, Gold and White
Summer Training Camp: William Jewell College, Liberty,
  Missouri 64068

KANSAS CITY CHIEFS 1985 SCHEDULE

PRE-SEASON
Aug.	10	at Cincinnati	7:00
Aug.	17	NEW ENGLAND	7:30
Aug.	24	at Houston	8:00
Aug.	31	ST. LOUIS	7:30

REGULAR SEASON
Sep.	8	at New Orleans	12:00
Sep.	12	LOS ANGELES RAIDERS	7:00
Sep.	22	at Miami	4:00
Sep.	29	SEATTLE	12:00
Oct.	6	at Los Angeles Raiders	1:00
Oct.	13	at San Diego	1:00
Oct.	20	LOS ANGELES RAMS	12:00
Oct.	27	DENVER	12:00
Nov.	3	at Houston	12:00
Nov.	10	PITTSBURGH	12:00
Nov.	17	at San Francisco	1:00
Nov.	24	INDIANAPOLIS	3:00
Dec.	1	at Seattle	1:00
Dec.	8	ATLANTA	12:00
Dec.	14	at Denver	2:00
Dec.	22	SAN DIEGO	12:00

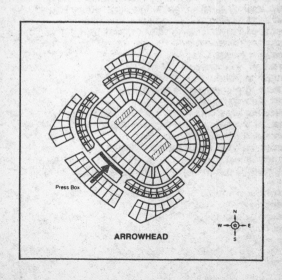

Press Box

ARROWHEAD

N
W ✦ E
S

KANSAS CITY CHIEFS
END OF SEASON DEPTH CHART

OFFENSE
WR   — 88 Carlos Carson, 83 Stephone Paige
OLT — 60 Matt Herkenhoff, 76 John Alt
OLG — 66 Brad Budde, 68 Scott Auer
C   — 53 Bob Rush, 62 Adam Lingner
ORG — 65 Tom Condon, 77 Rich Baldinger
ORT — 72 Dave Lutz, 70 Jim Rourke, 77 Rich Baldinger
TE   — 81 Willie Scott, 85 Ed Beckman, 87 Walt Arnold
WR   — 89 Henry Marshall, 82 Anthony Hancock
QB   — 9 Bill Kenney, 14 Todd Blackledge, 11 Sandy Osiecki
RB   — 44 Herman Heard, 27 Theotis Brown, 38 Michael Gunter
RB   — 40 Ken Lacy, 43 Billy Jackson

DEFENSE
DLE — 67 Art Still, 71 Dave Lindstrom, 93 Eric Holle
NT   — 63 Bill Maas, 91 Ken Kremer, 73 Mike Dawson
DRE — 71 Dave Lindstrom, 93 Eric Holle
LOLB — 94 Ken McAlister, 52 Ken Jolly
LILB — 57 Jerry Blanton, 97 Scott Radecic, 60 John Zamberlin
RILB — 59 Gary Spani, 97 Scott Radecic, 52 Ken Jolly
ROLB — 50 Calvin Daniels, 95 Jeff Paine, 52 Ken Jolly
LCB — 23 Greg Hill, 21 Kerry Parker, Skip Lane
RCB — 31 Kevin Ross, 23 Greg Hill, 21 Kerry Parker
SS   — 34 Lloyd Burruss, 30 Mark Robinson
FS   — 20 Deron Cherry, 30 Mark Robinson, 22 Van Jakes

SPECIAL TEAMS
P   — 6 Jim Arnold
K   — 8 Nick Lowery
H   — 9 Bill Kenney, 6 Jim Arnold
PR   — 44 Herman Heard, 82 Anthony Hancock
KR   — 83 Stephone Paige, 82 Anthony Hancock
LSN — 62 Adam Lingner, 53 Bob Rush

ALSO WITH THE KANSAS CITY CHIEFS
35 Ken Thomas (RB), 86 J.T. Smith (WR/PR), 55 Dave Klug (LB),
51 Charles Jackson (LB), 29 Albert Lewis (CB), 99 Mike Bell (DE)

KANSAS CITY CHIEFS

INDIVIDUAL RUSHERS

	Att	Yards	Avg	Long	TD
Heard, Herman	165	684	4.1	t69	4
Brown, Theotis	97	337	3.5	25	4
Jackson, Billy	50	225	4.5	16	1
Lacy, Kenneth	46	165	3.6	t24	2
Blackledge, Todd	18	102	5.7	26	1
Paige, Stephon	3	19	6.3	9	0
Gunter, Michael	15	12	0.8	4	0
Ricks, Lawrence	2	1	0.5	1	0
Arnold, Jim	1	0	0.0	0	0
Osiecki, Sandy	1	−2	−2.0	−2	0
Carson, Carlos	1	−8	−8.0	−8	0
Kenney, Bill	9	−8	−0.9	1	0

INDIVIDUAL PASSING

	Att	Comp	Pct Comp	Yds	Avg Gain	TD	Pct TD	Long	Int	Pct Int	Rating Points
Kenney, Bill	282	151	53.5	2098	7.44	15	5.3	t65	10	3.5	80.7
Blackledge, Todd	294	147	50.0	1707	5.81	6	2.0	t46	11	3.7	59.2
Osiecki, Sandy	17	7	41.2	64	3.76	0	0.0	19	1	5.9	27.6

INDIVIDUAL RECEIVERS

	No	Yards	Avg	Long	TD
Marshall, Henry	62	912	14.7	37	4
Carson, Carlos	57	1078	18.9	57	4
Brown, Theotis	38	236	6.2	17	0
Paige, Stephon	30	541	18.0	t65	4
Scott, Willie	28	253	9.0	27	3
Heard, Herman	25	223	8.9	17	0
Jackson, Billy	15	101	6.7	11	1
Lacy, Kenneth	13	87	6.7	20	2
Arnold, Walt, Wash.-K.C.	11	95	8.6	15	1
Hancock, Anthony	10	217	21.7	t46	1
Smith, J. T.	8	69	8.6	16	0
Beckman, Ed	7	44	6.3	9	1
Little, David	1	13	13.0	13	0

INDIVIDUAL INTERCEPTORS

	No	Yards	Avg	Long	TD
Cherry, Deron	7	140	20.0	67	0
Ross, Kevin	6	124	20.7	t71	1
Lewis, Albert	4	57	14.3	31	0
Radecic, Scott	2	54	27.0	35	1

	No	Yards	Avg	Long	TD
McAlister, Ken	2	33	16.5	22	0
Burruss, Lloyd	2	16	8.0	16	0
Daniels, Calvin	2	11	5.5	11	0
Hill, Greg	2	−1	−0.5	0	0
Jackson, Charles	1	16	16.0	16	0
Blanton, Jerry	1	14	14.0	14	0
Kremer, Ken	1	1	1.0	1	0

INDIVIDUAL KICKOFF RETURNERS

	No	Yards	Avg	Long	TD
Paige, Stephon	27	544	20.1	45	0
Smith, J.T.	19	391	20.6	39	0
Ricks, Lawrence	5	83	16.6	21	0
Hancock, Anthony	2	32	16.0	17	0
Scott, Willie	1	9	9.0	9	0
Carson, Carlos	1	2	2.0	2	0
Cherry, Deron	1	0	0.0	0	0

INDIVIDUAL PUNTERS

	No	Yards	Long	Avg	Total Punts	TB	Blk	Opp Ret	Ret Yds	In 20	Net Avg
Arnold, Jim	98	4397	63	44.9	98	13	0	60	461	22	37.5

INDIVIDUAL PUNT RETURNERS

	No	FC	Yards	Avg	Long	TD
Smith, J.T.	39	14	332	8.5	27	0
Hancock, Anthony	3	1	14	4.7	7	0

INDIVIDUAL SCORERS
KICKERS

	XP	XPA	FG	FGA	PTS
Lowery, Nick	35	35	23	33	104

NON-KICKERS

	TD	TDR	TDP	TDM	PTS
Brown, Theotis	4	4	0	0	24
Carson, Carlos	4	0	4	0	24
Heard, Herman	4	4	0	0	24
Lacy, Kenneth	4	2	2	0	24
Marshall, Henry	4	0	4	0	24
Paige, Stephon	4	0	4	0	24
Scott, Willie	3	0	3	0	18
Jackson, Billy	2	1	1	0	12
Arnold, Walt, Wash.-K.C.	1	0	1	0	6
Blackledge, Todd	1	1	0	0	6
Hancock, Anthony	1	0	1	0	6
Radecic, Scott	1	0	0	1	6
Ross, Kevin	1	0	0	1	6

LOS ANGELES RAIDERS
AFC Western Division

Address: 332 Center Street, El Segundo, California 90245
Telephone: (213) 322-3451

CLUB OFFICIALS
Managing General Partner: Al Davis
Executive Assistant: Al LoCasale
Head Coach: Tom Flores
Assistant Coaches: Sam Boghosian, Willie Brown, Chet Franklin,
   Larry Kennan, Earl Leggett, Bob Mischak, Steve Ortmayer,
   Art Shell, Tom Walsh, Ray Willsey, Bob Zeman
Player Personnel: Ron Wolf
Business Manager: Ken LaRue
Senior Administrators: Tom Grimes, Irv Kaze, John Herrera
Marketing/Promotions: Mike Ornstein
Ticket Operations: Peter Eiges
Comptroller: Peggy Ferguson
Trainers: George Anderson, H. Rod Martin
Equipment Manager: Richard Romanski

Stadium: Los Angeles Memorial Coliseum (Capacity 92,516)
Playing Surface: Grass
Stadium Address: 3911 South Figueroa Street, Los Angeles,
   California 90037
Colours: Silver and Black
Summer Training Camp: Hilton Hotel, Oxnard, California 93030

LOS ANGELES RAIDERS 1985 SCHEDULE

PRE-SEASON

Aug.	10	SAN FRANCISCO	6:00
Aug.	17	WASHINGTON	1:00
Aug.	24	MIAMI	6:00
Aug.	31	at Cleveland	7:30

REGULAR SEASON

Sep.	8	NEW YORK JETS	1:00
Sep.	12	at Kansas City	7:00
Sep.	22	SAN FRANCISCO	1:00
Sep.	29	at New England	1:00
Oct.	6	KANSAS CITY	1:00
Oct.	13	NEW ORLEANS	1:00
Oct.	20	at Cleveland	1:00
Oct.	28	SAN DIEGO	6:00
Nov.	3	at Seattle	1:00
Nov.	10	at San Diego	1:00
Nov.	17	CINCINNATI	1:00
Nov.	24	DENVER	1:00
Dec.	1	at Atlanta	4:00
Dec.	8	at Denver	2:00
Dec.	15	SEATTLE	1:00
Dec.	23	at Los Angeles Rams	6:00

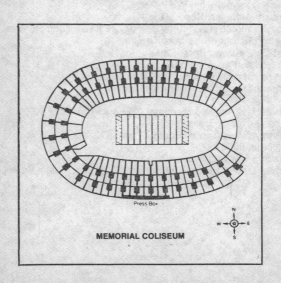

Press Box

MEMORIAL COLISEUM

LOS ANGELES RAIDERS
END OF SEASON DEPTH CHART

OFFENSE
WR — 21 Cliff Branch, 85 Dokie Williams, 88 Sam Seale
OLT — 79 Bruce Davis, 76 Ed Muransky
OLG — 60 Curt Marsh, 73 Charley Hannah
C — 50 Dave Dalby, 67 Dwight Wheeler
ORG — 65 Mickey Marvin, 73 Charley Hannah
ORT — 70 Henry Lawrence, 66 Warren Bryant
TE — 46 Todd Christensen, 87 Dave Casper,
  31 Derrick Jensen
WR — 80 Malcolm Barnwell, 85 Dokie Williams,
  28 Cleotha Montgomery
QB — 6 Marc Wilson, 16 Jim Plunkett, 8 Ray Guy
RB — 33 Kenny King, 27 Frank Hawkins, 31 Derrick Jensen
RB — 32 Marcus Allen, 34 Greg Pruitt, 38 Chester Willis

DEFENSE
DLE — 75 Howie Long, 93 Greg Townsend
NT — 62 Reggie Kinlaw, 71 Bill Pickel, 97 Richard Ackerman
DRE — 77 Lyle Alzado, 99 Sean Jones
LOLB — 91 Brad Van Pelt, 56 Jeff Barnes
LILB — 55 Matt Millen, 54 Darryl Byrd, 52 Mark Merrill
RILB — 58 Jack Squirek, 54 Darryl Byrd, 52 Mark Merrill
ROLB — 53 Rod Martin, 57 Tony Caldwell
LCB — 37 Lester Hayes, 45 James Davis
RCB — 22 Mike Haynes, 20 Ted Watts
SS — 36 Mike Davis, 30 Stacey Toran
FS — 26 Vann McElroy, 23 Odis McKinney

SPECIAL TEAMS
P — 8 Ray Guy, 10 Chris Bahr
K — 10 Chris Bahr, 8 Ray Guy
H — 6 Marc Wilson, 8 Ray Guy
PR — 28 Cleotha Montgomery, 34 Greg Pruitt, 20 Ted Watts
KR — 28 Cleotha Montgomery, 85 Dokie Williams,
  34 Greg Pruitt
LSN — 50 Dave Dalby, 73 Charley Hannah, 67 Dwight Wheeler

ALSO WITH THE LOS ANGELES RAIDERS
81 Andy Parker (TE), 43 Joe McCall (RB), 11 David Humm (QB),
72 Don Mosebar (T), 74 Shelby Jordan (T), 90 Larry McCoy (LB),
51 Bob Nelson (LB), 59 Stanley Adams (LB)

LOS ANGELES RAIDERS

INDIVIDUAL RUSHERS

	Att	Yards	Avg	Long	TD
Allen, Marcus	275	1168	4.2	t52	13
Hawkins, Frank	108	376	3.5	17	3
King, Kenny	67	254	3.8	18	0
Wilson, Marc	30	56	1.9	t14	1
Plunkett, Jim	16	14	0.9	9	1
Humm, David	2	7	3.5	9	0
Willis, Chester	5	4	0.8	2	0
Jensen, Derrick	3	3	1.0	2	1
McCall, Joe	1	3	3.0	3	0
Montgomery, Cleotha	1	1	1.0	1	0
Pruitt, Greg	8	0	0.0	3	0

INDIVIDUAL PASSING

	Att	Comp	Pct Comp	Yds	Avg Gain	TD	Pct TD	Long	Int	Pct Int	Rating Points
Wilson, Marc	282	153	54.3	2151	7.63	15	5.3	92	17	6.0	71.7
Plunkett, Jim	198	108	54.5	1473	7.44	6	3.0	t73	10	5.1	67.6
Allen, Marcus	4	1	25.0	38	9.50	0	0.0	38	0	0.0	66.7
Humm, David	7	4	57.1	56	8.00	0	0.0	21	1	14.3	43.5

INDIVIDUAL RECEIVERS

	No	Yards	Avg	Long	TD
Christensen, Todd	80	1007	12.6	38	7
Allen, Marcus	64	758	11.8	92	5
Barnwell, Malcolm	45	851	18.9	t51	2
Branch, Cliff	27	401	14.9	47	0
Williams, Dokie	22	509	23.1	t75	4
King, Kenny	14	99	7.1	15	0
Hawkins, Frank	7	51	7.3	15	0
Casper, Dave	4	29	7.3	13	2
Pruitt, Greg	2	12	6.0	8	0
Jensen, Derrick	1	1	1.0	t1	1

INDIVIDUAL INTERCEPTORS

	No	Yards	Avg	Long	TD
Haynes, Mike	6	220	36.7	t97	1
McElroy, Vann	4	42	10.5	31	0
Martin, Rod	2	31	15.5	17	1
Davis, Mike	2	11	5.5	11	0
Barnes, Jeff	1	15	15.0	15	0
Van Pelt, Brad	1	9	9.0	9	0
Davis, James	1	8	8.0	8	0
Hayes, Lester	1	3	3.0	3	0

	No	Yards	Avg	Long	TD
McKinney, Odis	1	0	0.0	0	0
Watts, Ted	1	0	0.0	0	0

INDIVIDUAL KICKOFF RETURNERS

	No	Yards	Avg	Long	TD
Williams, Dokie	24	621	25.9	62	0
Montgomery, Cleotha	26	555	21.3	42	0
Pruitt, Greg	3	16	5.3	13	0
Willis, Chester	1	13	13.0	13	0
Jensen, Derrick	1	11	11.0	11	0
McKinney, Odis	1	0	0.0	0	0

INDIVIDUAL PUNTERS

	No	Yards	Long	Avg	Total Punts	TB	Blk	Opp Ret	Ret Yds	In 20	Net Avg
Guy, Ray	91	3809	63	41.9	91	12	0	34	345	25	35.4

INDIVIDUAL PUNT RETURNERS

	No	FC	Yards	Avg	Long	TD
Pruitt, Greg	53	16	473	8.9	38	0
Montgomery, Cleotha	14	1	194	13.9	t69	1

INDIVIDUAL SCORERS

KICKERS	XP	XPA	FG	FGA	PTS
Bahr, Chris	40	42	20	27	100

NON-KICKERS	TD	TDR	TDP	TDM	PTS
Allen, Marcus	18	13	5	0	108
Christensen, Todd	7	0	7	0	42
Williams, Dokie	4	0	4	0	24
Hawkins, Frank	3	3	0	0	18
Martin, Rod	2	0	0	2	14
Barnwell, Malcolm	2	0	2	0	12
Casper, Dave	2	0	2	0	12
Jensen, Derrick	2	1	1	0	12
Haynes, Mike	1	0	0	1	6
Montgomery, Cleotha	1	0	0	1	6
Plunkett, Jim	1	1	0	0	6
Wilson, Marc	1	1	0	0	6

MIAMI DOLPHINS
AFC Eastern Division

Address: 4770 Biscayne Boulevard, Suite 1440, Miami,
  Florida 33137
Telephone: (305) 576-1000

CLUB OFFICIALS
President: Joseph Robbie
Vice President-General Manager: J. Michael Robbie
Vice President-Head Coach: Don Shula
Vice President/Special Projects and Development: Don Poss
Director of Player Personnel: Chuck Connor
Director of Pro Personnel: Charley Winner
Assistant Coaches: Tom Keane, Bob Matheson, John Sandusky,
  Mike Scarry, David Shula, Chuck Studley, Carl Taseff,
  Junior Wade
Director of Publicity: Chip Namias
Ticket Director: Steve Dangerfield
Controller: Howard F. Rieman
Trainer: Bob Lundy
Equipment Manager: Bob Monica

Stadium: Orange Bowl (Capacity: 75,206)
Playing Surface: Grass
Stadium Address: 1501 N.W. Third Street, Miami, Florida 33125
Colours: Aqua, Coral and White
Summer Training Camp: St. Thomas of Villanova,
  16400-D NW 32nd Avenue, Miami, Florida 33054

MIAMI DOLPHINS 1985 SCHEDULE

PRE-SEASON

Aug.	10	MINNESOTA	8:00
Aug.	17	BUFFALO	8:00
Aug.	24	at Los Angeles Raiders	6:00
Aug.	30	at Atlanta	8:00

REGULAR SEASON

Sep.	8	at Houston	12:00
Sep.	15	INDIANAPOLIS	1:00
Sep.	22	KANSAS CITY	4:00
Sep.	29	at Denver	2:00
Oct.	6	PITTSBURGH	1:00
Oct.	14	at New York Jets	9:00
Oct.	20	TAMPA BAY	4:00
Oct.	27	at Detroit	1:00
Nov.	3	at New England	1:00
Nov.	10	NEW YORK JETS	4:00
Nov.	17	at Indianapolis	1:00
Nov.	24	at Buffalo	1:00
Dec.	2	CHICAGO	9:00
Dec.	8	at Green Bay	12:00
Dec.	16	NEW ENGLAND	9:00
Dec.	22	BUFFALO	1:00

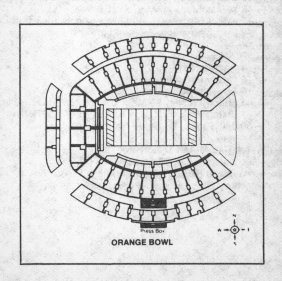

ORANGE BOWL

MIAMI DOLPHINS
END OF SEASON DEPTH CHART

OFFENSE

WR — 85 Mark Duper, 89 Nat Moore, 88 Vince Heflin
OLT — 79 Jon Giesler, 74 Cleveland Green
OLG — 61 Roy Foster, 60 Jeff Toews
C — 57 Dwight Stephenson, 60 Jeff Toews
ORG — 64 Ed Newman, 76 Steve Clark
ORT — 74 Cleveland Green, 72 Ronnie Lee
TE — 87 Dan Johnson, 84 Bruce Hardy, 80 Joe Rose
WR — 83 Mark Clayton, 81 Jimmy Cefalo, 11 Jim Jensen
QB — 13 Dan Marino, 10 Don Strock, 11 Jim Jensen
RB — 22 Tony Nathan, 23 Joe Carter, 31 Eddie Hill
RB — 34 Woody Bennett, 46 Pete Johnson

DEFENSE

DLE — 75 Doug Betters, 78 Charles Benson
NT — 73 Bob Baumhower, 70 Bill Barnett
DRE — 58 Kim Bokamper, 70 Bill Barnett, 71 Mike Charles
LOLB — 59 Bob Brudzinski
LILB — 77 A.J. Duhe, 53 Jay Brophy, 50 Jackie Shipp
RILB — 51 Mark Brown, 55 Earnest Rhone
ROLB — 56 Charles Bowser, 52 Sanders Shiver
LCB — 28 Don McNeal, 44 Paul Lankford, 41 Fulton Walker
RCB — 49 William Judson, 45 Robert Sowell
SS — 47 Glenn Blackwood, 40 Mike Kozlowski, 43 Bud Brown
FS — 42 Lyle Blackwood, 44 Paul Lankford

SPECIAL TEAMS

P — 4 Reggie Roby
K — 5 Uwe von Schamann
H — 10 Don Strock, 11 Jim Jensen
PR — 41 Fulton Walker, 83 Mark Clayton, 88 Vince Heflin
KR — 41 Fulton Walker, 23 Joe Carter, 88 Vince Heflin
LSN — 60 Jeff Toews, 84 Bruce Hardy

ALSO WITH THE MIAMI DOLPHINS

67 Bob Kuechenberg (G), 68 Eric Laakso (T),
32 Tommy Vigorito (RB), 37 Andra Franklin (RB),
53 Ron Hester (LB), 54 Rodell Thomas (LB)

MIAMI DOLPHINS

INDIVIDUAL RUSHERS

	Att	Yards	Avg	Long	TD
Bennett, Woody	144	606	4.2	23	7
Nathan, Tony	118	558	4.7	22	1
Carter, Joe	100	495	5.0	35	1
Johnson, Pete, S.D.-Mia.	87	205	2.4	9	12
Franklin, Andra	20	74	3.7	12	0
Clayton, Mark	3	35	11.7	30	0
Moore, Nat	1	3	3.0	3	0
Strock, Don	2	−5	−2.5	0	0
Marino, Dan	28	−7	−0.3	10	0

INDIVIDUAL PASSING

	Att	Comp	Pct Comp	Yds	Avg Gain	TD	Pct TD	Long	Int	Pct Int	Rating Points
Marino, Dan	564	362	64.2	5084	9.01	48	8.5	t80	17	3.0	108.9
Clayton, Mark	1	0	0.0	0	0.00	0	0.0	0	1	100.0	0.0
Jensen, Jim	1	1	100.0	35	35.00	1	100.0	t35	0	0.0	158.3
Strock, Don	6	4	66.7	27	4.50	0	0.0	12	0	0.0	76.4

INDIVIDUAL RECEIVERS

	No	Yards	Avg	Long	TD
Clayton, Mark	73	1389	19.0	t65	18
Duper, Mark	71	1306	18.4	t80	8
Nathan, Tony	61	579	9.5	26	2
Moore, Nat	43	573	13.3	t37	6
Johnson, Dan	34	426	12.5	42	3
Hardy, Bruce	28	257	9.2	19	5
Cefalo, Jimmy	18	185	10.3	t25	2
Jensen, Jim	13	139	10.7	20	2
Rose, Joe	12	195	16.3	t34	2
Carter, Joe	8	53	6.6	15	0
Bennett, Woody	6	44	7.3	20	1

INDIVIDUAL INTERCEPTORS

	No	Yards	Avg	Long	TD
Blackwood, Glenn	6	169	28.2	50	0
Judson, William	4	121	30.3	t60	1
McNeal, Don	3	41	13.7	30	1
Blackwood, Lyle	3	29	9.7	15	0
Lankford, Paul	3	25	8.3	22	0
Brown, Bud	1	53	53.0	53	0
Kozlowski, Mike	1	26	26.0	26	0
Duhe, A.J.	1	7	7.0	7	0
Sowell, Robert	1	7	7.0	7	0
Brudzinski, Bob	1	0	0.0	0	0

INDIVIDUAL KICKOFF RETURNERS

	No	Yards	Avg	Long	TD
Walker, Fulton	29	617	21.3	41	0
Heflin, Vince	9	130	14.4	26	0
Kozlowski, Mike	2	23	11.5	12	0
Clayton, Mark	2	15	7.5	14	0
Hill, Eddie	1	14	14.0	14	0
Duhe, A.J.	1	0	0.0	0	0

INDIVIDUAL PUNTERS

	No	Yards	Long	Avg	Total Punts	TB	Blk	Opp Ret	Ret Yds	In 20	Net Avg
Roby, Reggie	51	2281	69	44.7	51	10	0	17	138	15	38.1

INDIVIDUAL PUNT RETURNERS

	No	FC	Yards	Avg	Long	TD
Walker, Fulton	21	14	169	8.0	33	0
Clayton, Mark	8	2	79	9.9	22	0
Heflin, Vince	6	1	76	12.7	37	0
Kozlowski, Mike	4	4	41	10.3	20	0
Blackwood, Glenn	0	4	0	—	0	0
Blackwood, Lyle	0	2	0	—	0	0

INDIVIDUAL SCORERS

KICKERS

	XP	XPA	FG	FGA	PTS
von Schamann, Uwe	66	70	9	19	93

NON-KICKERS

	TD	TDR	TDP	TDM	PTS
Clayton, Mark	18	0	18	0	108
Johnson, Pete, S.D.-Mia.	12	12	0	0	72
Bennett, Woody	8	7	1	0	48
Duper, Mark	8	0	8	0	48
Moore, Nat	6	0	6	0	36
Hardy, Bruce	5	0	5	0	30
Johnson, Dan	3	0	3	0	18
Nathan, Tony	3	1	2	0	18
Cefalo, Jimmy	2	0	2	0	12
Jensen, Jim	2	0	2	0	12
Rose, Joe	2	0	2	0	12
Baumhower, Bob	1	0	0	1	6
Carter, Joe	1	1	0	0	6
Judson, William	1	0	0	1	6
McNeal, Don	1	0	0	1	6

NEW ENGLAND PATRIOTS
AFC Eastern Division

Address: Sullivan Stadium, Route 1, Foxboro,
  Massachusetts 02035
Telephone: (617) 543-7911, 262-1776

CLUB OFFICIALS
President: William H. Sullivan, Jr.
Executive Vice President: Charles W. Sullivan
Vice President: Francis J. (Bucko) Kilroy
General Manager: Patrick J. Sullivan
Director of Player Development: Dick Steinberg
Director of Pro Scouting: Bill McPeak
Director of College Scouting: Joe Mendes
Executive Director of Player Personnel: Darryl Stingley
Assistant Treasurer: Jeannette Keefe
Administrating Assistant to the General Manager: Judy Quimby
Business Manager: Phil Lynch
Director of Public Relations: Dave Wintergrass
Director of Promotions: Dave Wintergrass
Director of Ticket Sales: Peter Thompson
Director of Publicity: Jim Greenidge
Public Relations Assistant: Kris Erickson
Cheerleaders Director: Susan Ouellette
Head Coach: Raymond Berry
Assistant Coaches: Tommy Brasher, Cleve Bryant,
  LeBaron Caruthers, Steve Endicott, Lew Erber, Bill Muir,
  Rod Rust, Dante Scarnecchia, Steve Sidwell, Steve Walters
Trainer: Ron O'Neil

Stadium: Sullivan Stadium (Capacity: 61,000)
Playing Surface: Super Turf
Stadium Address: Route 1, Foxboro, Massachusetts 02035
Colours: Red, White and Blue
Summer Training Camp: Bryant College, Smithfield,
  Rhode Island 02917

NEW ENGLAND PATRIOTS 1985 SCHEDULE

PRE-SEASON

Aug.	10	NEW ORLEANS	3:30
Aug.	17	at Kansas City	7:30
Aug.	24	at Washington	8:00
Aug.	31	at Los Angeles Rams	7:00

REGULAR SEASON

Sep.	8	GREEN BAY	1:00
Sep.	15	at Chicago	12:00
Sep.	22	at Buffalo	1:00
Sep.	29	LOS ANGELES RAIDERS	1:00
Oct.	6	at Cleveland	1:00
Oct.	13	BUFFALO	1:00
Oct.	20	NEW YORK JETS	4:00
Oct.	27	at Tampa Bay	1:00
Nov.	3	MIAMI	1:00
Nov.	10	INDIANAPOLIS	1:00
Nov.	17	at Seattle	1:00
Nov.	24	at New York Jets	1:00
Dec.	1	at Indianapolis	1:00
Dec.	8	DETROIT	1:00
Dec.	16	at Miami	9:00
Dec.	22	CINCINNATI	1:00

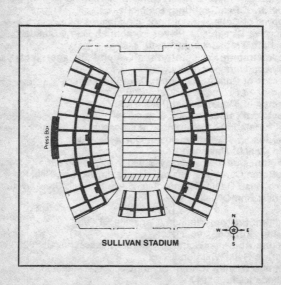

SULLIVAN STADIUM

NEW ENGLAND PATRIOTS
END OF SEASON DEPTH CHART

OFFENSE

WR — 86 Stanley Morgan, 82 Clarence Weathers,
       80 Irving Fryar
OLT — 76 Brian Holloway, 67 Steve Moore
OLG — 73 John Hannah, 75 Guy Morriss, 66 Paul Fairchild
C — 75 Guy Morriss, 58 Pete Brock
ORG — 61 Ron Wooten, 75 Guy Morriss, 66 Paul Fairchild
ORT — 68 Darryl Haley, 67 Steve Moore
TE — 87 Lin Dawson, 88 Derrick Ramsey, 41 Bo Robinson
WR — 81 Stephen Starring, 83 Cedric Jones,
       82 Clarence Weathers
QB — 11 Tony Eason, 14 Steve Grogan, 19 Mike Kerrigan
H-B — 88 Derrick Ramsey, 40 Greg Hawthorne,
       41 Bo Robinson
RB — 32 Craig James, 30 Mosi Tatupu, 33 Anthony Collins,
       24 Robert Weathers

DEFENSE

DLE — 77 Ken Sims, 65 Doug Rogers
NT — 98 Dennis Owens, 70 Luther Henson
DRE — 90 Toby Williams, 85 Julius Adams
LOLB — 56 Andre Tippett, 51 Brian Ingram, 50 Larry McGrew
LILB — 57 Steve Nelson, 52 Johnny Rembert, 59 Tim Golden
RILB — 50 Larry McGrew, 95 Ed Reynolds, 59 Tim Golden
ROLB — 55 Don Blackmon, 51 Brian Ingram, 54 Ed Williams
LCB — 43 Ernest Gibson, 42 Ronnie Lippett, 22 Keith Lee
RCB — 26 Ray Clayborn, 43 Ernest Gibson, 23 Rod McSwain
SS — 38 Roland James, 47 Paul Dombroski
FS — 25 Rick Sanford, 31 Fred Marion, 47 Paul Dombroski

SPECIAL TEAMS

P — 3 Rich Camarillo, 32 Craig James, 47 Paul Dombroski
K — 1 Tony Franklin
H — 11 Tony Eason, 32 Craig James
PR — 80 Irving Fryar, 81 Stephen Starring,
       82 Clarence Weathers
KR — 33 Anthony Collins, 40 Greg Hawthorne,
       83 Cedric Jones
LSN — 75 Guy Morriss, 65 Doug Rogers

ALSO WITH THE NEW ENGLAND PATRIOTS
44 Jon Williams (RB), 48 Darryal Wilson (WR),
72 Lester Williams (NT) 53 Clayton Weishuhn (LB)

NEW ENGLAND PATRIOTS

INDIVIDUAL RUSHERS

	Att	Yards	Avg	Long	TD
James, Craig	160	790	4.9	73	1
Tatupu, Mosi	133	553	4.2	t20	4
Collins, Anthony	138	550	4.0	21	5
Eason, Tony	40	154	3.9	t25	5
Grogan, Steve	7	12	1.7	1	0
Fryar, Irving	2	− 11	− 5.5	0	0
Starring, Stephen	2	− 16	− 8.0	0	0

INDIVIDUAL PASSING

	Att	Comp	Pct Comp	Yds	Avg Gain	TD	Pct TD	Long	Int	Pct Int	Rating Points
Eason, Tony	431	259	60.1	3228	7.49	23	5.3	t76	8	1.9	93.4
Grogan, Steve	68	32	47.1	444	6.53	3	4.4	t65	6	8.8	46.4
Kerrigan, Mike	1	1	100.0	13	13.00	0	0.0	13	0	0.0	118.8

INDIVIDUAL RECEIVERS

	No	Yards	Avg	Long	TD
Ramsey, Derrick	66	792	12.0	34	7
Starring, Stephen	46	657	14.3	t65	4
Dawson, Lin	39	427	10.9	27	4
Morgan, Stanley	38	709	18.7	t76	5
James, Craig	22	159	7.2	16	0
Jones, Cedric	19	244	12.8	22	2
Tatupu, Mosi	16	159	9.9	24	0
Collins, Anthony	16	100	6.3	19	0
Fryar, Irving	11	164	14.9	26	1
Weathers, Clarence	8	115	14.4	29	2
Hawthorne, Greg	7	127	18.1	26	0
Robinson, Bo	4	32	8.0	17	1

INDIVIDUAL INTERCEPTORS

	No	Yards	Avg	Long	TD
Clayborn, Ray	3	102	34.0	85	0
Lippett, Ronnie	3	23	7.7	13	0
Marion, Fred	2	39	19.5	26	0
James, Roland	2	14	7.0	14	0
Gibson, Ernest	2	4	2.0	4	0
Sanford, Rick	2	2	1.0	2	0
Dombroski, Paul	1	23	23.0	23	0
Blackmon, Don	1	3	3.0	3	0
Nelson, Steve	1	0	0.0	0	0

INDIVIDUAL KICKOFF RETURNERS

	No	Yards	Avg	Long	TD
Collins, Anthony	25	544	21.8	46	0
Williams, Jon	23	461	20.0	29	0
Fryar, Irving	5	95	19.0	22	0
Lee, Keith L.	3	43	14.3	17	0
Robinson, Bo	3	38	12.7	14	0
Jones, Cedric	1	20	20.0	20	0
Hawthorne, Greg	1	14	14.0	14	0
Tatupu, Mosi	1	9	9.0	9	0

INDIVIDUAL PUNTERS

	No	Yards	Long	Avg	Total Punts	TB	Blk	Opp Ret	Ret Yds	In 20	Net Avg
Prestridge, Luke	44	1884	89	42.8	44	5	0	21	228	8	35.4
Camarillo, Rich	48	2020	61	42.1	48	7	0	24	214	12	34.7

INDIVIDUAL PUNT RETURNERS

	No	FC	Yards	Avg	Long	TD
Fryar, Irving	36	10	347	9.6	55	0
Starring, Stephen	10	1	73	7.3	16	0
Gibson, Ernest	1	0	3	3.0	3	0
Weathers, Clarence	1	0	7	7.0	7	0
James, Roland	0	2	0	—	0	0
Sanford, Rick	0	2	0	—	0	0

INDIVIDUAL SCORERS

KICKERS

	XP	XPA	FG	FGA	PTS
Franklin, Tony	42	42	22	28	108

NON-KICKERS

	TD	TDR	TDP	TDM	PTS
Ramsey, Derrick	7	0	7	0	42
Collins, Anthony	5	5	0	0	30
Eason, Tony	5	5	0	0	30
Morgan, Stanley	5	0	5	0	30
Dawson, Lin	4	0	4	0	24
Starring, Stephen	4	0	4	0	24
Tatupu, Mosi	4	4	0	0	24
Jones, Cedric	3	0	2	1	18
Weathers, Clarence	2	0	2	0	12
Fryar, Irving	1	0	1	0	6
James, Craig	1	1	0	0	6
Robinson, Bo	1	0	1	0	6
James, Roland	0	0	0	0	2

NEW YORK JETS
AFC Eastern Division

Address: 598 Madison Avenue, New York, N.Y. 10022
Telephone: (212) 421-6600

CLUB OFFICIALS
Chairman of the Board: Leon Hess
President-Chief Operating Officer: Jim Kensil
Secretary and Administrative Manager: Steve Gutman
Director of Public Relations: Frank Ramos
Assistant Director of Public Relations: Ron Cohen
Director of Operations: Tim Davey
Travelling Secretary: Mike Kensil
Ticket Manager: Bob Parente
Head Coach: Joe Walton
Assistant Coaches: Bill Baird, Ralph Baker, Ray Callahan,
  Mike Faulkiner, Joe Gardi, Bobby Hammond, Rich Kotite,
  Larry Pasquale, Jim Ringo
Pro Personnel Director: Jim Royer
Director of Player Personnel: Mike Hickey
Talent Scouts: Joe Collins, Don Grammer, Sid Hall,
  Marv Sunderland
Trainer: Bob Reese
Assistant Trainer: Pepper Burruss
Equipment Manager: Bill Hampton

Stadium: Giants Stadium (Capacity 76,891)
Playing Surface: AstroTurf
Stadium Address: East Rutherford, New Jersey 07073
Colours: Kelly Green and White
Summer Training Camp: 1000 Fulton Avenue, Hempstead,
  N.Y. 11550
Telephone: (516) 538-6600

NEW YORK JETS 1985 SCHEDULE

PRE-SEASON

Aug.	10	PHILADELPHIA	8:00
Aug.	17	at Cincinnati	7:00
Aug.	24	at New York Giants	8:00
Aug.	31	at Green Bay	7:00

REGULAR SEASON

Sep.	8	at Los Angeles Raiders	1:00
Sep.	15	BUFFALO	1:00
Sep.	22	vs. Green Bay at Milwaukee	3:00
Sep.	29	INDIANAPOLIS	4:00
Oct.	6	at Cincinnati	4:00
Oct.	14	MIAMI	9:00
Oct.	20	at New England	4:00
Oct.	27	SEATTLE	1:00
Nov.	3	at Indianapolis	4:00
Nov.	10	at Miami	4:00
Nov.	17	TAMPA BAY	1:00
Nov.	24	NEW ENGLAND	1:00
Nov.	28	at Detroit	12:30
Dec.	8	at Buffalo	1:00
Dec.	14	CHICAGO	12:30
Dec.	22	CLEVELAND	1:00

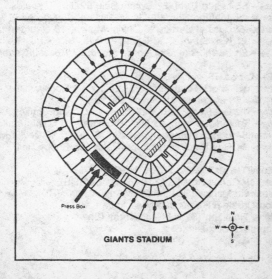

Press Box

GIANTS STADIUM

NEW YORK JETS
END OF SEASON DEPTH CHART

OFFENSE
WR — 85 Wesley Walker, 84 Bobby Humphery, 87 Kurt Sohn
OLT — 68 Reggie McElroy, 53 Jim Sweeney,
       70 Stan Waldemore
OLG — 70 Stan Waldemore, 53 Jim Sweeney,
       68 Reggie McElroy
C   — 65 Joe Fields, 64 Guy Bingham, 53 Jim Sweeney
ORG — 60 Dan Alexander, 63 Ted Banker, 53 Jim Sweeney
ORT — 79 Marvin Powell, 53 Jim Sweeney, 63 Ted Banker
TE — 82 Mickey Shuler, 86 Glenn Dennison, 89 Rocky Klever
WR — 80 Johnny Jones, 88 Chy Davidson, 83 Nick Bruckner
QB — 7 Ken O'Brien, 10 Pat Ryan, 17 Bob Avellini
RB — 34 Johnny Hector, 25 Cedric Minter
RB — 49 Tony Paige, 25 Cedric Minter, 31 Marion Barber

DEFENSE
DLE — 99 Mark Gastineau, 74 Ron Faurot, 76 Ben Rudolph
DLT — 78 Barry Bennett, 95 Tom Baldwin, 73 Joe Klecko
DRT — 93 Marty Lyons, 95 Tom Baldwin, 78 Barry Bennett
DRE — 73 Joe Klecko, 74 Ron Faurot, 76 Ben Rudolph
LLB — 51 Greg Buttle, 94 Rusty Guilbeau, 56 Lance Mehl
MLB — 59 Kyle Clifton, 57 John Woodring, 94 Rusty Guilbeau
RLB — 56 Lance Mehl, 58 Bobby Bell, 52 Jim Eliopulos
LCB — 29 Johnny Lynn, 20 Davlin Mullen, 38 George Floyd
RCB — 27 Russell Carter, 20 Davlin Mullen, 38 George Floyd
SS — 21 Kirk Springs, 38 George Floyd, 22 Mike Dennis
FS — 28 Darrol Ray, 38 George Floyd, 27 Russell Carter

SPECIAL TEAMS
P   — 15 Chuck Ramsey, 5 Pat Leahy, 89 Rocky Klever
K   — 5 Pat Leahy, 15 Chuck Ramsey
H   — 10 Pat Ryan, 7 Ken O'Brien, 15 Chuck Ramsey
PR — 21 Kirk Springs, 83 Nick Bruckner, 20 Davlin Mullen
KR — 84 Bobby Humphery, 21 Kirk Springs, 20 Davlin Mullen
LSN — 64 Guy Bingham, 65 Joe Fields, 58 Bobby Bell

ALSO WITH THE NEW YORK JETS
81 Derrick Gaffney (WR), 42 Bruce Harper (RB),
24 Freeman McNeil (RB), 35 Mike Augustyniak (RB),
50 Bob Crable (LB), 40 Bobby Jackson (CB),
39 Harry Hamilton (S), 48 Ken Schroy (S),
46 Fernanza Burgess (S)

NEW YORK JETS

INDIVIDUAL RUSHERS

	Att	Yards	Avg	Long	TD
McNeil, Freeman	229	1070	4.7	53	5
Hector, Johnny	124	531	4.3	64	1
Barber, Marion	31	148	4.8	18	2
Minter, Cedric	34	136	4.0	14	1
Paige, Tony	35	130	3.7	24	7
Ryan, Pat	23	92	4.0	16	0
Harper, Bruce	10	48	4.8	16	1
O'Brien, Ken	16	29	1.8	7	0
Dennison, Glenn	1	4	4.0	4	0
Walker, Wesley	1	1	1.0	1	0
Avellini, Bob, Chi.-Jets	3	−5	−1.7	0	0

INDIVIDUAL PASSING

	Att	Comp	Pct Comp	Yds	Avg Gain	TD	Pct TD	Long	Int	Pct Int	Rating Points
Ryan, Pat	285	156	54.7	1939	6.80	14	4.9	t44	14	4.9	72.0
O'Brien, Ken	203	116	57.1	1402	6.91	6	3.0	49	7	3.4	74.0
Avellini, Bob, Chi.-Jets	53	30	56.6	288	5.43	0	0.0	50	3	5.7	48.4

INDIVIDUAL RECEIVERS

	No	Yards	Avg	Long	TD
Shuler, Mickey	68	782	11.5	49	6
Walker, Wesley	41	623	15.2	t44	7
Jones, Lam	32	470	14.7	37	1
McNeil, Freeman	25	294	11.8	32	1
Hector, Johnny	20	182	9.1	26	0
Gaffney, Derrick	19	285	15.0	29	0
Dennison, Glenn	16	141	8.8	20	1
Humphery, Bobby	14	206	14.7	t44	1
Minter, Cedric	10	109	10.9	t39	1
Barber, Marion	10	79	7.9	17	0
Paige, Tony	6	31	5.2	10	1
Harper, Bruce	5	71	14.2	28	0
Klever, Rocky	3	29	9.7	13	1
Sohn, Kurt	2	28	14.0	16	0

INDIVIDUAL INTERCEPTORS

	No	Yards	Avg	Long	TD
Carter, Russell	4	26	6.5	19	0
Ray, Darrol	2	54	27.0	28	0
Lynn, Johnny	2	16	8.0	16	0
Schroy, Ken	2	13	6.5	13	0
Buttle, Greg	2	5	2.5	5	0
Mullen, Davlin	1	25	25.0	25	0
Springs, Kirk	1	13	13.0	13	0

	No	Yards	Avg	Long	TD
Bruckner, Nick...............................	1	11	11.0	11	0

INDIVIDUAL KICKOFF RETURNERS

	No	Yards	Avg	Long	TD
Humphery, Bobby............................	22	675	30.7	t97	1
Springs, Kirk..................................	23	521	22.7	73	0
Minter, Cedric.................................	10	224	22.4	52	0
Paige, Tony....................................	3	7	2.3	7	0
Mullen, Davlin	2	34	17.0	23	0
Bruckner, Nick................................	1	17	17.0	17	0
Davidson, Chy	1	9	9.0	9	0
Gaffney, Derrick	1	6	6.0	6	0
Banker, Ted	1	5	5.0	5	0
Shuler, Mickey...............................	1	0	0.0	0	0

INDIVIDUAL PUNTERS

	No	Yards	Long	Avg	Total Punts	TB	Blk	Opp Ret	Ret Yds	In 20	Net Avg
Ramsey, Chuck.............	74	2935	64	39.7	75	8	1	37	242	19	33.8

INDIVIDUAL PUNT RETURNERS

	No	FC	Yards	Avg	Long	TD
Springs, Kirk.................................	28	10	247	8.8	33	0
Minter, Cedric	4	2	44	11.0	18	0
Bruckner, Nick...............................	2	0	25	12.5	20	0
Mullen, Davlin...............................	1	0	8	8.0	8	0

INDIVIDUAL SCORERS

KICKERS	XP	XPA	FG	FGA	PTS
Leahy, Pat	38	39	17	24	89

NON-KICKERS	TD	TDR	TDP	TDM	PTS
Paige, Tony	8	7	1	0	48
Walker, Wesley........................	7	0	7	0	42
McNeil, Freeman	6	5	1	0	36
Shuler, Mickey.........................	6	0	6	0	36
Barber, Marion.........................	2	2	0	0	12
Humphery, Bobby.....................	2	0	1	1	12
Minter, Cedric	2	1	1	0	12
Buttle, Greg.............................	1	0	0	1	6
Dennison, Glenn	1	0	1	0	6
Gastineau, Mark	1	0	0	1	6
Harper, Bruce	1	1	0	0	6
Hector, Johnny	1	1	0	0	6
Jones, Lam	1	0	1	0	6
Klever, Rocky...........................	1	0	1	0	6
Ryan, Pat.................................	0	0	0	0	1

PITTSBURGH STEELERS
AFC Central Division

Address: Three Rivers Stadium, 300 Stadium Circle, Pittsburgh,
Pennsylvania 15212
Telephone: (412) 323-1200

CLUB OFFICIALS
Chairman of the Board: Arthur J. Rooney, Sr.
President: Daniel M. Rooney
Vice President: John R. McGinley
Vice President: Arthur J. Rooney, Jr.
Head Coach: Chuck Noll
Assistant Coaches: Ron Blackledge, Tony Dungy,
Dennis Fitzgerald, Dick Hoak, Jed Hughes, Jon Kolb,
Bill Meyers, Tom Moore.
Traveling Secretary: Jim Boston
Controller: Dennis P. Thimons
Publicity Director: Joe Gordon
Assistant Publicity Director: John Evenson
Director of Player Personnel: Dick Haley
Assistant Director of Player Personnel: William Nunn. Jr.
Pro Talent Scout: Tom Modrak
Talent Scout-West Coast: Bob Schmitz
Director of Ticket Sales: Geraldine R. Glenn
Trainer: Ralph Berlin
Equipment Manager: Anthony Parisi

Stadium: Three Rivers Stadium (Capacity 59,000)
Playing Surface: AstroTurf
Stadium Address: 300 Stadium Circle, Pittsburgh,
Pennsylvania 15212
Colours: Gold and Black
Summer Training Camp: St. Vincent College, Latrobe,
Pennsylvania 15650

PITTSBURGH STEELERS 1985 SCHEDULE

PRE-SEASON

Aug.	10	at Tampa Bay	8:00
Aug.	17	at Minnesota	7:00
Aug.	24	at St. Louis	7:30
Aug.	30	NEW YORK GIANTS	7:30

REGULAR SEASON

Sep.	8	INDIANAPOLIS	1:00
Sep.	16	at Cleveland	9:00
Sep.	22	HOUSTON	1:00
Sep.	30	CINCINNATI	9:00
Oct.	6	at Miami	1:00
Oct.	13	at Dallas	12:00
Oct.	20	ST. LOUIS	1:00
Oct.	27	at Cincinnati	4:00
Nov.	3	CLEVELAND	1:00
Nov.	10	at Kansas City	12:00
Nov.	17	at Houston	12:00
Nov.	24	WASHINGTON	1:00
Dec.	1	DENVER	1:00
Dec.	8	at San Diego	6:00
Dec.	15	BUFFALO	1:00
Dec.	21	at New York Giants	12:30

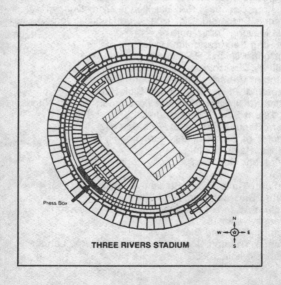

THREE RIVERS STADIUM

PITTSBURGH STEELERS
END OF SEASON DEPTH CHART

OFFENSE
WR   — 82 John Stallworth, 80 Wayne Capers,
            85 Calvin Sweeney
OLT   — 63 Pete Rostosky
OLG   — 73 Craig Wolfley, 61 Blake Wingle
C   — 52 Mike Webster, 60 Randy Rasmussen
ORG   — 61 Blake Wingle, 74 Terry Long, 60 Randy Rusmussen
ORT   — 62 Tunch Ilkin, 77 Steve August
TE   — 89 Bennie Cunningham, 81 Darrell Nelson
WR   — 83 Louis Lipps, 87 Weegie Thompson,
            80 Wayne Capers
QB   — 16 Mark Malone, 19 David Woodley, 10 Scott Campbell
RB   — 34 Walter Abercrombie, 24 Rich Erenberg,
            26 Fernadars Gillespie
RB   — 30 Frank Pollard, 38 Elton Veals, 40 Anthony Corley

DEFENSE
DLE   — 95 John Goodman, 64 Edmund Nelson, 93 Keith Willis
NT   — 67 Gary Dunn, 64 Edmund Nelson
DRE   — 92 Keith Gary, 64 Edmund Nelson, 78 Mark Catano
LOLB   — 57 Mike Merriweather, 59 Todd Seabaugh
LILB   — 58 Jack Lambert, 50 David Little, 90 Bob Kohrs
RILB   — 56 Robin Cole, 50 David Little, 90 Bob Kohrs
ROLB   — 53 Bryan Hinkle, 54 Craig Bingham, 59 Todd Seabaugh
LCB   — 49 Dwayne Woodruff, 23 Chris Brown, 21 Eric Williams
RCB   — 41 Sam Washington, 23 Chris Brown, 33 Harvey Clayton
SS   — 31 Donnie Shell, 29 Ron Johnson
FS   — 21 Eric Williams, 22 Rick Woods

SPECIAL TEAMS
P   — 5 Craig Colquitt
K   — 1 Gary Anderson
H   — 5 Craig Colquitt, 10 Scott Campbell
PR   — 83 Louis Lipps, 22 Rick Woods, 24 Rich Erenberg
KR   — 24 Rich Erenberg, 83 Louis Lipps,
            26 Fernadars Gillespie
LSN   — 52 Mike Webster, 60 Randy Rasmussen

ALSO WITH THE PITTSBURGH STEELERS
36 Todd Spencer (RB), 79 Larry Brown (T),
88 John Rodgers (TE), 84 Chris Kolodziejski (TE),
71 Emil Boures (G), 72 Ray Snell (T)

PITTSBURGH STEELERS

INDIVIDUAL RUSHERS

	Att	Yards	Avg	Long	TD
Pollard, Frank	213	851	4.0	52	6
Abercrombie, Walter	145	610	4.2	31	1
Erenberg, Rich	115	405	3.5	t31	2
Corley, Anthony	18	89	4.9	23	0
Veals, Elton	31	87	2.8	9	0
Lipps, Louis	3	71	23.7	t36	1
Malone, Mark	25	42	1.7	t13	3
Gillespie, Fernandars	7	18	2.6	9	0
Woodley, David	11	14	1.3	7	0
Colquitt, Craig	1	0	0.0	0	0
Spencer, Todd	1	0	0.0	0	0
Capers, Wayne	1	−3	−3.0	−3	0
Campbell, Scott	3	−5	−1.7	0	0

INDIVIDUAL PASSING

	Att	Comp	Pct Comp	Yds	Avg Gain	TD	Pct TD	Long	Int	Pct Int	Rating Points
Malone, Mark	272	147	54.0	2137	7.86	16	5.9	t61	17	6.3	73.4
Woodley, David	156	85	54.5	1273	8.16	8	5.1	t80	7	4.5	79.9
Campbell, Scott	15	8	53.3	109	7.27	1	6.7	t25	1	6.7	71.3

INDIVIDUAL RECEIVERS

	No	Yards	Avg	Long	TD
Stallworth, John	80	1395	17.4	51	11
Lipps, Louis	45	860	19.1	t80	9
Erenberg, Rich	38	358	9.4	25	1
Pollard, Frank	21	186	8.9	18	0
Thompson, Weegie	17	291	17.1	59	3
Abercrombie, Walter	16	135	8.4	59	0
Capers, Wayne	7	81	11.6	19	0
Kolodziejski, Chris	5	59	11.8	22	0
Cunningham, Bennie	4	64	16.0	29	1
Nelson, Darrell	2	31	15.5	19	0
Sweeney, Calvin	2	25	12.5	16	0
Gillespie, Fernandars	1	12	12.0	12	0

INDIVIDUAL INTERCEPTORS

	No	Yards	Avg	Long	TD
Shell, Donnie	7	61	8.7	t52	1
Washington, Sam	6	138	23.0	t69	2
Woodruff, Dwayne	5	56	11.2	t42	1
Hinkle, Bryan	3	77	25.7	43	0

	No	Yards	Avg	Long	TD
Williams, Eric	3	49	16.3	44	0
Merriweather, Mike	2	9	4.5	8	0
Woods, Rick	2	0	0.0	0	0
Brown, Chris	1	31	31.0	31	0
Cole, Robin	1	12	12.0	12	0
Clayton, Harvey	1	0	0.0	0	0

INDIVIDUAL KICKOFF RETURNERS

	No	Yards	Avg	Long	TD
Erenberg, Rich	28	575	20.5	47	0
Spencer, Todd	18	373	20.7	40	0
Veals, Elton	4	40	10.0	18	0
Corley, Anthony	1	15	15.0	15	0
Gillespie, Fernandars	1	12	12.0	12	0
Brown, Chris	1	11	11.0	11	0
Catano, Mark	1	0	0.0	0	0

INDIVIDUAL PUNTERS

	No	Yards	Long	Avg	Total Punts	TB	Blk	Opp Ret	Ret Yds	In 20	Net Avg
Colquitt, Craig	70	2883	62	41.2	70	5	0	37	351	21	34.7

INDIVIDUAL PUNT RETURNERS

	No	FC	Yards	Avg	Long	TD
Lipps, Louis	53	2	656	12.4	t76	1
Woods, Rick	6	0	40	6.7	14	0
Clayton, Harvey	1	0	0	0.0	0	0
Long, Terry	1	0	0	0.0	0	0

INDIVIDUAL SCORERS
KICKERS

	XP	XPA	FG	FGA	PTS
Anderson, Gary	45	45	24	32	117

NON-KICKERS	TD	TDR	TDP	TDM	PTS
Lipps, Louis	11	1	9	1	66
Stallworth, John	11	0	11	0	66
Pollard, Frank	6	6	0	0	36
Erenberg, Rich	3	2	1	0	18
Malone, Mark	3	3	0	0	18
Thompson, Weegie	3	0	3	0	18
Washington, Sam	2	0	0	2	12
Woodruff, Dwayne	2	0	0	2	12
Abercrombie, Walter	1	1	0	0	6
Cunningham, Bennie	1	0	1	0	6
Hinkle, Bryan	1	0	0	1	6
Shell, Donnie	1	0	0	1	6

SAN DIEGO CHARGERS
AFC Western Division

Address: San Diego Jack Murphy Stadium, PO Box 20666,
San Diego, California 92120
Telephone: (619) 280-2111

CLUB OFFICIALS
Chairman of the Board/President: Alex G. Spanos
General Manager: John R. Sanders
Assistant General Manager: Paul (Tank) Younger
Assistant to the President: Jack Teele
Head Coach: Don Coryell
Assistant Coaches: Tom Bass, Marv Braden, Earnel Durden,
Dave Levy, Al Saunders, Doug Shively, Jim Wagstaff,
Chuck Weber, Ernie Zampese
Administrative Assistant, Player Personnel: John Trump
Chief Scout: Aubrey (Red) Phillips
Director of Public Relations: Rick Smith
Business Manager: Pat Curran
Director of Marketing: Rich Israel
Assistant Director of Public Relations: Bill Johnston
Director of Ticket Operations: Joe Scott
Controller: Frances Beede
Trainer: Ric McDonald
Equipment Manager: Sid Brooks

Stadium: San Diego Jack Murphy Stadium (Capacity 60,100)
Playing Surface: Grass
Stadium Address: 9449 Friars Road, San Diego, California 92108
Colours: Royal Blue, Gold and White
Summer Training Camp: University of California-San Diego,
La Jolla, California 92037

SAN DIEGO CHARGERS 1985 SCHEDULE

PRE-SEASON

Aug.	10	CLEVELAND	6:00
Aug.	17	DALLAS	6:00
Aug.	24	at San Francisco	12:00
Aug.	30	NEW ORLEANS	7:00

REGULAR SEASON

Sep.	8	at Buffalo	4:00
Sep.	15	SEATTLE	1:00
Sep.	22	at Cincinnati	1:00
Sep.	29	CLEVELAND	1:00
Oct.	6	at Seattle	1:00
Oct.	13	KANSAS CITY	1:00
Oct.	20	at Minnesota	12:00
Oct.	28	at Los Angeles Raiders	6:00
Nov.	3	DENVER	1:00
Nov.	10	LOS ANGELES RAIDERS	1:00
Nov.	17	at Denver	2:00
Nov.	24	at Houston	12:00
Dec.	1	BUFFALO	1:00
Dec.	8	PITTSBURGH	6:00
Dec.	15	PHILADELPHIA	1:00
Dec.	22	at Kansas City	12:00

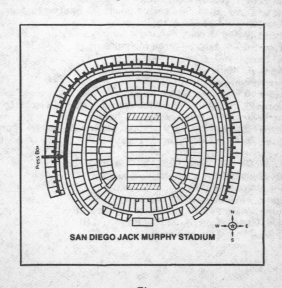

SAN DIEGO JACK MURPHY STADIUM

SAN DIEGO CHARGERS
END OF SEASON DEPTH CHART

OFFENSE

WR	—	18 Charlie Joiner, 86 Jesse Bendross
OLT	—	77 Sam Claphan, 64 Chuck Loewen
OLG	—	63 Doug Wilkerson, 69 Derrel Gofourth
C	—	62 Don Macek, 75 Andy Gissinger
ORG	—	60 Dennis McKnight, 69 Derrel Gofourth
ORT	—	67 Ed White, 75 Andy Gissinger
TE	—	85 Eric Sievers, 84 Ron Egloff
TE	—	88 Pete Holohan, 80 Bobby Micho
WR	—	89 Wes Chandler, 82 Bobby Duckworth
QB	—	14 Dan Fouts, 11 Ed Luther, 12 Bruce Mathison
RB	—	41 Earnest Jackson, 21 Buford McGee, 25 Wayne Morris, 26 Lionel James, 32 Jewerl Thomas

DEFENSE

DLE	—	78 Chuck Ehin, 99 Lee Williams
NT	—	68 Bill Elko, 73 Keith Guthrie
DRE	—	76 Keith Ferguson, 90 Fred Robinson
LOLB	—	57 Linden King, 55 Derrie Nelson
LILB	—	58 Mike Green, 59 Cliff Thrift
RILB	—	54 Billy Ray Smith, 56 Vince Osby
ROLB	—	51 Woodrow Lowe, 92 Eric Williams
LCB	—	22 Gill Byrd, 33 Lucious Smith, 20 Reuben Henderson
RCB	—	31 Bill Kay, 27 John Turner
SS	—	28 Ken Greene, 49 Andre Young
FS	—	48 Tim Fox, 24 Miles McPherson

SPECIAL TEAMS

P	—	7 Maury Buford
K	—	6 Rolf Benirschke, 85 Eric Sievers
H	—	11 Ed Luther, 12 Bruce Mathison, 88 Pete Holohan
PR	—	26 Lionel James, 89 Wes Chandler
KR	—	26 Lionel James, 21 Buford McGee, 32 Jewerl Thomas
LSN	—	75 Andy Gissinger, 60 Dennis McKnight, 62 Don Macek

ALSO WITH THE SAN DIEGO CHARGERS
Chuck Muncie (RB), Sherman Smith (RB),
80 Kellen Winslow (TE), Abdul Salaam (NT),
23 Danny Walters (CB), 43 Bob Gregor (S),
Johnny Ray Smith (CB), 50 Carlos Bradley (LB),
53 Mike Guendling (LB), 52 Ray Preston (LB)

SAN DIEGO CHARGERS

INDIVIDUAL RUSHERS

	Att	Yards	Avg	Long	TD
Jackson, Earnest	296	1179	4.0	t32	8
McGee, Buford	67	226	3.4	30	4
James, Lionel	25	115	4.6	20	0
Muncie, Chuck	14	51	3.6	11	0
Thomas, Jewerl	14	43	3.1	9	2
Morris, Wayne	5	12	2.4	5	1
Luther, Ed	4	11	2.8	7	0
Fouts, Dan	12	−29	−2.4	3	0

INDIVIDUAL PASSING

	Att	Comp	Pct Comp	Yds	Avg Gain	TD	Pct TD	Long	Int	Pct Int	Rating Points
Fouts, Dan	507	317	62.5	3740	7.38	19	3.7	t61	17	3.4	83.4
Luther, Ed	151	83	55.0	1163	7.70	5	3.3	t88	3	2.0	82.7
Holohan, Pete	2	1	50.0	25	12.50	1	50.0	t25	0	0.0	135.4
James, Lionel	2	0	0.0	0	0.00	0	0.0	0	1	50.0	0.0

INDIVIDUAL RECEIVERS

	No	Yards	Avg	Long	TD
Joiner, Charlie	61	793	13.0	41	6
Holohan, Pete	56	734	13.1	51	1
Winslow, Kellen	55	663	12.1	33	2
Chandler, Wes	52	708	13.6	t63	6
Sievers, Eric	41	438	10.7	32	3
Jackson, Earnest	39	222	5.7	21	1
Duckworth, Bobby	25	715	28.6	t88	4
James, Lionel	23	206	9.0	31	0
Bendross, Jesse	16	213	13.3	29	0
Egloff, Ron	11	92	8.4	17	0
McGee, Buford	9	76	8.4	43	2
Morris, Wayne	5	20	4.0	9	0
Muncie, Chuck	4	38	9.5	20	0
Johnson, Pete	2	7	3.5	7	0
Gissinger, Andy	1	3	3.0	3	0
Fouts, Dan	1	0	0.0	0	0

INDIVIDUAL INTERCEPTORS

	No	Yards	Avg	Long	TD
Byrd, Gill	4	157	39.3	t99	2
Lowe, Woodrow	3	61	20.3	t32	1
Smith, Billy Ray	3	41	13.7	21	0
King, Linden	2	52	26.0	37	0
Turner, John	2	43	21.5	43	0
Young, Andre	2	31	15.5	31	0
Williams, Lee	1	66	66.0	t66	1
Fox, Tim	1	36	36.0	36	0

	No	Yards	Avg	Long	TD
Gregor, Bob	1	12	12.0	12	0

INDIVIDUAL KICKOFF RETURNERS

	No	Yards	Avg	Long	TD
James, Lionel	43	959	22.3	55	0
McGee, Buford	14	315	22.5	35	0
Bird, Steve, St. L.-S.D.	11	205	18.6	28	0
Egloff, Ron	2	20	10.0	11	0
Jackson, Earnest	1	10	10.0	10	0
Gofourth, Derrel...............................	1	0	0.0	0	0

INDIVIDUAL PUNTERS

	No	Yards	Long	Avg	Total Punts	TB	Blk	Opp Ret	Ret Yds	In 20	Net Avg
Buford, Maury	66	2773	60	42.0	66	3	0	43	399	11	35.1

INDIVIDUAL PUNT RETURNERS

	No	FC	Yards	Avg	Long	TD
James, Lionel	30	9	208	6.9	t58	1
Bird, Steve, St.L.-S.D................	6	0	60	10.0	17	0
Henderson, Reuben	1	2	0	0.0	0	0
Smith, Lucious, Buff.-S.D...........	1	0	0	0.0	0	0
Chandler, Wes............................	0	1	0	—	0	0

INDIVIDUAL SCORERS

KICKERS	XP	XPA	FG	FGA	PTS
Benirschke, Rolf	41	41	17	26	92
Ricardo, Benny	5	6	3	3	14

NON-KICKERS	TD	TDR	TDP	TDM	PTS
Jackson, Earnest	9	8	1	0	54
Chandler, Wes	6	0	6	0	36
Joiner, Charlie	6	0	6	0	36
McGee, Buford	6	4	2	0	36
Duckworth, Bobby..................	4	0	4	0	24
Sievers, Eric	3	0	3	0	18
Byrd, Gill	2	0	0	2	12
Thomas, Jewerl	2	2	0	0	12
Winslow, Kellen	2	0	2	0	12
Holohan, Pete.........................	1	0	1	0	6
James, Lionel	1	0	0	1	6
Lowe, Woodrow	1	0	0	1	6
Morris, Wayne.........................	1	1	0	0	6
Williams, Lee	1	0	0	1	6

SEATTLE SEAHAWKS
AFC Western Division

Address: 5305 Lake Washington Blvd., Kirkland,
  Washington 98033
Telephone: (206) 827-9777

CLUB OFFICIALS
President/General Manager: Mike McCormack
Assistant General Manager: Chuck Allen
Business Manager: Mickey Loomis
Assistant Business Manager: Lynda Sides
Public Relations Director: Gary Wright
Assistant Public Relations Director: Dave Neubert
Head Coach: Chuck Knox
Assistant Coaches: Tom Catlin, George Dyer, Chick Harris,
  Ralph Hawkins, Ken Meyer, Steve Moore, Ray Prochaska,
  Rusty Tillman, Joe Vitt
Director of Player Personnel: Mike Allman
Ticket Manager: James Nagaoka
Trainer: Jim Whitesel
Equipment Manager: Walt Loeffler

Stadium: Kingdome (Capacity 64,984)
Playing Surface: AstroTurf
Stadium Address: 201 South King Street, Seattle,
  Washington 98104
Colours: Blue, Green and Silver
Summer Training Camp: Eastern Washington University,
  Cheney, Washington 99004

SEATTLE SEAHAWKS 1985 SCHEDULE

PRE-SEASON

Aug.	10	at Indianapolis	7:30
Aug.	17	DETROIT	7:30
Aug.	24	at Minnesota	7:00
Aug.	30	SAN FRANCISCO	6:00

REGULAR SEASON

Sep.	8	at Cincinnati	1:00
Sep.	15	at San Diego	1:00
Sep.	23	LOS ANGELES RAMS	6:00
Sep.	29	at Kansas City	12:00
Oct.	6	SAN DIEGO	1:00
Oct.	13	ATLANTA	1:00
Oct.	20	at Denver	2:00
Oct.	27	at New York Jets	1:00
Nov.	3	LOS ANGELES RAIDERS	1:00
Nov.	10	at New Orleans	12:00
Nov.	17	NEW ENGLAND	1:00
Nov.	25	at San Francisco	6:00
Dec.	1	KANSAS CITY	1:00
Dec.	8	CLEVELAND	1:00
Dec.	15	at Los Angeles Raiders	1:00
Dec.	20	DENVER	5:00

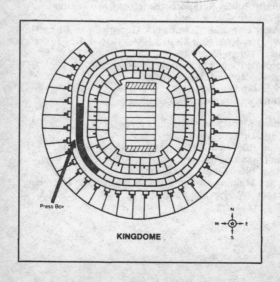

Press Box

KINGDOME

N W R E S

SEATTLE SEAHAWKS
END OF SEASON DEPTH CHART

OFFENSE
WR   — 81 Daryl Turner, 83 Chris Castor, 82 Paul Skansi
OLT   — 64 Ron Essink, 69 Sid Abramowitz
OLG   — 67 Reggie McKenzie, 75 Adam Schreiber
C   — 59 Blair Bush, 62 Kani Kauahi
ORG   — 61 Bob Pratt, 75 Adam Schreiber
ORT   — 78 Bob Cryder, 71 Bryan Millard
TE   — 87 Charle Young, 86 Mike Tice, 88 Pete Metzelaars
WR   — 80 Steve Largent, 89 Byron Walker
QB   — 17 Dave Krieg, 10 Jim Zorn
RB   — 33 Dan Doornink, 43 Randall Morris, 37 Eric Lane,
            31 Zachary Dixon
RB   — 46 David Hughes, 32 Cullen Bryant

DEFENSE
DLE   — 79 Jacob Green, 74 Mike Fanning
NT   — 72 Joe Nash, 73 Dino Mangiero
DRE   — 77 Jeff Bryant, 68 Randy Edwards
LOLB — 58 Bruce Scholtz, 60 John Kaiser
LILB — 57 Shelton Robinson, 60 John Kaiser
RILB — 53 Keith Butler, 51 Sam Merriman
ROLB — 55 Michael Jackson, 56 Greg Gaines, 50 Fredd Young
LCB   — 42 Keith Simpson, 20 Terry Taylor
RCB   — 22 Dave Brown, 24 Terry Jackson
SS   — 45 Kenny Easley, 35 Don Dufek
FS   — 44 John Harris, 21 Paul Moyer

SPECIAL TEAMS
P   — 8 Jeff West
K   — 9 Norm Johnson
H   — 10 Jim Zorn, 80 Steve Largent
PR   — 45 Kenny Easley, 82 Paul Skansi
KR   — 31 Zachary Dixon, 43 Randall Morris
LSN — 62 Kani Kauahi, 59 Blair Bush

ALSO WITH THE SEATTLE SEAHAWKS
28 Curt Warner (RB), 85 Paul Johns (WR),
84 Dwight Scales (WR), 65 Edwin Bailey (G),
54 Eugene Williams (LB), 96 Chuck Butler (LB),
63 Mark Hicks (LB), 52 Joe Norman (LB)

SEATTLE SEAHAWKS

INDIVIDUAL RUSHERS

	Att	Yards	Avg	Long	TD
Hughes, David	94	327	3.5	14	1
Lane, Eric	80	299	3.7	t40	4
Doornink, Dan	57	215	3.8	25	0
Morris, Randall	58	189	3.3	16	0
Krieg, Dave	46	186	4.0	t37	3
Harris, Franco	68	170	2.5	16	0
Dixon, Zachary	52	149	2.9	17	2
Bryant, Cullen	20	58	2.9	8	0
Warner, Curt	10	40	4.0	9	0
Largent, Steve	2	10	5.0	6	0
Young, Charle	1	5	5.0	5	0
Zorn, Jim	7	−3	−0.4	7	0

INDIVIDUAL PASSING

QUALIFIERS	Att	Comp	Pct Comp	Yds	Avg Gain	TD	Pct TD	Long	Int	Pct Int	Rating Points
Krieg, Dave	480	276	57.5	3671	7.65	32	6.7	t80	24	5.0	83.3
Zorn, Jim	17	7	41.2	80	4.71	0	0.0	21	2	11.8	16.4
Morris, Randall	0	0	—	0	—	0	—	0	0	—	0.0

INDIVIDUAL RECEIVERS

	No	Yards	Avg	Long	TD
Largent, Steve	74	1164	15.7	65	12
Turner, Daryl	35	715	20.4	t80	10
Young, Charle	33	337	10.2	31	1
Doornink, Dan	31	365	11.8	32	2
Hughes, David	22	121	5.5	25	1
Johns, Paul	17	207	12.2	32	1
Walker, Byron	13	236	18.2	41	1
Lane, Eric	11	101	9.2	t55	1
Morris, Randall	9	61	6.8	18	0
Tice, Mike	8	90	11.3	30	3
Castor, Chris	8	89	11.1	21	0
Skansi, Paul	7	85	12.1	27	0
Metzelaars, Pete	5	80	16.0	25	0
Bryant, Cullen	3	20	6.7	11	0
Scales, Dwight	2	22	11.0	11	0
Dixon, Zachary	2	6	3.0	6	0
Pratt, Bob	1	30	30.0	30	0
Warner, Curt	1	19	19.0	19	0
Harris, Franco	1	3	3.0	3	0

INDIVIDUAL INTERCEPTORS

	No	Yards	Avg	Long	TD
Easley, Ken	10	126	12.6	t58	2
Brown, Dave	8	179	22.4	t90	2

	No	Yards	Avg	Long	TD
Harris, John	6	79	13.2	29	0
Simpson, Keith	4	138	34.5	t76	2
Jackson, Terry	4	78	19.5	t62	1
Taylor, Terry	3	63	21.0	37	0
Gaines, Greg	1	18	18.0	18	0
Scholtz, Bruce	1	15	15.0	15	0
Bryant, Jeff	1	1	1.0	1	0

INDIVIDUAL KICKOFF RETURNERS

	No	Yards	Avg	Long	TD
Dixon, Zachary	25	446	17.8	36	0
Hughes, David	17	348	20.5	38	0
Morris, Randall	8	153	19.1	34	0
Bryant, Cullen	3	53	17.7	21	0
Harris, John	1	7	7.0	7	0

INDIVIDUAL PUNTERS

	No	Yards	Long	Avg	Total Punts	TB	Blk	Opp Ret	Ret Yds	In 20	Net Avg
West, Jeff	95	3567	60	37.5	95	10	0	32	205	24	33.3

INDIVIDUAL PUNT RETURNERS

	No	FC	Yards	Avg	Long	TD
Skansi, Paul	16	2	145	9.1	16	0
Easley, Ken	16	5	194	12.1	42	0
Johns, Paul	11	4	140	12.7	t47	1
Dixon, Zachary	1	0	5	5.0	5	0

INDIVIDUAL SCORERS

KICKERS

	XP	XPA	FG	FGA	PTS
Johnson, Norm	50	51	20	24	110

NON-KICKERS

	TD	TDR	TDP	TDM	PTS
Largent, Steve	12	0	12	0	72
Turner, Daryl	10	0	10	0	60
Lane, Eric	5	4	1	0	30
Krieg, Dave	3	3	0	0	18
Tice, Mike	3	0	3	0	18
Brown, Dave	2	0	0	2	12
Dixon, Zachary	2	2	0	0	12
Doornink, Dan	2	0	2	0	12
Easley, Ken	2	0	0	2	12
Hughes, David	2	1	1	0	12
Johns, Paul	2	0	1	1	12
Simpson, Keith	2	0	0	2	12
Jackson, Terry	1	0	0	1	6
Nash, Joe	1	0	0	1	6
Walker, Byron	1	0	1	0	6
Young, Charle	1	0	1	0	6
Bryant, Jeff	0	0	0	0	2

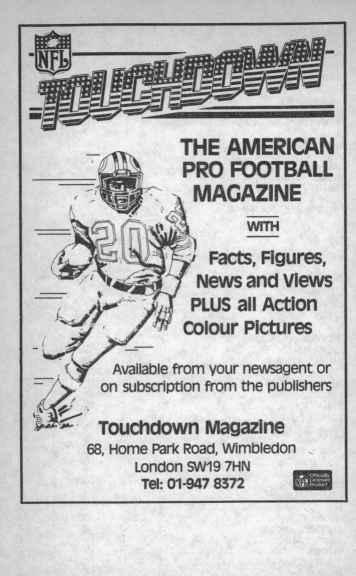

NATIONAL FOOTBALL CONFERENCE

Atlanta Falcons
Chicago Bears
Dallas Cowboys
Detroit Lions
Green Bay Packers
Los Angeles Rams
Minnesota Vikings
New Orleans Saints
New York Giants
Philadelphia Eagles
St. Louis Cardinals
San Francisco 49ers
Tampa Bay Buccaneers
Washington Redskins

ATLANTA FALCONS
NFC Western Division

Address: Suwanee Road at 1-85, Suwanee, Georgia 30174
Telephone: (404) 588-1111

CLUB OFFICIALS
Chairman of the Board: Rankin M. Smith, Sr.
President: Rankin Smith, Jr.
Executive Vice President: Eddie LeBaron
General Manager: Tom Braatz
Corporate Secretary: Taylor Smith
Chief Financial Officer: Jim Hay
Head Coach: Dan Henning
Assistant Coaches: Steve Crosby, George Dostal, Sam Elliott,
  Ted Fritsch, Bob Fry, Bob Harrison, Bobby Jackson,
  John Marshall, Garry Puetz, Dan Sekanovich, Jack Stanton
Director of Pro Personnel: Bill Jobko
Ticket Manager: Ken Grantham
Public Relations Director: Charlie Dayton
Assistant Director of Public Relations: Bob Dickinson
Assistant Director of Community Affairs: Carol Henderson
Head Trainer: Jerry Rhea
Assistant Trainer: Billy Brooks
Equipment Manager: Whitey Zimmerman
Assistant Equipment Manager: Horace Daniel
Scouts: Bob Cegelski, Bob Fry, John Jelacic, Bob Riggle,
  Bill Striegel

Stadium: Atlanta-Fulton County Stadium (Capacity 60,748)
Playing Surface: Grass
Stadium Address: 521 Capitol Avenue S.W., Atlanta, Georgia
  30312
Colours: Red, Black, White and Silver
Summer Training Camp: Suwanee Road at 1-85, Suwanee,
  Georgia 30174

ATLANTA FALCONS 1985 SCHEDULE

PRE-SEASON

Aug.	10	WASHINGTON	8:00
Aug.	17	at Tampa Bay	8:00
Aug.	24	Green Bay Packers at Milwaukee	7:00
Aug.	30	MIAMI	8:00

REGULAR SEASON

Sep.	8	DETROIT	1:00
Sep.	15	at San Francisco	1:00
Sep.	22	DENVER	1:00
Sep.	29	at Los Angeles Rams	1:00
Oct.	6	SAN FRANCISCO	1:00
Oct.	13	at Seattle	1:00
Oct.	20	NEW ORLEANS	1:00
Oct.	27	at Dallas	12:00
Nov.	3	WASHINGTON	1:00
Nov.	10	at Philadelphia	1:00
Nov.	17	LOS ANGELES RAMS	1:00
Nov.	24	at Chicago	12:00
Dec.	1	LOS ANGELES RAIDERS	4:00
Dec.	8	at Kansas City	12:00
Dec.	15	MINNESOTA	1:00
Dec.	22	at New Orleans	12:00

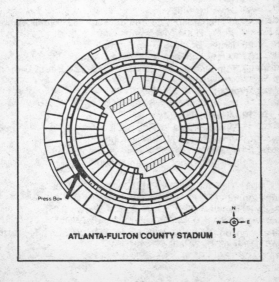

ATLANTA-FULTON COUNTY STADIUM

ATLANTA FALCONS
END OF SEASON DEPTH CHART

OFFENSE

WR — 85 Alfred Jackson, 83 Floyd Hodge, 89 Willie Curran
OLT — 78 Mike Kenn, 71 Dan Dufour
OLG — 68 R.C. Thielemann, 57 Jeff Van Note,
       70 Mike Chapman
C — 57 Jeff Van Note, 64 Joe Pellegrini, 71 Dan Dufour
ORG — 61 John Scully, 57 Jeff Van Note, 70 Mike Chapman
ORT — 71 Dan Dufour, 62 Brett Miller
TE — 88 Arthur Cox, 80 Mike Landrum
WR — 82 Stacey Bailey, 86 Perry Tuttle, 41 Virgil Seay
QB — 15 Mike Moroski, 16 David Archer, 8 Bob Holly
H-B — 87 Cliff Benson, 83 Floyd Hodge, 89 Willie Curran
RB — 42 Gerald Riggs, 21 Lynn Cain, 39 Cliff Austin,
       32 Tim Tyrell

DEFENSE

DLE — 79 Jeff Yeates, 72 Andrew Provence
DLT — 73 Gary Burley, 69 Dan Benish
DRT — 77 Rick Bryan, 75 Roy Harris
DRE — 65 Don Smith, 72 Andrew Provence
LLB — 58 David Frye, 53 Thomas Benson, 96 Johnny Taylor
MLB — 50 Buddy Curry, 54 Fulton Kuykendall,
       55 Dave Levenick
RLB — 56 Al Richardson, 51 Jeff Jackson, 52 Rydell Malancon
LCB — 23 Bobby Butler, 26 James Britt
RCB — 26 James Britt, 48 Gerald Small
LS — 37 Kenny Johnson, 34 Blane Gaison
RS — 27 Tom Pridemore, 25 Scott Case, 34 Blane Gaison

SPECIAL TEAMS

P — 1 Ralph Giacomarro
K — 18 Mick Luckhurst
H — 15 Mike Moroski, 1 Ralph Giacomarro
PR — 41 Virgil Seay, 37 Kenny Johnson
KR — 89 Willie Curran, 37 Kenny Johnson
LSN — 64 Joe Pellegrini, 71 Dan Dufour

ALSO WITH THE ATLANTA FALCONS
67 Eric Sanders (T), 49 Allama Matthews (H-B),
10 Steve Bartkowski (QB), 31 William Andrews (RB),
44 Rodney Tate (RB), 84 Sylvester Stamps (WR),
81 Billy Johnson (WR), 59 John Rade (LB), 30 Steve Haworth (S),
20 Earl Jones (CB), 74 Mike Pitts (DE)

ATLANTA FALCONS

INDIVIDUAL RUSHERS

	Att	Yards	Avg	Long	TD
Riggs, Gerald	353	1486	4.2	57	13
Cain, Lynn	77	276	3.6	t31	3
Moroski, Mike	21	98	4.7	17	0
Archer, David	6	38	6.3	12	0
Bartkowski, Steve	15	34	2.3	8	0
Hodge, Floyd	2	17	8.5	9	0
Stamps, Sylvester	3	15	5.0	8	0
Benson, Cliff	3	8	2.7	6	0
Johnson, Billy	3	8	2.7	11	0
Austin, Cliff	4	7	1.8	3	0
Pridemore, Tom	1	7	7.0	7	0
Giacomarro, Ralph	1	0	0.0	0	0

INDIVIDUAL PASSING

	Att	Comp	Pct Comp	Yds	Avg Gain	TD	Pct TD	Long	Int	Pct Int	Rating Points
Bartkowski, Steve	269	181	67.3	2158	8.02	11	4.1	61	10	3.7	89.7
Archer, David	18	11	61.1	181	10.06	1	5.6	34	1	5.6	90.3
Moroski, Mike	191	102	53.4	1207	6.32	2	1.0	t48	9	4.7	56.8

INDIVIDUAL RECEIVERS

	No	Yards	Avg	Long	TD
Bailey, Stacey	67	1138	17.0	61	6
Jackson, Alfred	52	731	14.1	t50	2
Riggs, Gerald	42	277	6.6	21	0
Cox, Arthur	34	329	9.7	t23	3
Benson, Cliff	26	244	9.4	30	0
Johnson, Billy	24	371	15.5	t45	3
Hodge, Floyd	24	234	9.8	26	0
Cain, Lynn	12	87	7.3	18	0
Landrum, Mike	6	66	11.0	30	0
Stamps, Sylvester	4	48	12.0	31	0
Curran, Willie	1	7	7.0	7	0
Matthews, Allama	1	7	7.0	7	0
Tuttle, Perry, T.B.-Atl	1	7	7.0	7	0

INDIVIDUAL INTERCEPTORS

	No	Yards	Avg	Long	TD
Johnson, Kenny	5	75	15.0	28	0
Butler, Bobby	2	25	12.5	25	0
Pridemore, Tom	2	0	0.0	0	0
Jackson, Jeff	1	35	35.0	t35	1
Britt, James	1	10	10.0	10	0
Small, Gerald	1	2	2.0	2	0

INDIVIDUAL KICKOFF RETURNERS

	No	Yards	Avg	Long	TD
Stamps, Sylvester	19	452	23.8	50	0
Johnson, Kenny	19	359	18.9	27	0
Curran, Willie	11	219	19.9	42	0
Tate, Rodney	9	148	16.4	31	0
Seay, Virgil, Wash.-Atl.	5	108	21.6	28	0
Austin, Cliff	4	77	19.3	23	0
Johnson, Billy	2	39	19.5	21	0
Gaison, Blane	1	15	15.0	15	0
Matthews, Allama	1	3	3.0	3	0
Malancon, Rydell	1	0	0.0	0	0
Tyrrell, Tim	1	0	0.0	0	0

INDIVIDUAL PUNTERS

	No	Yards	Long	Avg	Total Punts	TB	Blk	Opp Ret	Ret Yds	In 20	Net Avg
Giacomarro, Ralph	68	2855	58	42.0	70	6	2	42	450	12	32.6

INDIVIDUAL PUNT RETURNERS

	No	FC	Yards	Avg	Long	TD
Johnson, Billy	15	1	152	10.1	37	0
Johnson, Kenny	10	1	79	7.9	14	0
Curran, Willie	9	1	21	2.3	10	0
Seay, Virgil, Wash.-Atl.	8	1	10	1.3	7	0

INDIVIDUAL SCORERS

KICKERS	XP	XPA	FG	FGA	PTS
Luckhurst, Mick	31	31	20	27	91

NON-KICKERS	TD	TDR	TDP	TDM	PTS
Riggs, Gerald	13	13	0	0	78
Bailey, Stacey	6	0	6	0	36
Cain, Lynn	3	3	0	0	18
Cox, Arthur	3	0	3	0	18
Johnson, Billy	3	0	3	0	18
Jackson, Alfred	2	0	2	0	12
Jackson, Jeff	1	0	0	1	6
Bryan, Rick	0	0	0	0	2
Case, Scott	0	0	0	0	2

CHICAGO BEARS
NFC Central Division

Corporate Headquarters: Halas Hall, 250 North Washington, Lake Forest, Illinois 60045
Telephone: (312) 295-6600

CLUB OFFICIALS
Chairman of the Board: Edward W. McCaskey
President and Chief Executive Officer: Michael B. McCaskey
Vice President, General Manager and Treasurer: Jerome R. Vainisi
Vice President: Charles A. Brizzolara
Secretary: Virginia H. McCaskey
Head Coach: Mike Ditka
Assistant Coaches: Jim Dooley, Dale Haupt, Ed Hughes, Jim LaRue, Ted Plumb, Johnny Roland, Buddy Ryan, Dick Stanfel
Director of Player Personnel: Bill Tobin
Director of Community Involvement: Pat McCaskey
Director of Marketing/Communications: Bill McGrane
Coordinator of Media Relations: Ken Valdiserri
Ticket Manager: George Arneson
Trainer: Fred Caito
Strength Coordinator: Clyde Emrich
Equipment Manager: Ray Earley
Scouts: Jim Parmer, Rod Graves, Don King

Stadium: Soldier Field (Capacity 65,790)
Playing Surface: AstroTurf
Stadium Address: 425 McFetridge Place, Chicago, Illinois 60605
Colours: Navy Blue, Orange and White
Summer Training Camp: Wisconsin-Platteville, Platteville, Wisconsin 53818

CHICAGO BEARS 1985 SCHEDULE

PRE-SEASON

Aug.	10	at St. Louis	7:30
Aug.	17	INDIANAPOLIS	6:00
Aug.	24	at Dallas	7:00
Aug.	31	BUFFALO	6:00

REGULAR SEASON

Sep.	8	TAMPA BAY	12:00
Sep.	15	NEW ENGLAND	12:00
Sep.	19	at Minnesota	7:00
Sep.	29	WASHINGTON	12:00
Oct.	6	at Tampa Bay	1:00
Oct.	13	at San Francisco	1:00
Oct.	21	GREEN BAY	8:00
Oct.	27	MINNESOTA	12:00
Nov.	3	at Green Bay	12:00
Nov.	10	DETROIT	12:00
Nov.	17	at Dallas	12:00
Nov.	24	ATLANTA	12:00
Dec.	2	at Miami	9:00
Dec.	8	INDIANAPOLIS	12:00
Dec.	14	at New York Jets	12:30
Dec.	22	at Detroit	1:00

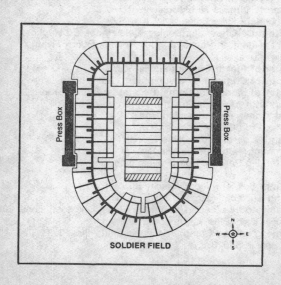

SOLDIER FIELD

CHICAGO BEARS
END OF SEASON DEPTH CHART

OFFENSE
WR   — 83 Willie Gault, 30 Jack Cameron, 86 Brad Anderson
OLT   — 74 Jimbo Covert, 71 Andy Frederick
OLG   — 62 Mark Bortz, 64 Rob Fada
C   — 63 Jay Hilgenberg, 60 Tom Andrews
ORG   — 79 Kurt Becker
ORT   — 78 Keith Van Horne, 71 Andy Frederick
TE   — 87 Emery Moorehead, 88 Pat Dunsmore, 81 Jay Saldi,
           89 Mitch Krenk
WR   — 85 Dennis McKinnon, 84 Brian Baschnagel,
           86 Brad Anderson
QB   — 4 Steve Fuller, 12 Rusty Lisch, Greg Landry
RB   — 26 Matt Suhey, 33 Calvin Thomas
RB   — 34 Walter Payton, 29 Dennis Gentry,
           32 Anthony Hutchison

DEFENSE
DLE   — 73 Mike Hartenstine, 98 Tyrone Keys
DLT   — 76 Steve McMichael, 68 Jim Osborne,
           70 Henry Waechter
DRT   — 99 Dan Hampton, 95 Richard Dent, 70 Henry Waechter
DRE   — 95 Richard Dent, 98 Tyrone Keys
LLB   — 55 Otis Wilson, 59 Ron Rivera, 53 Dan Rains
MLB   — 50 Mike Singletary, 54 Brian Cabral
RLB   — 90 Al Harris, 58 Wilber Marshall
LCB   — 27 Mike Richardson, 44 Terry Schmidt
RCB   — 21 Leslie Frazier
SS   — 25 Todd Bell, 24 Jeff Fisher, 20 Kevin Potter
FS   — 45 Gary Fencik, 22 Dave Duerson, 24 Jeff Fisher

SPECIAL TEAMS
P   — 15 Dave Finzer
K   — 16 Bob Thomas, 15 Dave Finzer
H   — 84 Brian Baschnagel, 15 Dave Finzer
PR   — 24 Jeff Fisher, 85 Dennis McKinnon, 30 Jack Cameron
KR   — 30 Jack Cameron, 29 Dennis Gentry,
           32 Anthony Hutchison
LSN   — 63 Jay Hilgenberg, 53 Dan Rains, 59 Ron Rivera

ALSO WITH THE CHICAGO BEARS
9 Jim McMahon (QB), 82 Ken Margerum (WR),
80 Rickey Watts (WR), 49 Donald Jordan (RB),
75 Stefan Humphries (G), 23 Shaun Gayle (CB)

CHICAGO BEARS

INDIVIDUAL RUSHERS

	Att	Yards	Avg	Long	TD
Payton, Walter	381	1684	4.4	t72	11
Suhey, Matt	124	424	3.4	21	4
McMahon, Jim	39	276	7.1	30	2
Thomas, Calvin	40	186	4.7	37	1
Lisch, Rusty	18	121	6.7	31	0
Fuller, Steve	15	89	5.9	26	1
Gentry, Dennis	21	79	3.8	28	1
Jordan, Donald	11	70	6.4	29	0
Hutchison, Anthony	14	39	2.8	6	1
McKinnon, Dennis	2	12	6.0	21	0
Landry, Greg	2	1	0.5	t1	1
Baschnagel, Brian	1	0	0.0	0	0
Finzer, David	2	0	0.0	5	0
Moorehead, Emery	1	−2	−2.0	−2	0

INDIVIDUAL PASSING

	Att	Comp	Pct Comp	Yds	Avg Gain	TD	Pct TD	Long	Int	Pct Int	Rating Points
Fuller, Steve	78	53	67.9	595	7.63	3	3.8	31	0	0.0	103.3
McMahon, Jim	143	85	59.4	1146	8.01	8	5.6	t61	2	1.4	97.8
Landry, Greg	20	11	55.0	199	9.95	1	5.0	t55	3	15.0	66.5
Lisch, Rusty	85	43	50.6	413	4.86	0	0.0	23	6	7.1	35.1
Baschnagel, Brian	2	1	50.0	7	3.50	0	0.0	7	0	0.0	58.3
Payton, Walter	8	3	37.5	47	5.88	2	25.0	42	1	12.5	57.8
Suhey, Matt	1	0	0.0	0	0.0	0	0.0	0	0	0.0	39.6

INDIVIDUAL RECEIVERS

	No	Yards	Avg	Long	TD
Payton, Walter	45	368	8.2	31	0
Suhey, Matt	42	312	7.4	23	2
Gault, Willie	34	587	17.3	t61	6
Moorehead, Emery	29	497	17.1	50	1
McKinnon, Dennis	29	431	14.9	t32	3
Dunsmore, Pat	9	106	11.8	25	1
Saldi, Jay	9	90	10.0	20	0
Thomas, Calvin	9	39	4.3	9	0
Baschnagel, Brian	6	53	8.8	17	0
Gentry, Dennis	4	29	7.3	13	0
Anderson, Brad	3	77	25.7	t49	1
Krenk, Mitch	2	31	15.5	24	0
McMahon, Jim	1	42	42.0	42	0
Cameron, Jack	1	13	13.0	13	0
Cabral, Brian	1	7	7.0	7	0
Hutchison, Anthony	1	7	7.0	7	0
Jordan, Donald	1	6	6.0	6	0

INDIVIDUAL INTERCEPTORS

	No	Yards	Avg	Long	TD
Fencik, Gary	5	102	20.4	61	0
Frazier, Leslie	5	89	17.8	33	0
Bell, Todd	4	46	11.5	t36	1
Richardson, Mike	2	7	3.5	7	0
Harris, Al	1	34	34.0	34	0
Duerson, Dave	1	9	9.0	9	0
Singletary, Mike	1	4	4.0	4	0
Schmidt, Terry	1	0	0.0	0	0
Gayle, Shaun	1	−1	−1.0	−1	0

INDIVIDUAL KICKOFF RETURNERS

	No	Yards	Avg	Long	TD
Cameron, Jack	26	485	18.7	40	0
Gentry, Dennis	11	209	19.0	33	0
Jordan, Donald	5	62	12.4	22	0
Duerson, Dave	4	95	23.8	26	0
Bell, Todd	2	33	16.5	17	0
Gault, Willie	1	12	12.0	12	0

INDIVIDUAL PUNTERS

	No	Yards	Long	Avg	Total Punts	TB	Blk	Opp Ret	Ret Yds	In 20	Net Avg
Finzer, David	83	3328	87	40.1	85	4	2	41	249	26	35.3

INDIVIDUAL PUNT RETURNERS

	No	FC	Yards	Avg	Long	TD
Fisher, Jeff	57	11	492	8.6	28	0
McKinnon, Dennis	5	0	62	12.4	18	0
Duerson, Dave	1	0	4	4.0	4	0

INDIVIDUAL SCORERS

KICKERS

	XP	XPA	FG	FGA	PTS
Thomas, Bob	35	37	22	28	101

NON-KICKERS

	TD	TDR	TDP	TDM	PTS
Payton, Walter	11	11	0	0	66
Gault, Willie	6	0	6	0	36
Suhey, Matt	6	4	2	0	36
McKinnon, Dennis	3	0	3	0	18
McMahon, Jim	2	2	0	0	12
Anderson, Brad	1	0	1	0	6
Bell, Todd	1	0	0	1	6
Dunsmore, Pat	1	0	1	0	6
Fuller, Steve	1	1	0	0	6
Gentry, Dennis	1	1	0	0	6
Hutchison, Anthony	1	1	0	0	6
Landry, Greg	1	1	0	0	6
Moorehead, Emery	1	0	1	0	6
Thomas, Calvin	1	1	0	0	6

DALLAS COWBOYS
NFC Eastern Division

Address: One Cowboy Parkway, Irving, Texas 75063
Telephone: (214) 369-8000

CLUB OFFICIALS
General Partner: H. R. Bright
President-General Manager: Texas E. Schramm
Head Coach: Tom Landry
Assistant Coaches: Neill Armstrong, Al Lavan, Alan Lowry,
   Jim Myers, Dick Nolan, Jim Shofner, Gene Stallings,
   Ernie Stautner, Jerry Tubbs, Bob Ward
Vice President-Personnel Development: Gil Brandt
Vice President-Treasurer: Don Wilson
Vice President-Administration: Joe Bailey
Director of Public Relations: Doug Todd
Ticket Manager: Steve Orsini
Equipment Manager: William T. (Buck) Buchanan
Cheerleaders Director: Suzanne Mitchell

Stadium: Texas Stadium (Capacity 63,749)
Playing Surface: Texas Turf
Stadium Address: Irving, Texas 75062
Colours: Royal Blue, Metallic Silver Blue and White
Summer Training Camp: California Lutheran College,
   Thousand Oaks, California 91360

DALLAS COWBOYS 1985 SCHEDULE

PRE-SEASON

Aug.	10	GREEN BAY	8:00
Aug.	17	at San Diego	6:00
Aug.	24	CHICAGO	7:00
Aug.	30	HOUSTON	8:00

REGULAR SEASON

Sep.	9	WASHINGTON	8:00
Sep.	15	at Detroit	1:00
Sep.	22	CLEVELAND	12:00
Sep.	29	at Houston	12:00
Oct.	6	at New York Giants	9:00
Oct.	13	PITTSBURGH	12:00
Oct.	20	at Philadelphia	1:00
Oct.	27	ATLANTA	12:00
Nov.	4	at St. Louis	8:00
Nov.	10	at Washington	4:00
Nov.	17	CHICAGO	12:00
Nov.	24	PHILADELPHIA	3:00
Nov.	28	ST. LOUIS	3:00
Dec.	8	at Cincinnati	1:00
Dec.	15	NEW YORK GIANTS	12:00
Dec.	22	at San Francisco	1:00

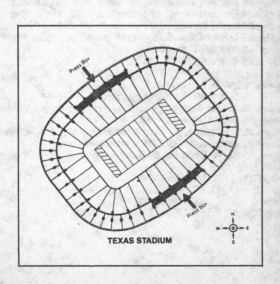

TEXAS STADIUM

DALLAS COWBOYS
END OF SEASON DEPTH CHART

OFFENSE

WR — 80 Tony Hill, 86 Duriel Harris, 81 Kirk Phillips
OLT — 68 Herbert Scott, 63 Glen Titensor, 79 John Hunt
OLG — 63 Glen Titensor, 76 Dowe Aughtman, 79 John Hunt
C — 64 Tom Rafferty, 62 Brian Baldinger, 63 Glen Titensor
ORG — 65 Kurt Petersen, 62 Brian Baldinger, 73 Syd Kitson
ORT — 75 Phil Pozderac, 62 Brian Baldinger, 79 John Hunt
TE — 84 Doug Cosbie, 85 Fred Cornwell, 89 Brian Salonen
WR — 83 Doug Donley, 82 Mike Renfro, 81 Kirk Phillips
QB — 11 Danny White, 14 Gary Hogeboom, 16 Steve Pelluer
RB — 33 Tony Dorsett, 23 James Jones, 35 Chuck McSwain,
      31 Gary Allen
RB — 30 Tim Newsome, 20 Ron Springs, 28 Norm Granger

DEFENSE

DLE — 72 Ed Jones, 71 Mark Tuinei, 60 Don Smerek
DLT — 78 John Dutton, 60 Don Smerek, 71 Mark Tuinei
DRT — 54 Randy White, 60 Don Smerek, 71 Mark Tuinei
DRE — 77 Jim Jeffcoat, 71 Mark Tuinei, 60 Don Smerek
LLB — 58 Mike Hegman, 50 Jeff Rohrer, 57 Jimmie Turner
MBL — 56 Eugene Lockhart, 55 Steve DeOssie, 50 Jeff Rohrer
RLB — 51 Anthony Dickerson, 50 Jeff Rohrer, 57 Jimmie Turner
LCB — 24 Everson Walls, 22 Victor Scott, 32 Dennis Thurman
RCB — 27 Ron Fellows, 22 Victor Scott, 32 Dennis Thurman
SS — 47 Dextor Clinkscale, 40 Bill Bates, 36 Vince Albritton
FS — 26 Michael Downs, 32 Dennis Thurman,
      36 Vince Albritton

SPECIAL TEAMS

P — 11 Danny White, 5 John Warren
K — 1 Rafael Septien, 5 John Warren, 11 Danny White
H — 14 Gary Hogeboom, 16 Steve Pelluer
PR — 31 Gary Allen, 35 Chuck McSwain, 27 Ron Fellows
KR — 31 Gary Allen, 35 Chuck McSwain
LSN — 55 Steve DeOssie, 64 Tom Rafferty, 62 Brian Baldinger

ALSO WITH THE DALLAS COWBOYS

61 Jim Cooper (T), 66 Chris Schultz (T),
70 Howard Richards (T/G), 21 Carl Howard (CB),
53 Bob Breunig (LB), 52 Billy Cannon Jr. (LB)

DALLAS COWBOYS

INDIVIDUAL RUSHERS

	Att	Yards	Avg	Long	TD
Dorsett, Tony	302	1189	3.9	t31	6
Newsome, Tim	66	268	4.1	30	5
Springs, Ron	68	197	2.9	16	1
White, Danny	6	21	3.5	8	0
Hogeboom, Gary	15	19	1.3	11	0
Jones, James	8	13	1.6	6	0
Hill, Tony	1	7	7.0	7	0
Donley, Doug	2	5	2.5	6	0
Smith, Waddell	1	−5	−5.0	−5	0

INDIVIDUAL PASSING

	Att	Comp	Pct Comp	Yds	Avg Gain	TD	Pct TD	Long	Int	Pct Int	Rating Points
White, Danny	233	126	54.1	1580	6.78	11	4.7	t66	11	4.7	71.5
Hogeboom, Gary	367	195	53.1	2366	6.45	7	1.9	t68	14	3.8	63.7
Dorsett, Tony	1	0	0.0	0	0.0	0	0.0	0	1	100.0	0.0
Renfro, Mike	2	1	50.0	49	24.50	1	50.0	t49	0	0.0	135.4
Springs, Ron	1	0	0.0	0	-0.00	0	0.0	0	0	0.0	39.6

INDIVIDUAL RECEIVERS

	No	Yards	Avg	Long	TD
Cosbie, Doug	60	789	13.2	36	4
Hill, Tony	58	864	14.9	t66	5
Dorsett, Tony	51	459	9.0	t68	1
Springs, Ron	46	454	9.9	t57	3
Renfro, Mike	35	583	16.7	t60	2
Harris, Duriel, Clev.-Dall.	33	521	15.8	43	2
Donley, Doug	32	473	14.8	t49	2
Newsome, Tim	26	263	10.1	29	0
Jones, James	7	57	8.1	19	1
Cornwell, Fred	2	23	11.5	13	1
Carmichael, Harold	1	7	7.0	7	0
Smith, Waddell	1	7	7.0	7	0
Phillips, Kirk	1	6	6.0	6	0
Pozderac, Phil	1	1	1.0	1	0

INDIVIDUAL INTERCEPTORS

	No	Yards	Avg	Long	TD
Downs, Mike	7	126	18.0	t27	1
Thurman, Dennis	5	81	16.2	43	1
Clinkscale, Dextor	3	32	10.7	23	0
Walls, Everson	3	12	4.0	12	0
Fellows, Ron	3	3	1.0	3	0
Hegman, Mike	3	3	1.0	3	0
Lockhart, Eugene	1	32	32.0	32	0

	No	Yards	Avg	Long	TD
Scott, Victory	1	5	5.0	5	0
Bates, Bill	1	3	3.0	3	0
Dickerson, Anthony	1	0	0.0	0	0

INDIVIDUAL KICKOFF RETURNERS

	No	Yards	Avg	Long	TD
Allen, Gary	33	666	20.2	34	0
McSwain, Chuck	20	403	20.2	32	0
Fellows, Ron	6	94	15.7	23	0
Salonen, Brian	2	30	15.0	22	0
Granger, Norm	2	6	3.0	5	0

INDIVIDUAL PUNTERS

	No	Yards	Long	Avg	Total Punts	TB	Blk	Opp Ret	Ret Yds	In 20	Net Avg
White, Danny	82	3151	54	38.4	82	8	0	38	156	21	34.6
Warren, John	21	799	48	38.0	21	3	0	13	47	3	33.0
Miller, Jim	5	173	41	34.6	5	0	0	4	27	1	29.2

INDIVIDUAL PUNT RETURNERS

	No	FC	Yards	Avg	Long	TD
Allen, Gary	54	15	446	8.3	18	0
Harris, Duriel, Clev.-Dall.	9	0	73	8.1	13	0

INDIVIDUAL SCORERS
KICKERS

	XP	XPA	FG	FGA	PTS
Septien, Rafael	33	34	23	29	102

NON-KICKERS

	TD	TDR	TDP	TDM	PTS
Dorsett, Tony	7	6	1	0	42
Hill, Tony	5	0	5	0	30
Newsome, Tim	5	5	0	0	30
Cosbie, Doug	4	0	4	0	24
Springs, Ron	4	1	3	0	24
Donley, Doug	2	0	2	0	12
Harris, Duriel, Clev.-Dall.	2	0	2	0	12
Renfro, Mike	2	0	2	0	12
Cornwell, Fred	1	0	1	0	6
Downs, Mike	1	0	0	1	6
Jeffcoat, Jim	1	0	0	1	6
Jones, James	1	0	1	0	6
Thurman, Dennis	1	0	0	1	6
Dutton, John	0	0	0	0	2

DETROIT LIONS
NFC Central Division

Address: Pontiac Silverdome, 1200 Featherstone Road,
   Box 4200, Pontiac, Michigan 48057
Telephone: (313) 335-4131 (Office)
   (313) 335-4151 (Tickets)

CLUB OFFICIALS
Owner and President: William Clay Ford
Executive Vice President/General Manager: Russell Thomas
Director of Football Operations/Head Coach: Darryl Rogers
Controller: Charles Schmidt
Ticket Manager: Fred Otto
Director of Public Relations: George Heddleston
Publicity Assistant: Brian Muir
Director of Player Personnel: T.B.A.
Assistant Coaches: Ed Beard, Don Doll, Fred Hoaglin,
   Bill Johnson, Ed Khayat, Joe Madden, Bill Nelsen, Mel Phillips,
   Larry Seiple
Strength and Conditioning: Don Clemons
Administrative Coordinator: Mike Working
Trainer: Kent Falb
Equipment Manager: Dan Jaroshewich
College Scouts: Joe Bushofsky, Dirk Dierking, Ron Hughes,
   Jim Owen

Stadium: Pontiac Silverdome (Capacity 80,638)
Playing Surface: AstroTurf
Stadium Address: 1200 Featherstone Road, Box 4200, Pontiac,
   Michigan 48057
Colours: Honolulu Blue and Silver
Summer Training Camp: Oakland University, Rochester,
   Michigan 48063

DETROIT LIONS 1985 SCHEDULE

PRE-SEASON

Aug.	10	BUFFALO	8:00
Aug.	17	at Seattle	7:30
Aug.	24	CINCINNATI	8:00
Aug.	29	at Philadelphia	7:30

REGULAR SEASON

Sep.	8	at Atlanta	1:00
Sep.	15	DALLAS	1:00
Sep.	22	at Indianapolis	12:00
Sep.	29	TAMPA BAY	1:00
Oct.	6	at Green Bay	12:00
Oct.	13	at Washington	1:00
Oct.	20	SAN FRANCISCO	1:00
Oct.	27	MIAMI	1:00
Nov.	3	at Minnesota	12:00
Nov.	10	at Chicago	12:00
Nov.	17	MINNESOTA	4:00
Nov.	24	at Tampa Bay	1:00
Nov.	28	NEW YORK JETS	12:30
Dec.	8	at New England	1:00
Dec.	15	GREEN BAY	1:00
Dec.	22	CHICAGO	1:00

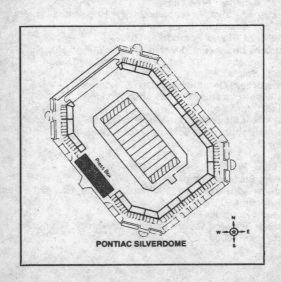

PONTIAC SILVERDOME

DETROIT LIONS
END OF SEASON DEPTH CHART

OFFENSE
WR   — 86 Mark Nichols, 89 Jeff Chadwick, 82 Pete Mandley
OLT — 73 Don Laster, 61 Homer Elias, 72 Chris Dieterich
OLG — 72 Chris Dieterich, 61 Homer Elias, 64 Larry Lee
C   — 65 Amos Fowler, 64 Larry Lee, 51 David Jones
ORG — 67 Don Greco, 64 Larry Lee, 68 Steve Baack
ORT — 70 Keith Dorney, 72 Chris Dieterich, 73 Don Laster
TE   — 87 David Lewis, 84 Rob Rubick, 81 Reese McCall
WR   — 39 Leonard Thompson, 83 Robbie Martin, 80 Carl Bland
QB   — 16 Gary Danielson, 18 John Witkowski,
          14 Mike Machurek
RB   — 31 Ken Jenkins, 24 Dexter Bussey
RB   — 30 James Jones, 44 Dave D'Addio, 36 Mike Meade

DEFENSE
DLE — 66 Mike Cofer, 63 Martin Moss
DLT — 62 Curtis Green, 76 Eric Williams
DRT — 78 Doug English, 76 Eric Williams
DRE — 79 William Gay, 63 Martin Moss
LLB — 53 Gary Cobb, 92 Angelo King, 93 Kirk Dodge
MLB — 57 Ken Fantetti, 58 Steve Doig, 50 August Curley
RLB — 59 Jimmy Williams, 54 Roosevelt Barnes
LCB — 27 Bobby Watkins, 26 William Frizzell
RCB — 29 Bruce McNorton, 43 Al Latimer
LS   — 33 William Graham, 21 Demetrious Johnson
RS   — 35 Alvin Hall, 21 Demetrious Johnson

SPECIAL TEAMS
P   — 11 Mike Black, 3 Ed Murray
K   — 3 Ed Murray, 11 Mike Black
H   — 16 Gary Danielson, 11 Mike Black
PR   — 82 Pete Mandley, 35 Alvin Hall, 83 Robbie Martin
KR   — 82 Pete Mandley, 35 Alvin Hall, 83 Robbie Martin
LSN — 51 David Jones, 64 Larry Lee, 65 Amos Fowler

ALSO WITH THE DETROIT LIONS
71 Rich Strenger (T), 17 Eric Hipple (QB), 20 Billy Sims (RB),
52 Steve Mott (C), 55 Terry Tautolo (LB)

DETROIT LIONS
INDIVIDUAL RUSHERS

	Att	Yards	Avg	Long	TD
Sims, Billy	130	687	5.3	81	5
Jones, James	137	532	3.9	34	3
Jenkins, Ken	78	358	4.6	t25	1
Danielson, Gary	41	218	5.3	40	3
Bussey, Dexter	32	91	2.8	18	0
D'Addio, Dave	7	46	6.6	14	0
Witkowski, John	7	33	4.7	10	0
Nichols, Mark	3	27	9.0	13	0
Martin, Robbie	1	14	14.0	14	0
Chadwick, Jeff	1	12	12.0	t12	1
Machurek, Mike	1	9	9.0	9	0
Hipple, Eric	2	3	1.5	2	0
Black, Mike	3	−6	−2.0	4	0
Thompson, Leonard	3	−7	−2.3	4	0

INDIVIDUAL PASSING

	Att	Comp	Pct Comp	Yds	Avg Gain	TD	Pct TD	Long	Int	Pct Int	Rating Points
Danielson, Gary	410	252	61.5	3076	7.50	17	4.1	t77	15	3.7	83.1
Hipple, Eric	38	16	42.1	246	6.47	1	2.6	40	1	2.6	62.0
Witkowski, John	34	13	38.2	210	6.18	0	0.0	39	0	0.0	59.7
Machurek, Mike	43	14	32.6	193	4.49	0	0.0	48	6	14.0	8.3
Jenkins, Ken	1	0	0.0	0	0.00	0	0.0	0	0	0.0	39.6
Jones, James	5	3	60.0	62	12.40	1	20.0	27	0	0.0	143.3

INDIVIDUAL RECEIVERS

	No	Yards	Avg	Long	TD
Jones, James	77	662	8.6	39	5
Thompson, Leonard	50	773	15.5	t66	6
Chadwick, Jeff	37	540	14.6	46	2
Nichols, Mark	34	744	21.9	t77	1
Sims, Billy	31	239	7.7	20	0
Jenkins, Ken	21	246	11.7	68	0
Lewis, David	16	236	14.8	58	3
Rubick, Rob	14	188	13.4	29	1
Bussey, Dexter	9	63	7.0	19	0
Mandley, Pete	3	38	12.7	19	0
McCall, Reese	3	15	5.0	7	0
Danielson, Gary	1	22	22.0	t22	1
D'Addio, Dave	1	12	12.0	12	0
Martin, Robbie	1	9	9.0	9	0

INDIVIDUAL INTERCEPTORS

	No	Yards	Avg	Long	TD
Watkins, Bobby	6	0	0.0	0	0
Graham, William	3	22	7.3	15	0

	No	Yards	Avg	Long	TD
Hall, Alvin	2	64	32.0	36	0
McNorton, Bruce	2	0	0.0	0	0
Fantetti, Ken	1	1	1.0	1	0

INDIVIDUAL KICKOFF RETURNERS

	No	Yards	Avg	Long	TD
Mandley, Pete	22	390	17.7	32	0
Hall, Alvin	19	385	20.3	46	0
Jenkins, Ken	18	396	22.0	32	0
Martin, Robbie	10	144	14.4	23	0
Meade, Mike	4	32	8.0	15	0
D'Addio, Dave	1	0	0.0	0	0

INDIVIDUAL PUNTERS

	No	Yards	Long	Avg	Total Punts	TB	Blk	Opp Ret	Ret Yds	In 20	Net Avg
Black, Mike	76	3164	63	41.6	76	8	0	49	516	13	32.7

INDIVIDUAL PUNT RETURNERS

	No	FC	Yards	Avg	Long	TD
Martin, Robbie	25	8	210	8.4	23	0
Hall, Alvin	7	1	30	4.3	11	0
Mandley, Pete	2	2	0	0.0	0	0
Johnson, Demetrious	1	0	0	0.0	0	0
Jenkins, Ken	1	0	1	1.0	1	0

INDIVIDUAL SCORERS
KICKERS

	XP	XPA	FG	FGA	PTS
Murray, Ed	31	31	20	27	91

NON-KICKERS

	TD	TDR	TDP	TDM	PTS
Jones, James	8	3	5	0	48
Thompson, Leonard	6	0	6	0	36
Sims, Billy	5	5	0	0	30
Danielson, Gary	4	3	1	0	24
Chadwick, Jeff	3	1	2	0	18
Lewis, David	3	0	3	0	18
Jenkins, Ken	1	1	0	0	6
Nichols, Mark	1	0	1	0	6
Rubick, Rob	1	0	1	0	6

GREEN BAY PACKERS
NFC Central Division

Address: 1265 Lombardi Avenue, Green Bay,
   Wisconsin 54307-0628
Telephone: (414) 494-2351

CLUB OFFICIALS
Chairman of the Board: Dominic Olejniczak
President, CEO: Robert J. Parins
Vice President: Tony Canadeo
Secretary: John Torinus
Assistant to the President: Bob Harlan
Assistant to the President: Tom Miller
Director of Public Relations: Lee Remmel
Executive Assistant: Phil Pionek
Ticket Director: Mark Wagner
Head Coach: Forrest Gregg
Assistant Coaches: Lew Carpenter, Virgil Knight,
   Dick Modzelewski, Herb Patera, Ken Riley, George Sefcik,
   Bob Schnelker, Jerry Wampfler
Director of Player Personnel: Dick Corrick
Director of Pro Personnel: Burt Gustafson
Scouting: Billy Atkins, Red Cochran, Lloyd Eaton, Dave Hanner,
   Baby Ray, Tom Tipps
Equipment Manager: Bob Noel
Trainer: Domenic Gentile

Stadiums: (I) Lambeau Field (Capacity 56,928)
                (II) Milwaukee County Stadium (Capacity 55,976)
Playing Surfaces: Grass
Stadiums Addresses: (I) P.O. Box 10628,
   1265 Lombardi Avenue, Green Bay, Wisconsin 54307-0628
   (II) Highway 1-94, Milwaukee, Wisconsin 53214
Colours: Dark Green, Gold and White
Summer Training Camp: St. Norbert College, DePere,
   Wisconsin 54115

GREEN BAY PACKERS 1985 SCHEDULE

PRE-SEASON

Aug.	10	at Dallas	8:00
Aug.	17	at New York Giants	8:00
Aug.	24	ATLANTA at Milwaukee	3:00
Aug.	31	NEW YORK JETS	7:00

REGULAR SEASON

Sep.	8	at New England	1:00
Sep.	15	NEW YORK GIANTS	3:00
Sep.	22	NEW YORK JETS at Milwaukee	3:00
Sep.	29	at St. Louis	12:00
Oct.	6	DETROIT	12:00
Oct.	13	MINNESOTA at Milwaukee	12:00
Oct.	21	at Chicago	8:00
Oct.	27	at Indianapolis	1:00
Nov.	3	CHICAGO	12:00
Nov.	10	at Minnesota	12:00
Nov.	17	NEW ORLEANS at Milwaukee	12:00
Nov.	24	at Los Angeles Rams	1:00
Dec.	1	TAMPA BAY	12:00
Dec.	8	MIAMI	12:00
Dec.	15	at Detroit	1:00
Dec.	22	at Tampa Bay	1:00

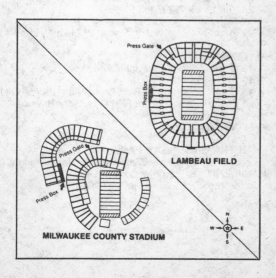

LAMBEAU FIELD

MILWAUKEE COUNTY STADIUM

GREEN BAY PACKERS
END OF SEASON DEPTH CHART

OFFENSE
WR — 80 James Lofton, 88 Ron Cassidy, Lenny Taylor
OLT — 67 Karl Swanke, 74 Tim Huffman, 68 Greg Koch
OLG — 74 Tim Huffman, 61 Dave Drechsler, 60 Blake Moore
C — 60 Blake Moore, 58 Mark Cannon
ORG — 65 Ron Hallstrom, 70 Keith Uecker, 60 Blake Moore
ORT — 68 Greg Koch, 65 Ron Hallstrom
TE — 82 Paul Coffman, 86 Ed West
WR — 85 Phillip Epps, 88 Ron Cassidy, 89 John Jefferson
QB — 12 Lynn Dickey, 19 Rich Campbell
RB — 40 Eddie Lee Ivery, 25 Harlan Huckleby, 35 Del Rodgers
RB — 31 Gerry Ellis, 21 Ray Crouse

DEFENSE
DLE — 76 Alphonso Carreker, 94 Charles Martin
NT — 63 Terry Jones, 77 Bill Neill, 94 Charles Martin,
Tony DeLuca
DRE — 79 Donnie Humphrey, 93 Robert Brown
LOLB — 59 John Anderson, 51 Guy Prather
LILB — 55 Randy Scott, 50 Rich Wingo
RILB — 52 George Cumby, 99 John Dorsey
ROLB — 53 Mike Douglass, 56 Cliff Lewis
LCB — 22 Mark Lee, 27 Gary Hayes
RCB — 26 Tim Lewis, 38 Estus Hood
SS — 37 Mark Murphy, 43 Daryll Jones, 24 Johnnie Gray
FS — 41 Tom Flynn, 43 Daryll Jones, 28 Mike McLeod

SPECIAL TEAMS
P — 13 Bucky Scribner, 59 John Anderson
K — 10 Al Del Greco
H — 13 Bucky Scribner, 19 Rich Campbell, 12 Lynn Dickey
PR — 85 Phillip Epps, 41 Tom Flynn, 27 Gary Hayes
KR — 35 Del Rodgers, 25 Harlan Huckleby
LSN — 58 Mark Cannon

ALSO WITH THE GREEN BAY PACKERS
81 Gary Lewis (TE), 33 Jessie Clark (RB), 16 Randy Wright (QB),
69 Leotis Harris (G), 54 Larry McCarren (C),
90 Ezra Johnson (DE), 29 Mike McCoy (CB)

GREEN BAY PACKERS
INDIVIDUAL RUSHERS

	Att	Yards	Avg	Long	TD
Ellis, Gerry	123	581	4.7	50	4
Ivery, Eddie Lee	99	552	5.6	49	6
Clark, Jessie	87	375	4.3	t43	4
Crouse, Ray	53	169	3.2	14	0
Huckleby, Harlan	35	145	4.1	23	0
Rodgers, Del	25	94	3.8	15	0
Lofton, James	10	82	8.2	26	0
Wright, Randy	8	11	1.4	5	0
Dickey, Lynn	18	6	0.3	9	3
Campbell, Rich	2	2	1.0	5	0
West, Ed	1	2	2.0	t2	1

INDIVIDUAL PASSING

	Att	Comp	Pct Comp	Yds	Avg Gain	TD	Pct TD	Long	Int	Pct Int	Rating Points
Dickey, Lynn	401	237	59.1	3195	7.97	25	6.2	t79	19	4.7	85.6
Campbell, Rich	38	16	42.1	218	5.74	3	7.9	t43	5	13.2	47.8
Wright, Randy	62	27	43.5	310	5.00	2	3.2	56	6	9.7	30.4
Ellis, Gerry	4	1	25.0	17	4.25	0	0.0	17	0	0.0	44.8
Scribner, Bucky	1	0	0.0	0	0.00	0	0.0	0	0	0.0	39.6

INDIVIDUAL RECEIVERS

	No	Yards	Avg	Long	TD
Lofton, James	62	1361	22.0	t79	7
Coffman, Paul	43	562	13.1	t44	9
Ellis, Gerry	36	312	8.7	22	2
Clark, Jessie	29	234	8.1	20	2
Epps, Phillip	26	435	16.7	56	3
Jefferson, John	26	339	13.0	33	0
Ivery, Eddie Lee	19	141	7.4	18	1
Crouse, Ray	9	93	10.3	25	1
Huckleby, Harlan	8	65	8.1	13	0
West, Ed	6	54	9.0	t29	4
Rodgers, Del	5	56	11.2	22	0
Childs, Henry	4	32	8.0	17	0
Lewis, Gary	4	29	7.3	15	0
Cassidy, Ron	2	16	8.0	10	0
Taylor, Lenny	1	8	8.0	8	0
Moore, Blake	1	3	3.0	t3	1

INDIVIDUAL INTERCEPTORS

	No	Yards	Avg	Long	TD
Flynn, Tom	9	106	11.8	31	0
Lewis, Tim	7	151	21.6	t99	1
Lee, Mark	3	33	11.0	14	0
Anderson, John	3	24	8.0	22	0

	No	Yards	Avg	Long	TD
Hood, Estus	1	8	8.0	8	0
Cumby, George	1	7	7.0	7	0
Brown, Robert	1	5	5.0	t5	0
Murphy, Mark	1	4	4.0	4	0
McLeod, Mike	1	0	0.0	0	0

INDIVIDUAL KICKOFF RETURNERS

	No	Yards	Avg	Long	TD
Rodgers, Del	39	843	21.6	t97	1
Huckleby, Harlan	14	261	18.6	54	0
Epps, Phillip	12	232	19.3	47	0
Jones, Daryll	1	19	19.0	19	0
Prather, Guy	1	7	7.0	7	0

INDIVIDUAL PUNTERS

	No	Yards	Long	Avg	Total Punts	TB	Blk	Opp Ret	Ret Yds	In 20	Net Avg
Scribner, Bucky	85	3596	61	42.3	85	12	0	46	368	18	35.2

INDIVIDUAL PUNT RETURNERS

	No	FC	Yards	Avg	Long	TD
Epps, Phillip	29	10	199	6.9	39	0
Flynn, Tom	15	4	128	8.5	20	0
Hayes, Gary	4	0	24	6.0	10	0
Murphy, Mark	0	2	0	—	0	0

INDIVIDUAL SCORERS

KICKERS

	XP	XPA	FG	FGA	PTS
Del Greco, Al	34	34	9	12	61
Garcia, Eddie	14	15	3	9	23

NON-KICKERS	TD	TDR	TDP	TDM	PTS
Coffman, Paul	9	0	9	0	54
Ivery, Eddie Lee	7	6	1	0	42
Lofton, James	7	0	7	0	42
Clark, Jessie	6	4	2	0	36
Ellis, Gerry	6	4	2	0	36
West, Ed	5	1	4	0	30
Dickey, Lynn	3	3	0	0	18
Epps, Phillip	3	0	3	0	18
Brown, Robert	1	0	0	1	6
Crouse, Ray	1	0	1	0	6
Lewis, Tim	1	0	0	1	6
Moore, Blake	1	0	1	0	6
Rodgers, Del	1	0	0	1	6

LOS ANGELES RAMS
NFC Western Division

Address: 2327 West Lincoln Ave., Anaheim, California 92801
Telephone: (714) 535-7267 or (213) 585-5400

CLUB OFFICIALS
President: Georgia Frontiere
Vice President, Finance: John Shaw
Administrator, Football Operations: Jack Faulkner
Director of Operations: Dick Beam
Director of Player Personnel: John Math
Head Coach: John Robinson
Assistant Coaches: Bob Baker, Marv Goux, Gil Haskell,
  Hudson Houck, Jimmy Raye, Steve Shafer, Fritz Shurmur,
  Bruce Snyder, Fred Whittingham
Director of Public Relations: Pete Donovan
Director of Community Relations: Marshall Klein
Trainers: Jim Anderson, Garrett Giemont, George Menefee
Equipment Manager: Don Hewitt

Stadium: Anaheim Stadium (Capacity 69,007)
Playing Surface: Grass
Stadium Address: 1900 State College Blvd., Anaheim,
  California 92806
Colours: Royal Blue, Gold and White
Summer Training Camp: California State University, Fullerton,
  California 92634

LOS ANGELES RAMS 1985 SCHEDULE

PRE-SEASON

Aug.	10	HOUSTON	7:00
Aug.	15	ST. LOUIS	7:00
Aug.	24	vs. Philadelphia	7:30
Aug.	31	NEW ENGLAND	7:00

REGULAR SEASON

Sep.	8	DENVER	1:00
Sep.	15	at Philadelphia	1:00
Sep.	23	at Seattle	6:00
Sep.	29	ATLANTA	1:00
Oct.	6	MINNESOTA	1:00
Oct.	13	at Tampa Bay	1:00
Oct.	20	at Kansas City	12:00
Oct.	27	SAN FRANCISCO	1:00
Nov.	3	NEW ORLEANS	1:00
Nov.	10	at New York Giants	1:00
Nov.	17	at Atlanta	1:00
Nov.	24	GREEN BAY	1:00
Dec.	1	at New Orleans	12:00
Dec.	9	at San Francisco	6:00
Dec.	15	ST. LOUIS	1:00
Dec.	23	LOS ANGELES RAIDERS	6:00

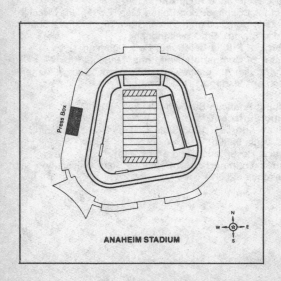

ANAHEIM STADIUM

LOS ANGELES RAMS
END OF SEASON DEPTH CHART

OFFENSE
WR   — 87 Drew Hill, 89 Ron Brown
OLT   — 75 Irv Pankey, 73 Russ Bolinger
OLG   — 72 Kent Hill, 73 Russ Bolinger
C   — 56 Doug Smith, 64 Joe Shearin
ORG   — 60 Dennis Harrah, 73 Russ Bolinger
ORT   — 62 Bill Bain, 73 Russ Bolinger
TE   — 81 David Hill, 86 Mike Barber, 83 James McDonald
WR   — 80 Henry Ellard, 82 Otis Grant, 84 George Farmer
QB   — 9 Jeff Kemp, 8 Steve Dils, 15 Vince Ferragamo
H-B   — 44 Mike Guman, 81 David Hill, 46 John Kamana
RB   — 29 Eric Dickerson, 30 Barry Redden,
           45 Dwayne Crutchfield

DEFENSE
DLE   — 85 Jack Youngblood, 77 Gary Jeter, 93 Doug Reed
NT   — 69 Greg Meisner, 70 Charles DeJurnett
DRE   — 71 Reggie Doss, 77 Gary Jeter, 66 Booker Reese
LOLB — 58 Mel Owens, 51 Norwood Vann
LILB — 55 Carl Ekern, 90 Ed Brady, 63 Mike McDonald
RILB — 50 Jim Collins, 59 Mark Jerue, 57 Jim Laughlin
ROLB — 54 Mike Wilcher, 53 Jim Youngblood
LCB   — 27 Gary Green, 28 David Croudip
RCB   — 47 LeRoy Irvin, 28 David Croudip
SS   — 22 Vince Newsome, 37 Ivory Sully
FS   — 20 Johnnie Johnson, 37 Ivory Sully, 43 Mike Pleasant

SPECIAL TEAMS
P   — 6 John Misko
K   — 1 Mike Lansford
H   — 8 Steve Dils, 9 Jeff Kemp
PR   — 80 Henry Ellard, 47 LeRoy Irvin, 20 Johnnie Johnson
KR   — 30 Barry Redden, 87 Drew Hill, 44 Mike Guman
LSN   — 63 Mike McDonald, 90 Ed Brady, 56 Doug Smith

ALSO WITH THE LOS ANGELES RAMS
88 Chris Faulkner (TE), 76 Gary Kowalski (T), 78 Jackie Slater (T),
61 Tony Slaton (C), 21 Nolan Cromwell (S), 26 Eric Harris (CB),
52 George Andrews (LB), 96 Doug Barnett (DE),
98 Shawn Miller (DE)

LOS ANGELES RAMS

INDIVIDUAL RUSHERS

	Att	Yards	Avg	Long	TD
Dickerson, Eric	379	2105	5.6	66	14
Crutchfield, Dwayne	73	337	4.6	36	1
Redden, Barry	45	247	5.5	35	0
Kemp, Jeff	34	153	4.5	23	1
Brown, Ron	2	25	12.5	16	0
Guman, Mike	1	2	2.0	2	0
Ferragamo, Vince	4	0	0.0	2	0
Ellard, Henry	3	−5	−1.7	5	0

INDIVIDUAL PASSING

	Att	Comp	Pct Comp	Yds	Avg Gain	TD	Pct TD	Long	Int	Pct Int	Rating Points
Kemp, Jeff	284	143	50.4	2021	7.12	13	4.6	t63	7	2.5	78.7
Ferragamo, Vince	66	29	43.9	317	4.80	2	3.0	68	8	12.1	29.2
Dickerson, Eric	1	0	0.0	0	0.00	0	0.0	0	1	100.0	0.0
Dils, Steve, Minn.-Rams	7	4	57.1	44	6.29	1	14.3	t14	1	14.3	75.9

INDIVIDUAL RECEIVERS

	No	Yards	Avg	Long	TD
Ellard, Henry	34	622	18.3	t63	6
Hill, David	31	300	9.7	26	1
Brown, Ron	23	478	20.8	54	4
Dickerson, Eric	21	139	6.6	19	0
Guman, Mike	19	161	8.5	29	0
Hill, Drew	14	390	27.9	68	4
Grant, Otis,	9	64	7.1	15	0
Farmer, George	7	75	10.7	23	0
Barber, Mike	7	42	6.0	11	0
McDonald, James	4	55	13.8	22	0
Redden, Barry	4	39	9.8	6	0
Crutchfield, Dwayne	2	11	5.5	7	1
Faulkner, Chris	1	6	6.0	6	0

INDIVIDUAL INTERCEPTORS

	No	Yards	Avg	Long	TD
Irvin, LeRoy	5	166	33.2	t81	2
Green, Gary	3	88	29.3	60	0
Cromwell, Nolan	3	54	18.0	t33	1
Collins, Jim	2	43	21.5	40	0
Johnson, Johnnie	2	21	10.5	21	0
Newsome, Vince	1	31	31.0	31	0
Owens, Mel	1	−4	−4.0	−4	0

INDIVIDUAL KICKOFF RETURNERS

	No	Yards	Avg	Long	TD
Redden, Barry	23	530	23.0	40	0
Hill, Drew	26	543	20.9	40	0
Pleasant, Mike	2	48	24.0	29	0
Irvin, LeRoy	2	33	16.5	22	0
Ellard, Henry	2	24	12.0	12	0
Guman, Mike	1	43	43.0	t43	1
Crutchfield, Dwayne	1	20	20.0	20	0
Sully, Ivory	1	3	3.0	3	0

INDIVIDUAL PUNTERS

	No	Yards	Long	Avg	Total Punts	TB	Blk	Opp Ret	Ret Yds	In 20	Net Avg
Misko, John	74	2866	58	38.7	74	9	0	35	196	21	33.6

INDIVIDUAL PUNT RETURNERS

	No	FC	Yards	Avg	Long	TD
Ellard, Henry	30	3	403	13.4	t83	2
Irvin, LeRoy	9	0	83	9.2	22	0
Johnson, Johnnie	1	1	3	3.0	3	0

INDIVIDUAL SCORERS

KICKERS

	XP	XPA	FG	FGA	PTS
Lansford, Mike	37	38	25	33	112

NON-KICKERS

	TD	TDR	TDP	TDM	PTS
Dickerson, Eric	14	14	0	0	84
Ellard, Henry	8	0	6	2	48
Brown, Ron	4	0	4	0	24
Hill, Drew	4	0	4	0	24
Crutchfield, Dwayne	2	1	1	0	12
Irvin, LeRoy	2	0	0	2	12
Cromwell, Nolan	1	0	0	1	6
Guman, Mike	1	0	0	1	6
Hill, David	1	0	1	0	6
Kemp, Jeff	1	1	0	0	6
Sully, Ivory	0	0	0	0	2
Vann, Norwood	0	0	0	0	2

MINNESOTA VIKINGS
NFC Central Division

Address: 9520 Viking Drive, Eden Prairie, Minnesota 55344
Telephone: (612) 828-6500

CLUB OFFICIALS
President: Max Winter
Vice President/General Manager: Mike Lynn
Head Coach: Bud Grant
Assistant Coaches: Tom Batta, Bud Bjornaraa, Dean Brittenham
 Jerry Burns, Tom Cecchini, Ross Fichtner, Bob Holloway,
 Bus Mertes, John Michels, Dan Radakovich, Floyd Reese
 Mike Sweatman
Director of Administration: Harley Peterson
Assistant to the General Manager/Director of Operations:
 Jeff Diamond
Ticket Manager: Harry Randolph
Director of Football Operations: Jerry Reichow
Director of Player Personnel: Frank Gilliam
Head Scout: Ralph Kohl
Assistant Head Scout: Don Deisch
Scout: John Carson
Director of Public Relations: Merrill Swanson
Director of Communications and Community Relations:
 Kernal Buhler
Public Relations Assistant: Katie Hogan
Trainer: Fred Zamberletti
Equipment Manager: Dennis Ryan

Stadium: Hubert H. Humphrey Metrodome (Capacity 62,212)
Playing Surface: SuperTurf
Stadium Address: 500 11th Avenue, So. Minneapolis,
 Minnesota 55415
Colours: Purple, Gold and White
Summer Training Camp: Mankato State University, Mankato,
 Minnesota 56001

MINNESOTA VIKINGS 1985 SCHEDULE

PRE-SEASON

Aug.	10	at Miami	8:00
Aug.	17	PITTSBURGH	7:00
Aug.	24	SEATTLE	7:00
Aug.	30	at Denver	7:00

REGULAR SEASON

Sep.	8	SAN FRANCISCO	12:00
Sep.	15	at Tampa Bay	4:00
Sep.	19	CHICAGO	7:00
Sep.	29	at Buffalo	1:00
Oct.	6	at Los Angeles Rams	1:00
Oct.	13	vs. Green Bay at Milwaukee	12:00
Oct.	20	SAN DIEGO	12:00
Oct.	27	at Chicago	12:00
Nov.	3	DETROIT	12:00
Nov.	10	GREEN BAY	12:00
Nov.	17	at Detroit	4:00
Nov.	24	NEW ORLEANS	12:00
Dec.	1	at Philadelphia	1:00
Dec.	8	TAMPA BAY	3:00
Dec.	15	at Atlanta	1:00
Dec.	22	PHILADELPHIA	12:00

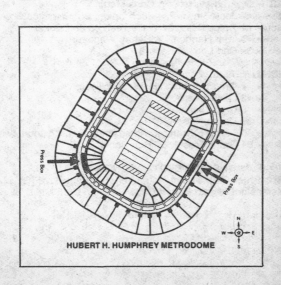

HUBERT H. HUMPHREY METRODOME

MINNESOTA VIKINGS
END OF SEASON DEPTH CHART

OFFENSE

WR	—	87 Leo Lewis, 85 Sammy White
OLT	—	78 Steve Riley, 60 Matt Hernandez
OLG	—	68 Curtis Rouse, 61 Wes Hamilton
C	—	67 Ron Sams, 64 Grant Feasel
ORG	—	66 Terry Tausch, 61 Wes Hamilton
ORT	—	76 Tim Irwin, 64 Grant Feasel
TE	—	83 Steve Jordan, 86 Mike Mularkey, 88 Don Hasselbeck, 81 Joe Senser
WR	—	89 Mike Jones, 84 Dwight Collins
QB	—	9 Tommy Kramer, 11 Wade Wilson, 4 Archie Manning
RB	—	46 Alfred Anderson, 23 Ted Brown, 24 Maurice Turner
RB	—	20 Darrin Nelson, 23 Ted Brown, 36 Allen Rice

DEFENSE

DLE	—	79 Doug Martin, 73 Neil Elshire, 90 John Haines
NT	—	65 Charlie Johnson, 91 Greg Smith
DRE	—	73 Neil Elshire, 91 Greg Smith, 69 Hasson Arbubakkr
LOLB	—	59 Matt Blair, 57 Robin Sendlein
LILB	—	52 Dennis Johnson, 58 Walker Ashley
RILB	—	55 Scott Studwell, 50 Dennis Fowlkes
ROLB	—	54 Fred McNeil, 56 Chris Martin
LCB	—	47 Joey Browner, 43 Jeff Colter, 25 Marcellus Greene
RCB	—	21 Rufus Bess, 37 Willie Teal, 43 Jeff Colter
SS	—	45 Tom Hannon, 34 Danny Wagoner
FS	—	39 Carl Lee, 29 John Swain

SPECIAL TEAMS

P	—	8 Greg Coleman, 11 Wade Wilson
K	—	3 Jan Stenerud
H	—	8 Greg Coleman, 87 Leo Lewis
PR	—	20 Darrin Nelson, 87 Leo Lewis
KR	—	20 Darrin Nelson, 46 Alfred Anderson, 87 Leo Lewis
LSN	—	64 Grant Feasel, 67 Ron Sams

ALSO WITH THE MINNESOTA VIKINGS
82 Bob Bruer (TE), 51 Jim Hough (G), 62 Brent Boyd (G),
49 Keith Nord (S), 63 Robert Cobb (DE), 77 Mark Mullaney (DE)

MINNESOTA VIKINGS

INDIVIDUAL RUSHERS

	Att	Yards	Avg	Long	TD
Anderson, Alfred	201	773	3.8	23	2
Brown, Ted	98	442	4.5	19	3
Nelson, Darrin	80	406	5.1	39	3
Rice, Allen	14	58	4.1	16	1
Jones, Mike	4	45	11.3	36	0
Manning, Archie	11	42	3.8	16	0
Wilson, Wade	9	30	3.3	12	0
Waddy, Billy	3	24	8.0	11	0
Coleman, Greg	2	11	5.5	13	0
Lewis, Leo	2	11	5.5	6	0
Kramer, Tommy	15	9	0.6	14	0
Jordan, Steve	1	4	4.0	t4	1
Nelson, David	1	3	3.0	3	0
Collins, Dwight	3	−14	−4.7	1	0

INDIVIDUAL PASSING

	Att	Comp	Pct Comp	Yds	Avg Gain	TD	Pct TD	Long	Int	Pct Int	Rating Points
Kramer, Tommy	236	124	52.5	1678	7.11	9	3.8	t70	10	4.2	70.6
Manning, Archie	94	52	55.3	545	5.80	2	2.1	56	3	3.2	66.1
Wilson, Wade	195	102	52.3	1019	5.23	5	2.6	38	11	5.6	52.5
Anderson, Alfred	7	3	42.9	95	13.57	2	28.6	t43	1	14.3	89.9
Coleman, Greg	1	0	0.0	0	0.00	0	0.0	0	0	0.0	39.6

INDIVIDUAL RECEIVERS

	No	Yards	Avg	Long	TD
Lewis, Leo	47	830	17.7	56	4
Brown, Ted	46	349	7.6	35	3
Jones, Mike	38	591	15.6	t70	1
Jordan, Steve	38	414	10.9	26	2
Nelson, Darrin	27	162	6.0	17	1
White, Sammy	21	399	19.0	47	1
Anderson, Alfred	17	102	6.0	t28	1
Senser, Joe	15	110	7.3	26	0
Mularkey, Mike	14	134	9.6	26	2
Collins, Dwight	11	143	13.0	t43	1
Rice, Allen	4	59	14.8	24	1
Kramer, Tommy	1	20	20.0	t20	1
LeCount, Terry	1	14	14.0	14	0
Hasselbeck, Don	1	10	10.0	10	0

INDIVIDUAL INTERCEPTORS

	No	Yards	Avg	Long	TD
Bess, Rufus	3	7	2.3	7	0
Swain, John	2	20	10.0	11	0

	No	Yards	Avg	Long	TD
Teal, Willie	1	53	53.0	t53	1
Browner, Joey	1	20	20.0	20	0
Studwell, Scott	1	20	20.0	20	0
Hannon, Tom	1	0	0.0	0	0
Lee, Carl	1	0	0.0	0	0
McNeill, Fred	1	0	0.0	0	0

INDIVIDUAL KICKOFF RETURNERS

	No	Yards	Avg	Long	TD
Nelson, Darrin	39	891	22.8	47	0
Anderson, Alfred	30	639	21.3	41	0
Waddy, Billy	3	64	21.3	31	0
Bess, Rufus	3	47	15.7	19	0
Rice, Allen	3	34	11.3	13	0
Smith, Greg	2	26	13.0	15	0
Rouse, Curtis	2	22	11.0	15	0
Turner, Maurice	2	21	10.5	14	0
Lewis, Leo	1	31	31.0	31	0
Nelson, David	1	0	0.0	0	0

INDIVIDUAL PUNTERS

	No	Yards	Long	Avg	Total Punts	TB	Blk	Opp Ret	Ret Yds	In 20	Net Avg
Coleman, Greg	82	3473	62	42.4	82	2	0	49	435	16	36.6

INDIVIDUAL PUNT RETURNERS

	No	FC	Yards	Avg	Long	TD
Nelson, Darrin	23	9	180	7.8	21	0
Lewis, Leo	4	1	31	7.8	13	0
Bess, Rufus	2	0	9	4.5	7	0
Waddy, Billy	1	0	-3	-3.0	-3	0
Teal, Willie	1	0	0	0.0	0	0

INDIVIDUAL SCORERS

KICKERS	XP	XPA	FG	FGA	PTS
Stenerud, Jan	30	31	20	23	90

NON-KICKERS	TD	TDR	TDP	TDM	PTS
Brown, Ted	6	3	3	0	36
Lewis, Leo	4	0	4	0	24
Nelson, Darrin	4	3	1	0	24
Anderson, Alfred	3	2	1	0	18
Jordan, Steve	3	1	2	0	18
Mularkey, Mike	2	0	2	0	12
Rice, Allen	2	1	1	0	12
Browner, Joey	1	0	0	1	6
Collins, Dwight	1	0	1	0	6
Jones, Mike	1	0	1	0	6
Kramer, Tommy	1	0	1	0	6
Martin, Chris	1	0	0	1	6
Teal, Willie	1	0	0	1	6
White, Sammy	1	0	1	0	6

NEW ORLEANS SAINTS
NFC Western Division

Address: 1500 Poydras Street, New Orleans, Louisiana 70112
Telephone: (504) 522-1500

CLUB OFFICIALS
Managing General Partner: Tom Benson, Jr.
President: Eddie Jones
Vice President-Administration: Fred Williams
Director of Football Operations: Pat Peppler
Head Coach/General Manager: O.A. (Bum) Phillips
Assistant Coaches: Andy Everest, King Hill, John Levra,
   Carl Mauck, Lamar McHan, Russell Paternostro,
   Wade Phillips, Harold Richardson, Joe Spencer,
   Lance Van Zandt, John Paul Young, Willie Zapalac
Director of Scouting: Bob Whitman
Director of Public Relations: Greg Suit
Assistant Director of Public Relations: Rusty Kasmiersky
Public Relations Assistant: Sylvia Alfortish
Ticket Manager: Sandy King
Director of Marketing: Barra Birrcher
Administrative Assistant: Jack Cherry
Trainer: Dean Kleinschmidt
Equipment Manager: Dan Simmons

Stadium: Louisiana Superdome (Capacity 71,647)
Playing Surface: AstroTurf
Stadium Address: 1500 Poydras Street, New Orleans, Louisiana
   70112
Colours: Old Gold, Black and White
Summer Training Camp: Louisiana Tech University, Ruston,
   Louisiana 71272

NEW ORLEANS SAINTS 1985 SCHEDULE

PRE-SEASON

Aug.	10	at New England	3:30
Aug.	17	HOUSTON	7:00
Aug.	24	TAMPA BAY	7:00
Aug.	30	at San Diego	7:00

REGULAR SEASON

Sep.	8	KANSAS CITY	12:00
Sep.	15	at Denver	2:00
Sep.	22	TAMPA BAY	12:00
Sep.	29	at San Francisco	1:00
Oct.	6	PHILADELPHIA	12:00
Oct.	13	at Los Angeles Raiders	1:00
Oct.	20	at Atlanta	1:00
Oct.	27	NEW YORK GIANTS	3:00
Nov.	3	at Los Angeles Rams	1:00
Nov.	10	SEATTLE	12:00
Nov.	17	vs. Green Bay at Milwaukee	12:00
Nov.	24	at Minnesota	12:00
Dec.	1	LOS ANGELES RAMS	12:00
Dec.	8	at St. Louis	12:00
Dec.	15	SAN FRANCISCO	12:00
Dec.	22	ATLANTA	12:00

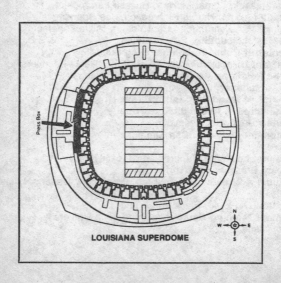

LOUISIANA SUPERDOME

NEW ORLEANS SAINTS
END OF SEASON DEPTH CHART

OFFENSE
WR — 86 Jeff Groth, 88 Eugene Goodlow, 19 Guido Merkens
OLT — 72 Chris Ward, 76 Jim Pietrzak
OLG — 63 Brad Edelman, 68 Kelvin Clark
C — 62 John Hill, 76 Jim Pietrzak, 65 David Carter
ORG — 60 Steve Korte, 66 Louis Oubre
ORT — 68 Kelvin Clark, 76 Jim Pietrzak
TE — 85 Hoby Brenner, 84 Junior Miller, 87 Larry Hardy
WR — 89 Tyrone Young, 80 Lindsay Scott
QB — 11 Richard Todd, 18 Dave Wilson, 19 Guido Merkens
RB — 38 George Rogers, 35 Earl Campbell, 30 Wayne Wilson, 22 Tyrone Anthony, 41 Jimmy Rogers
RB — 46 Hokie Gajan, 30 Wayne Wilson

DEFENSE
DLE — 75 Bruce Clark, 97 James Geathers
NT — 99 Tony Elliott, 73 Frank Warren
DRE — 94 Jim Wilks, 98 Reggie Lewis
LOLB — 57 Rickey Jackson, 53 Scott Pelluer
LILB — 56 Dennis Winston, 92 James Haynes
RILB — 52 Jim Kovach, 58 Glen Redd
ROLB — 51 Whitney Paul, 53 Scott Pelluer
LCB — 44 Dave Waymer, 29 Rodney Lewis
RCB — 25 Johnnie Poe, 26 Jitter Fields
SS — 20 Russell Gary, 34 Bobby Johnson
FS — 49 Frank Wattelet, 24 Terry Hoage, 28 Greg Harding

SPECIAL TEAMS
P — 10 Brian Hansen
K — 7 Morten Andersen
H — 19 Guido Merkens, 86 Jeff Groth
PR — 26 Jitter Fields, 86 Jeff Groth
KR — 22 Tyrone Anthony, 26 Jitter Fields
LSN — 76 Jim Pietrzak, 62 John Hill, 65 David Carter

ALSO WITH THE NEW ORLEANS SAINTS
64 Dave Lafary (T), 67 Stan Brock (T), 83 Kenny Duckett (WR), 82 John Tice (TE), 45 Tim Wilson (RB), 61 Joel Hilgenberg (C), 96 Don Thorp (NT), 74 Derland Moore (NT), 93 Gary Lewis (NT)

NEW ORLEANS SAINTS

INDIVIDUAL RUSHERS

	Att	Yards	Avg	Long	TD
Rogers, George	239	914	3.8	28	2
Gajan, Hokie	102	615	6.0	t62	5
Campbell, Earl, Hou.-N.O.	146	468	3.2	22	4
Wilson, Wayne	74	261	3.5	36	1
Todd, Richard	28	111	4.0	15	0
Anthony, Tyrone	20	105	5.3	19	1
Wilson, Tim	2	8	4.0	5	0
Goodlow, Eugene	1	5	5.0	5	0
Stabler, Ken	1	−1	−1.0	−1	0
Duckett, Kenny	1	−3	−3.0	−3	0
Wilson, Dave	3	−7	−2.3	−2	0
Hansen, Brian	2	−27	−13.5	−12	0

INDIVIDUAL PASSING

	Att	Comp	Pct Comp	Yds	Avg Gain	TD	Pct TD	Long	Int	Pct Int	Rating Points
Todd, Richard	312	161	51.6	2178	6.98	11	3.5	74	19	6.1	60.6
Wilson, Dave	93	51	54.8	647	6.96	7	7.5	154	4	4.3	83.9
Stabler, Ken	70	33	47.1	339	4.84	2	2.9	29	5	7.1	41.3
Gajan, Hokie	1	1	100.0	34	34.00	1	100.0	t34	0	0.0	158.3

INDIVIDUAL RECEIVERS

	No	Yards	Avg	Long	TD
Gajan, Hokie	35	288	8.2	51	2
Groth, Jeff	33	487	14.8	31	0
Wilson, Wayne	33	314	9.5	t34	3
Young, Tyrone	29	597	20.6	74	3
Brenner, Hoby	28	554	19.8	57	6
Goodlow, Eugene	22	281	12.8	23	3
Scott, Lindsay	21	278	13.2	37	1
Anthony, Tyrone	12	113	9.4	32	0
Rogers, George	12	76	6.3	15	0
Miller, Junior	8	81	10.1	22	1
Tice, John	6	55	9.2	17	1
Hardy, Larry	4	50	12.5	t28	1
Campbell, Earl, Hou.-N.O.	3	27	9.0	15	0
Duckett, Kenny	3	24	8.0	11	0

INDIVIDUAL INTERCEPTORS

	No	Yards	Avg	Long	TD
Waymer, Dave	4	9	2.3	9	0
Winston, Dennis	2	90	45.0	t47	2
Wattelet, Frank	2	52	26.0	t35	1

	No	Yards	Avg	Long	TD
Kovach, Jim	1	16	16.0	16	0
Poe, Johnnie	1	16	16.0	16	0
Jackson, Rickey	1	14	14.0	14	0
Clark, Bruce	1	9	9.0	9	0
Johnson, Bobby	1	7	7.0	7	0

INDIVIDUAL KICKOFF RETURNERS

	No	Yards	Avg	Long	TD
Anthony, Tyrone	22	490	22.3	64	0
Duckett, Kenny	29	580	20.0	39	0
Fields, Jitter	19	356	18.7	31	0
Wilson, Wayne	1	23	23.0	23	0
Wilson, Tim	1	16	16.0	16	0

INDIVIDUAL PUNTERS

	No	Yards	Long	Avg	Total Punts	TB	Blk	Opp Ret	Ret Yds	In 20	Net Avg
Hansen, Brian	69	3020	66	43.8	70	7	1	47	550	9	33.3

INDIVIDUAL PUNT RETURNERS

	No	FC	Yards	Avg	Long	TD
Fields, Jitter	27	6	236	8.7	61	0
Groth, Jeff	6	12	32	5.3	9	0

INDIVIDUAL SCORERS

KICKERS

	XP	XPA	FG	FGA	PTS
Andersen, Morten	34	34	20	27	94

NON-KICKERS

	TD	TDR	TDP	TDM	PTS
Gajan, Hokie	7	5	2	0	42
Brenner, Hoby	6	0	6	0	36
Campbell, Earl, Hou.-N.O.	4	4	0	0	24
Wilson, Wayne	4	1	3	0	24
Goodlow, Eugene	3	0	3	0	18
Young, Tyrone	3	0	3	0	18
Rogers, George	2	2	0	0	12
Wattelet, Frank	2	0	0	2	12
Winston, Dennis	2	0	0	2	12
Anthony, Tyrone	1	1	0	0	6
Hardy, Larry	1	0	1	0	6
Miller, Junior	1	0	1	0	6
Scott, Lindsay	1	0	1	0	6
Tice, John	1	0	1	0	6

NEW YORK GIANTS
NFC Eastern Division

Address: Giants Stadium, East Rutherford, New Jersey 07073
Telephone: (201) 935-8111

CLUB OFFICIALS
President: Wellington T. Mara
Vice President-Treasurer: Timothy J. Mara
Vice President-Secretary: Raymond J. Walsh
Vice President-General Manager: George Young
Assistant General Manager: Harry Hulmes
Head Coach: Bill Parcells
Assistant Coaches: Bill Belichick, Tom Bresnahan,
   Romeo Crennell, Ron Erhardt, Len Fontes, Ron Handley,
   Pat Hodgson, Lamar Leachman, Johnny Parker, Mike Pope,
   Steve Schnall
Controller: John Pasquali
Director of Player Personnel: Tom Boisture
Director of Pro Personnel: Tim Rooney
Director of Media Services: Ed Croke
Director of Promotions: Tom Power
Director of Special Projects: Victor Del Guercio
Box Office Treasurer: Jim Gleason
Trainers Emeritus: John Dziegiel
Head Trainer: Ronnie Barnes
Assistant Trainers: Dave Barringer, John Johnson
Equipment Manager: Ed Wagner, Jr.

Stadium: Giants Stadium (Capacity 76,891)
Playing Surface: AstroTurf
Stadium Address: East Rutherford, New Jersey 07073
Colours: Blue, Red and White
Summer Training Camp: Pace University, Pleasantville,
   N.Y. 10570

NEW YORK GIANTS 1985 SCHEDULE

PRE-SEASON

Aug.	3	vs. Houston Oilers (Hall of Fame Game)	2:30
Aug.	10	at Denver	7:00
Aug.	17	GREEN BAY	8:00
Aug.	24	NEW YORK JETS	8:00
Aug.	30	at Pittsburgh	7:30

REGULAR SEASON

Sep.	8	PHILADELPHIA	1:00
Sep.	15	at Green Bay	3:00
Sep.	22	ST. LOUIS	1:00
Sep.	29	at Philadelphia	1:00
Oct.	6	DALLAS	9:00
Oct.	13	at Cincinnati	1:00
Oct.	20	WASHINGTON	1:00
Oct.	27	at New Orleans	3:00
Nov.	3	TAMPA BAY	1:00
Nov.	10	LOS ANGELES RAMS	1:00
Nov.	18	at Washington	9:00
Nov.	24	at St. Louis	3:00
Dec.	1	CLEVELAND	1:00
Dec.	8	at Houston	3:00
Dec.	15	at Dallas	12:00
Dec.	21	PITTSBURGH	12:30

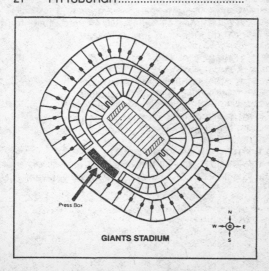

Press Box

GIANTS STADIUM

NEW YORK GIANTS
END OF SEASON DEPTH CHART

OFFENSE
WR   — 83 Earnest Gray, 86 Lionel Manuel, 85 John Mistler
OLT   — 60 Brad Benson, 66 Bill Roberts, 62 Conrad Goode
OLG   — 69 David Jordan
C   — 73 Kevin Belcher, 59 Rich Umphrey
ORG   — 61 Chris Godfrey, 69 David Jordan
ORT   — 63 Karl Nelson, 62 Conrad Goode
TE   — 84 Zeke Mowatt, 81 Tom Mullady
WR   — 88 Bob Johnson, 87 Byron Williams
QB   — 11 Phil Simms, 17 Jeff Rutledge, 15 Jeff Hostetler
RB   — 25 Butch Woolfolk, 20 Joe Morris
RB   — 26 Rob Carpenter, 30 Tony Galbreath,
            31 Frank Cephous

DEFENSE
DLE   — 76 Curtis McGriff, 75 George Martin
NT   — 64 Jim Burt, 78 Jerome Sally
DRE   — 79 Dee Hardison, 70 Leonard Marshall, 71 Casey Merrill
LOLB — 58 Carl Banks, 57 Byron Hunt, 54 Andy Headen
LILB   — 55 Gary Reasons, 52 Joe McLaughlin, 51 Robbie Jones
RILB   — 53 Harry Carson, 52 Joe McLaughlin
ROLB— 56 Lawrence Taylor, 58 Carl Banks
LCB   — 24 Kenny Daniel, 33 LeCharls McDaniel
RCB   — 23 Perry Williams, 34 Elvis Patterson
SS   — 29 Bill Currier, 48 Kenny Hill, 44 Pete Shaw
FS   — 43 Terry Kinard, 37 Larry Flowers

SPECIAL TEAMS
P   — 13 Dave Jennings
K   — 6 Ali Haji-Sheikh, 30 Tony Galbreath
H   — 17 Jeff Rutledge, 15 Jeff Hostetler
PR   — 44 Pete Shaw, 86 Lionel Manuel
KR   — 31 Frank Cephous, 86 Lionel Manuel
LSN   — 59 Rich Umphrey

ALSO WITH THE NEW YORK GIANTS
72 Gordon King (T), 80 Phil McConkey (WR),
38 John Tuggle (RB), 67 Billy Ard (G), 36 Mark Haynes (CB)

NEW YORK GIANTS

INDIVIDUAL RUSHERS

	Att	Yards	Avg	Long	TD
Carpenter, Rob	250	795	3.2	22	7
Morris, Joe	133	510	3.8	28	4
Simms, Phil	42	162	3.9	21	0
Galbreath, Tony	22	97	4.4	11	0
Woolfolk, Butch	40	92	2.3	17	1
Cephous, Frank	3	2	0.7	2	0
Manuel, Lionel	3	2	0.7	11	0

INDIVIDUAL PASSING

	Att	Comp	Pct Comp	Yds	Avg Gain	TD	Pct TD	Long	Int	Pct Int	Rating Points
Simms, Phil	533	286	53.7	4044	7.59	22	4.1	t65	18	3.4	78.1
Galbreath, Tony	1	1	100.0	13	13.00	0	0.0	13	0	0.0	118.8
Rutledge, Jeff	1	1	100.0	9	9.00	0	0.0	9	0	0.0	104.2

INDIVIDUAL RECEIVERS

	No	Yards	Avg	Long	TD
Johnson, Bob	48	795	16.6	45	7
Mowatt, Zeke	48	698	14.5	34	6
Gray, Earnest	38	529	13.9	31	2
Galbreath, Tony	37	357	9.6	37	0
Manuel, Lionel	33	619	18.8	53	4
Carpenter, Rob	26	209	8.0	19	1
Williams, Byron	24	471	19.6	t65	2
Morris, Joe	12	124	10.3	26	0
Woolfolk, Butch	9	53	5.9	13	0
McConkey, Phil	8	154	19.3	39	0
Mullady, Tom	2	35	17.5	22	0
Simms, Phil	1	13	13.0	13	0
Mistler, John, Buff-Giants	1	5	5.0	5	0
Belcher, Kevin	1	4	4.0	4	0

INDIVIDUAL INTERCEPTORS

	No	Yards	Avg	Long	TD
Haynes, Mark	7	90	12.9	22	0
Williams, Perry	3	7	2.3	7	0
Kinard, Terry	2	29	14.5	29	0
Reasons, Gary	2	26	13.0	26	0
Hunt, Byron	1	14	14.0	14	0
Currier, Bill	1	7	7.0	7	0
Carson, Harry	1	6	6.0	6	0
Headen, Andy	1	4	4.0	4	0
Taylor, Lawrence	1	−1	−1.0	−1	0

INDIVIDUAL KICKOFF RETURNERS

	No	Yards	Avg	Long	TD
McConkey, Phil	28	541	19.3	33	0
Woolfolk, Butch	14	232	16.6	27	0
Cephous, Frank	9	178	19.8	30	0
Morris, Joe,	6	69	11.5	14	0
McLaughlin, Jim	2	18	9.0	11	0
Daniel, Kenny	1	52	52.0	52	0
Hill, Ken	1	27	27.0	27	0

INDIVIDUAL PUNTERS

	No	Yards	Long	Avg	Total Punts	TB	Blk	Opp Ret	Ret Yds	In 20	Net Avg
Jennings, Dave	90	3598	54	40.0	93	10	3	50	479	22	31.4
Haji-Sheikh, Ali	0	0	0	—	1	0	1	0	0	0	0.0

INDIVIDUAL PUNT RETURNERS

	No	FC	Yards	Avg	Long	TD
McConkey, Phil	46	15	306	6.7	31	0
Manuel, Lionel	8	3	62	7.8	22	0
Kinard, Terry	1	0	0	0.0	0	0

INDIVIDUAL SCORERS

KICKERS

	XP	XPA	FG	FGA	PTS
Haji-Sheikh, Ali	32	35	17	33	83

NON-KICKERS

	TD	TDR	TDP	TDM	PTS
Carpenter, Rob	8	7	1	0	48
Johnson, Bob	7	0	7	0	42
Mowatt, Zeke	6	0	6	0	36
Manuel, Lionel	4	0	4	0	24
Morris, Joe	4	4	0	0	24
Gray, Earnest	2	0	2	0	12
Williams, Byron	2	0	2	0	12
Headen, Andy	1	0	0	1	6
McConkey, Phil	1	0	0	1	6
Woolfolk, Butch	1	1	0	0	6

PHILADELPHIA EAGLES
NFC Eastern Division

Address: Philadelphia Veterans Stadium, Broad Street and
   Pattison Avenue, Philadelphia, Pennsylvania 19148
Telephone: (215) 463-2500

CLUB OFFICIALS
Owner and President: Norman Braman
Co-owner: Ed Leibowitz
Vice President-Legal Counsel: Susan Fletcher
Head Coach: Marion Campbell
Assistant Coaches: Fred Bruney, Chuck Clausen, Tom Coughlin,
   Frank Gansz, George Hill, Ken Iman, Ted Marchibroda,
   Billie Matthews
Director of Public Relations: Jim Gallagher
Director of Communications: Ed Wisneski
Business Manager: Mimi Box
Director of Sales and Marketing: Bob Caesar
Ticket Manager: Hugh Ortman
Director of Player Personnel: Lynn Stiles
Assistant Director of Player Personnel: Jackie Graves
Talent Scouts: Bill Baker, Lou Blumling
Trainer: Otho Davis
Strength and Conditioning Coordinator: Tim Jorgensen
Equipment Manager: Rusty Sweeney

Stadium: Philadelphia Veterans Stadium (Capacity 71,640)
Playing Surface: AstroTurf
Stadium Address: Broad Street and Pattison Avenue,
   Philadelphia, Pennsylvania 19148
Colours: Kelly Green, Silver and White
Summer Training Camp: West Chester University, West Chester,
   Pennsylvania 19380

PHILADELPHIA EAGLES 1985 SCHEDULE

PRE-SEASON

Aug.	10	at New York Jets	8:30
Aug.	17	at Cleveland	7:30
Aug.	24	vs. Los Angeles Rams	7:30
Aug.	29	DETROIT	7:30

REGULAR SEASON

Sep.	8	at New York Giants	1:00
Sep.	15	LOS ANGELES RAMS	1:00
Sep.	22	at Washington	1:00
Sep.	29	NEW YORK GIANTS	1:00
Oct.	6	at New Orleans	12:00
Oct.	13	at St. Louis	12:00
Oct.	20	DALLAS	1:00
Oct.	27	BUFFALO	1:00
Nov.	3	at San Francisco	1:00
Nov.	10	ATLANTA	1:00
Nov.	17	ST. LOUIS	1:00
Nov.	24	at Dallas	3:00
Dec.	1	MINNESOTA	1:00
Dec.	8	WASHINGTON	1:00
Dec.	15	at San Diego	1:00
Dec.	22	at Minnesota	12:00

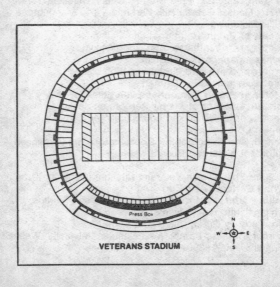

Press Box

N
W E
S

VETERANS STADIUM

PHILADELPHIA EAGLES
END OF SEASON DEPTH CHART

OFFENSE

WR — 82 Mike Quick, 83 Tony Woodruff, 85 Mel Hoover,
       86 Gregg Garrity
OLT — 64 Dean Miraldi, 79 Rusty Russell, 74 Leonard Mitchell
OLG — 73 Steve Kenney, 62 Petey Perot, 72 Dave Pacella
C — 65 Mark Dennard, 67 Gerry Feehery
ORG — 63 Ron Baker, 67 Gerry Feehery, 72 Dave Pacella,
       62 Petey Perot
ORT — 74 Leonard Mitchell, 63 Ron Baker, 79 Rusty Russell
TE — 88 John Spagnola, 84 Vyto Kab,
       87 Lawrence Sampleton
WR — 81 Kenny Jackson, 85 Mel Hoover, 86 Gregg Garrity
QB — 9 Joe Pisarcik, 5 Dean May, Jeff Christensen
RB — 31 Wilbert Montgomery, 32 Michael Williams,
       47 Andre Hardy
RB — 34 Hubert Oliver, 26 Michael Haddix, 39 Major Everett

DEFENSE

DLE — 68 Dennis Harrison, 94 Byron Darby,
       93 Thomas Strauthers
NT — 71 Ken Clarke, 96 Harvey Armstrong, 94 Byron Darby
DRE — 98 Greg Brown, 94 Byron Darby, 93 Thomas Strauthers
LOLB — 51 Reggie Wilkes, 53 Jody Schulz, 52 Rich Kraynak
LILB — 56 Jerry Robinson, 55 Mike Reichenbach,
       52 Rich Kraynak
RILB — 58 Anthony Griggs, 55 Mike Reichenbach,
       52 Rich Kraynak
ROLB — 59 Joel Williams, 52 Rich Kraynak, 53 Jody Schulz
LCB — 29 Elbert Foules, 43 Roynell Young, 22 Brenard Wilson,
       20 Andre Waters
RCB — 46 Herman Edwards, 43 Roynell Young,
       22 Brenard Wilson, 21 Evan Cooper
SS — 24 Ray Ellis, 22 Brenard Wilson
FS — 48 Wes Hopkins, 22 Brenard Wilson, 21 Evan Cooper

SPECIAL TEAMS

P — 2 Michael Horan
K — 8 Paul McFadden
H — 9 Joe Pisarcik, 2 Michael Horan
PR — 21 Evan Cooper, 20 Andre Waters, 81 Kenny Jackson
KR — 20 Andre Waters, 21 Evan Cooper, 24 Ray Ellis,
       39 Major Everett
LSN — 72 Dave Pacella, 68 Mark Dennard, 67 Gerry Feehery

ALSO WITH THE PHILADELPHIA EAGLES
80 Joe Hayes (WR/KR), 76 Jerry Sisemore (T),
7 Ron Jaworski (QB), 57 Bill Cowher (LB)

PHILADELPHIA EAGLES

INDIVIDUAL RUSHERS

	Att	Yards	Avg	Long	TD
Montgomery, Wilbert	201	789	3.9	27	2
Oliver, Hubert	72	263	3.7	17	0
Haddix, Michael	48	130	2.7	21	1
Williams, Mike	33	83	2.5	8	0
Hardy, Andre	14	41	2.9	10	0
Pisarcik, Joe	7	19	2.7	16	2
Jaworski, Ron	5	18	3.6	10	1
Quick, Mike	1	−5	−5.0	−5	0

INDIVIDUAL PASSING

	Att	Comp	Pct Comp	Yds	Avg Gain	TD	Pct TD	Long	Int	Pct Int	Rating Points
Jaworski, Ron	427	234	54.8	2754	6.45	16	3.7	t90	14	3.3	73.5
Pisarcik, Joe	176	96	54.5	1036	5.89	3	1.7	40	3	1.7	70.6
May, Dean	1	1	100.0	33	33.00	0	0.0	33	0	0.0	118.8
Montgomery, Wilbert	2	0	0.0	0	0.00	0	0.0	0	0	0.0	39.6

INDIVIDUAL RECEIVERS

	No	Yards	Avg	Long	TD
Spagnola, John	65	701	10.8	34	1
Quick, Mike	61	1052	17.2	t90	9
Montgomery, Wilbert	60	501	8.4	28	0
Haddix, Michael	33	231	7.0	22	0
Oliver, Hubert	32	142	4.4	21	0
Woodruff, Tony	30	484	16.1	38	3
Jackson, Kenny	26	398	15.3	t83	1
Kab, Vyto	9	102	11.3	26	3
Williams, Mike	7	47	6.7	15	0
Hoover, Mel	6	143	23.8	44	2
Garrity, Gregg, Pitt.-Phil.	2	22	11.0	12	0
Hardy, Andre	2	22	11.0	13	0

INDIVIDUAL INTERCEPTORS

	No	Yards	Avg	Long	TD
Ellis, Ray	7	119	17.0	31	0
Hopkins, Wes	5	107	21.4	33	0
Foules, Elbert	4	27	6.8	20	0
Edwards, Herman	2	0	0.0	0	0
Wilson, Brenard	1	28	28.0	28	0
Wilkes, Reggie	1	6	6.0	6	0

INDIVIDUAL KICKOFF RETURNERS

	No	Yards	Avg	Long	TD
Hayes, Joe	22	441	20.0	44	0
Cooper, Evan	17	299	17.6	48	0
Waters, Andre	13	319	24.5	t89	1
Everett, Major	3	40	13.3	18	0
Ellis, Ray	2	25	12.5	15	0
Hardy, Andre	1	20	20.0	20	0
Strauthers, Thomas	1	12	12.0	12	0

INDIVIDUAL PUNTERS

	No	Yards	Long	Avg	Total Punts	TB	Blk	Opp Ret	Ret Yds	In 20	Net Avg
Horan, Mike	92	3880	69	42.2	92	6	0	58	486	21	35.6

INDIVIDUAL PUNT RETURNERS

	No	FC	Yards	Avg	Long	TD
Cooper, Evan	40	19	250	6.3	16	0

INDIVIDUAL SCORERS

KICKERS

	XP	XPA	FG	FGA	PTS
McFadden, Paul	26	27	30	37	116

NON-KICKERS

	TD	TDR	TDP	TDM	PTS
Quick, Mike	9	0	9	0	54
Kab, Vyto	3	0	3	0	18
Woodruff, Tony	3	0	3	0	18
Hoover, Mel	2	0	2	0	12
Montgomery, Wilbert	2	2	0	0	12
Pisarcik, Joe	2	2	0	0	12
Haddix, Michael	1	1	0	0	6
Jackson, Kenny	1	0	1	0	6
Jaworski, Ron	1	1	0	0	6
Kraynak, Rich	1	0	0	1	6
Spagnola, John	1	0	1	0	6
Waters, Andre	1	0	0	1	6

ST. LOUIS CARDINALS
NFC Eastern Division

Address: Busch Stadium, Box 888, St. Louis, Missouri 63188
Telephone: (314) 421-0777

CLUB OFFICIALS
Chairman of the Board, CEO: William V. Bidwill
President: Bing Devine
Vice President/Administration: Curt Mosher
Director of Pro Personnel: Larry Wilson
Treasurer: Charley Schlegel
Head Coach: Jim Hanifan
Assistant Coaches: Chuck Banker, Tom Bettis, Don Brown, Rudy Feldman, Dick Jamieson, Tom Lovat, Leon McLaughlin, Floyd Peters, Emmitt Thomas
Director of Player Personnel: George Boone
Director of Public Relations: Michael Menchel
Media Coordinator: Greg Gladysiewski
Director of Community Relations: Adele Harris
Ticket Manager: Steve Walsh
Trainer: John Omohundro
Assistant Trainers: Jim Shearer, Ed Fleming
Equipment Manager: Bill Simmons
Assistant Equipment Managers: Mark Ahlmeier, Eric Youngstrom

Stadium: Busch Memorial Stadium (Capacity 51,392)
Playing Surface: AstroTurf
Stadium Address: 200 Stadium Plaza, St. Louis, Missouri 63102
Colours: Cardinal Red, Black and White
Summer Training Camp: Eastern Illinois University, Charleston, Illinois 61920

ST. LOUIS CARDINALS 1985 SCHEDULE

PRE-SEASON

Aug.	10	CHICAGO	7:30
Aug.	15	at Los Angeles Rams	7:00
Aug.	24	PITTSBURGH	7:30
Aug.	31	at Kansas City	7:30

REGULAR SEASON

Sep.	8	at Cleveland	1:00
Sep.	15	CINCINNATI	12:00
Sep.	22	at New York Giants	1:00
Sep.	29	GREEN BAY	12:00
Oct.	7	at Washington	9:00
Oct.	13	PHILADELPHIA	12:00
Oct.	20	at Pittsburgh	1:00
Oct.	27	HOUSTON	12:00
Nov.	4	DALLAS	8:00
Nov.	10	at Tampa Bay	1:00
Nov.	17	at Philadelphia	1:00
Nov.	24	NEW YORK GIANTS	3:00
Nov.	28	at Dallas	3:00
Dec.	8	NEW ORLEANS	12:00
Dec.	15	at Los Angeles Rams	1:00
Dec.	21	WASHINGTON	3:00

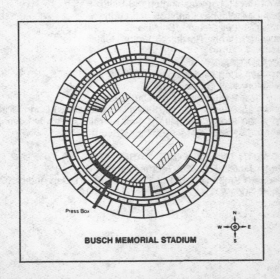

Press Box

BUSCH MEMORIAL STADIUM

N
W — E
S

ST. LOUIS CARDINALS
END OF SEASON DEPTH CHART

OFFENSE
WR — 81 Roy Green, 85 Danny Pittman, 86 Clyde Duncan
OLT — 67 Luis Sharpe, 70 Art Plunkett
OLG — 68 Terry Stieve, 66 Doug Dawson
C — 64 Randy Clark, 56 Carlos Scott
ORG — 71 Joe Bostic, 64 Randy Clark
ORT — 63 Tootie Robbins, 70 Art Plunkett
TE — 80 Doug Marsh, 89 Greg LaFleur, 84 John Goode
WR — 83 Pat Tilley, 82 Cedric Mack
QB — 15 Neil Lomax, 14 Rick McIvor, 12 Kyle Mackey
RB — 32 Ottis Anderson, 30 Stump Mitchell, 39 Willard Harrell,
       36 Perry Harrington
RB — 31 Earl Ferrell, 40 Randy Love

DEFENSE
DLE — 60 Al Baker
DLT — 62 Ramsey Dardar, 78 Elois Grooms
DRT — 65 David Galloway, 72 Dan Ralph
DRE — 75 Curtis Greer, 76 Stafford Mays, 57 Falaniko Noga
LLB — 59 Thomas Howard, 58 Dave Ahrens
MLB — 54 E.J. Junior, 51 Kurt Allerman
RLB — 52 Charles Baker, 50 Bob Harris, 57 Falaniko Noga
LCB — 48 Lionel Washington, 46 Victor Heflin
RCB — 44 Wayne Smith, 35 Jeff Griffin
SS — 38 Lee Nelson, Billy Davis
FS — 23 Benny Perrin, 46 Victor Heflin

SPECIAL TEAMS
P — 18 Carl Birdsong
K — 11 Neil O'Donoghue
H — 23 Benny Perrin, 18 Carl Birdsong
PR — 30 Stump Mitchell, 39 Willard Harrell, 85 Danny Pittman
KR — 30 Stump Mitchell, 31 Earl Ferrell, 40 Randy Love
LSN — 64 Randy Clark, 56 Carlos Scott

ALSO WITH THE ST. LOUIS CARDINALS
87 Eddie McGill (TE), 26 George Schmitt (S),
45 Leonard Smith (S), 42 Bill Whitaker (S), 61 Dan Audick (G),
73 Mark Duda (DT)

ST. LOUIS CARDINALS

INDIVIDUAL RUSHERS

	Att	Yards	Avg	Long	TD
Anderson, Ottis	289	1174	4.1	24	6
Mitchell, Stump	81	434	5.4	39	9
Ferrell, Earl	41	190	4.6	25	1
Lomax, Neil	35	184	5.3	20	3
Love, Randy	25	90	3.6	13	1
Harrell, Willard	9	20	2.2	7	1
Harrington, Perry	3	6	2.0	5	0
McIvor, Rick	3	5	1.7	6	0
Marsh, Doug	1	−5	−5.0	−5	0
Green, Roy	1	−10	−10.0	−10	0

INDIVIDUAL PASSING

	Att	Comp	Pct Comp	Yds	Avg Gain	TD	Pct TD	Long	Int	Pct Int	Rating Points
Lomax, Neil	560	345	61.6	4614	8.24	28	5.0	t83	16	2.9	92.5
McIvor, Rick	4	0	0.0	0	0.00	0	0.0	0	0	0.0	39.6
Mitchell, Stump	1	1	100.0	20	20.00	0	0.0	20	0	0.0	118.8
Perrin, Benny	1	1	100.0	0	0.00	0	0.0	0	0	0.0	79.2

INDIVIDUAL RECEIVERS

	No	Yards	Avg	Long	TD
Green, Roy	78	1555	19.9	t83	12
Anderson, Ottis	70	611	8.7	57	2
Tilley, Pat	52	758	14.6	42	5
Marsh, Doug	39	608	15.6	47	5
Mitchell, Stump	26	318	12.2	t44	2
Ferrell, Earl	26	218	8.4	21	1
LaFleur, Greg	17	198	11.6	23	0
Harrell, Willard	14	106	7.6	15	0
Pittman, Danny	10	145	14.5	50	0
Love, Randy	7	33	4.7	16	1
Mack, Cedric	5	61	12.2	22	0
Goode, John	3	23	7.7	10	0

INDIVIDUAL INTERCEPTORS

	No	Yards	Avg	Long	TD
Washington, Lionel	5	42	8.4	18	0
Smith, Wayne	4	35	8.8	23	0
Perrin, Benny	4	22	5.5	22	0
Smith, Leonard	2	31	15.5	t25	1
Griffin, Jeff	2	0	0.0	0	0
Howard, Thomas	2	−4	−2.0	1	0
Heflin, Victor	1	19	19.0	19	0
Junior, E.J.	1	18	18.0	18	0

INDIVIDUAL KICKOFF RETURNERS

	No	Yards	Avg	Long	TD
Mitchell, Stump	35	804	23.0	56	0
Pittman, Danny, St. L	14	319	22.8	43	0
Harrell, Willard	13	231	17.8	28	0
Green, Roy	1	18	18.0	18	0
Love, Randy	1	1	1.0	1	0
Ferrell, Earl	1	0	0.0	0	0

INDIVIDUAL PUNTERS

	No	Yards	Long	Avg	Total Punts	TB	Blk	Opp Ret	Ret Yds	In 20	Net Avg
Birdsong, Carl	67	2594	59	38.7	68	8	1	27	239	19	32.3

INDIVIDUAL PUNT RETURNERS

	No	FC	Yards	Avg	Long	TD
Mitchell, Stump	38	3	333	8.8	39	0
Pittman, Danny	4	1	10	2.5	5	0
Green, Roy	0	1	0	—	0	0

INDIVIDUAL SCORERS

KICKERS

	XP	XPA	FG	FGA	PTS
O'Donoghue, Neil	48	51	23	35	117

NON-KICKERS

	TD	TDR	TDP	TDM	PTS
Green, Roy	12	0	12	0	72
Mitchell, Stump	11	9	2	0	66
Anderson, Ottis	8	6	2	0	48
Marsh, Doug	5	0	5	0	30
Tilley, Pat	5	0	5	0	30
Lomax, Neil	3	3	0	0	18
Ferrell, Earl	2	1	1	0	12
Love, Randy	2	1	1	0	12
Harrell, Willard	1	1	0	0	6
Howard, Thomas	1	0	0	1	6
Smith, Leonard	1	0	0	1	6

SAN FRANCISCO 49ERS
NFC Western Division

Address: 711 Nevada St., Redwood City, California 94061
Telephone: (415) 365-3420

CLUB OFFICIALS
Owner and Chairman of the Board: Edward J. DeBartolo, Jr.
President/Head Coach: Bill Walsh
Vice President/General Manager: John McVay
Assistant Coaches: Jerry Attaway, Paul Hackett, Norb Hecker, Sherman Lewis, Bobb McKittrick, Bill McPherson, Ray Rhodes, George Siefert
Vice President of Marketing and Community Affairs: Ken Flower
Director of Pro Scouting: Alan Webb
Director of College Scouting: Tony Razzano
Director of Publicity and Media Relations: Jerry Walker
Business Manager: Keith Simon
Ticket Manager: Ken Dargel
Trainer: Lindsy McLean
Assistant Trainer: John Miller
Equipment Manager: Bronco Hinek

Stadium: Candlestick Park (Capacity 61,413)
Playing Surface: Grass
Stadium Address: San Francisco, California 94124
Colours: Forty Niners Gold and Scarlet
Summer Training Camp: Sierra Community College, Rocklin, California 95677

SAN FRANCISCO 49ERS 1985 SCHEDULE

PRE-SEASON

Aug.	10	at Los Angeles Raiders	6:00
Aug.	19	DENVER	6:00
Aug.	24	SAN DIEGO	12:00
Aug.	30	at Seattle	6:00

REGULAR SEASON

Sep.	8	at Minnesotta	12:00
Sep.	15	ATLANTA	1:00
Sep.	22	at Los Angeles Raiders	1:00
Sep.	29	NEW ORLEANS	1:00
Oct.	6	at Atlanta	1:00
Oct.	13	CHICAGO	1:00
Oct.	20	at Detroit	1:00
Oct.	27	at Los Angeles Rams	1:00
Nov.	3	PHILADELPHIA	1:00
Nov.	11	at Denver	7:00
Nov.	17	KANSAS CITY	1:00
Nov.	25	SEATTLE	6:00
Dec.	1	at Washington	4:00
Dec.	9	LOS ANGELES RAMS	6:00
Dec.	15	at New Orleans	12:00
Dec.	22	DALLAS	1:00

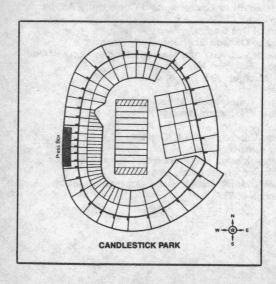

CANDLESTICK PARK

SAN FRANCISCO 49ERS
END OF SEASON DEPTH CHART

OFFENSE

WR   — 87 Dwight Clark, 83 Renaldo Nehemiah
OLT — 77 Bubba Paris, 67 Billy Shields
OLG — 68 John Ayers, 62 Guy McIntyre
C   — 56 Fred Quillan, 51 Randy Cross
ORG — 51 Randy Cross, 62 Guy McIntyre
ORT — 71 Keith Fahnhorst, 66 Allan Kennedy
TE   — 81 Russ Francis, 89 Earl Cooper, 86 John Frank
WR   — 88 Freddie Solomon, 85 Mike Wilson
QB   — 16 Joe Montana, 6 Matt Cavanaugh
RB   — 26 Wendell Tyler, 32 Carl Monroe, 24 Derrick Harmon
RB   — 33 Roger Craig, 30 Bill Ring

DEFENSE

DLE — 79 Jim Stuckey, 65 Lawrence Pillers, 72 Jeff Stover
NT   — 78 Manu Tuiasosopo, 94 Louie Kelcher,
         95 Michael Carter
DRE — 76 Dwaine Board, 97 Gary Johnson, 74 Fred Dean
LOLB — 57 Dan Bunz, 53 Milt McColl, 52 Blanchard Montgomery
LILB — 50 Riki Ellison, 99 Mike Walter
RILB — 64 Jack Reynolds, 99 Mike Walter
ROLB — 58 Keena Turner, 90 Todd Shell
LCB — 42 Ronnie Lott, 29 Mario Clark
RCB — 21 Eric Wright, 43 Dana McLemore
SS   — 27 Carlton Williamson, 49 Jeff Fuller
FS   — 22 Dwight Hicks, 28 Tom Holmoe

SPECIAL TEAMS

P   — 4 Max Runager
K   — 14 Ray Wersching
H   — 16 Joe Montana, 6 Matt Cavanaugh,
         88 Freddie Solomon
PR   — 43 Dana McLemore, 24 Derrick Harmon,
         88 Freddie Solomon
KR   — 32 Carl Monroe, 24 Derrick Harmon, 30 Bill Ring
LSN — 51 Randy Cross, 56 Fred Quillan, 68 John Ayers

ALSO WITH THE SAN FRANCISCO 49ERS
75 John Harty (NT), 54 Ron Ferrari (LB), 55 Jim Fahnhorst (LB),
47 Tim Collier (S)

SAN FRANCISCO 49ERS

INDIVIDUAL RUSHERS

	Att	Yards	Avg	Long	TD
Tyler, Wendell	246	1262	5.1	40	7
Craig, Roger	155	649	4.2	28	7
Harmon, Derrick	39	192	4.9	19	1
Ring, Bill	38	162	4.3	34	3
Montana, Joe	39	118	3.0	15	2
Solomon, Freddie	6	72	12.0	47	1
Cooper, Earl	3	13	4.3	7	0
Monroe, Carl	3	13	4.3	7	0
Runager, Max	1	−5	−5.0	−5	0
Cavanaugh, Matt	4	−11	−2.8	−1	0

INDIVIDUAL PASSING

	Att	Comp	Pct Comp	Yds	Avg Gain	TD	Pct TD	Long	Int	Pct Int	Rating Points
Montana, Joe	432	279	64.6	3630	8.40	28	6.5	t80	10	2.3	102.9
Cavanaugh, Matt	61	33	54.1	449	7.36	4	6.6	t51	0	0.0	99.7
Clark, Dwight	1	0	0.0	0	0.00	0	0.0	0	0	0.0	39.6
Harmon, Derrick	2	0	0.0	0	0.00	0	0.0	0	0	0.0	39.6

INDIVIDUAL RECEIVERS

	No	Yards	Avg	Long	TD
Craig, Roger	71	675	9.5	t64	3
Clark, Dwight	52	880	16.9	t80	6
Cooper, Earl	41	459	11.2	26	4
Solomon, Freddie	40	737	18.4	t64	10
Tyler, Wendell	28	230	8.2	t26	2
Francis, Russ	23	285	12.4	32	2
Nehemiah, Renaldo	18	357	19.8	t59	2
Wilson, Mike	17	245	14.4	44	1
Monroe, Carl	11	139	12.6	47	1
Frank, John	7	60	8.6	21	1
Ring, Bill	3	10	3.3	15	0
Harmon, Derrick	1	2	2.0	2	0

INDIVIDUAL INTERCEPTORS

	No	Yards	Avg	Long	TD
Turner, Keena	4	51	12.8	21	0
Lott, Ronnie	4	26	6.5	15	0
Shell, Todd	3	81	27.0	t53	1
Hicks, Dwight	3	42	14.0	29	0
McLemore, Dana	2	54	27.0	t54	1
Williamson, Carlton	2	42	21.0	26	0

	No	Yards	Avg	Long	TD
Fahnhorst, Jim	2	9	4.5	9	0
Wright, Eric	2	0	0.0	0	0
Fuller, Jeff	1	38	38.0	38	0
Bunz, Dan	1	2	2.0	2	0
Clark, Mario	1	0	0.0	0	0

INDIVIDUAL KICKOFF RETURNERS

	No	Yards	Avg	Long	TD
Monroe, Carl	27	561	20.8	44	0
Harmon, Derrick	13	357	27.5	51	0
McLemore, Dana	3	80	26.7	50	0
Ring, Bill	1	27	27.0	27	0
Wilson, Mike	1	14	14.0	14	0
Cooper, Earl	1	0	0.0	0	0
McIntyre, Guy	1	0	0.0	0	0

INDIVIDUAL PUNTERS

	No	Yards	Long	Avg	Total Punts	TB	Blk	Opp Ret	Ret Yds	In 20	Net Avg
Runager, Max	56	2341	59	41.8	57	12	1	26	176	18	33.8
Orosz, Tom	5	195	55	39.0	5	0	0	4	14	1	36.2

INDIVIDUAL PUNT RETURNERS

	No	FC	Yards	Avg	Long	TD
McLemore, Dana	45	11	521	11.6	t79	1

INDIVIDUAL SCORERS

KICKERS

	XP	XPA	FG	FGA	PTS
Wersching, Ray	56	56	25	35	131

NON-KICKERS

	TD	TDR	TDP	TDM	PTS
Solomon, Freddie	11	1	10	0	66
Craig, Roger	10	7	3	0	60
Tyler, Wendell	9	7	2	0	54
Clark, Dwight	6	0	6	0	36
Cooper, Earl	4	0	4	0	24
Ring, Bill	3	3	0	0	18
Francis, Russ	2	0	2	0	12
McLemore, Dana	2	0	0	2	12
Montana, Joe	2	2	0	0	12
Nehemiah, Renaldo	2	0	2	0	12
Johnson, Gary, S.D.-S.F.	1	0	0	1	8
Frank, John	1	0	1	0	6
Harmon, Derrick	1	1	0	0	6
Monroe, Carl	1	0	1	0	6
Shell, Todd	1	0	0	1	6
Wilson, Mike	1	0	1	0	6

TAMPA BAY BUCCANEERS
NFC Central Division

Address: One Buccaneer Place, Tampa, Florida 33607
Telephone: (813) 870-2700

CLUB OFFICIALS
Owner: Hugh F. Culverhouse
President: John McKay
Vice President: Joy Culverhouse
Secretary/Treasurer: Ward Holland
Director of Administration: Herbert M. Gold
Assistant to the Owner: Phil Krueger
Director of Player Personnel: Jim Gruden
Director of Public Relations: Rick Odioso
Director of Marketing/Advertising: Bob Passwaters
Assistant Director-Community Relations: Sandy Cottrell
Assistant Director-Media Relations: John Gerdes
Head Coach: Leeman Bennett
Assistant Coaches: John Brunner, Joe Diange, Boyd Dowler,
  Wayne Fontes, Abe Gibron, Kim Helton, Chip Myers,
  Jimmy Raye, Doug Shively, Howard Tippett
Director of Pro Personnel: Erik Widmark
Director of Ticket Operations: Terry Wooten
Controller: Edward Easom
Trainer: Jay Shoop
Assistant Trainer: Scott Anderson
Equipment Manager: Frank Pupello
Assistant Equipment Manager: Carl Melchior

Stadium: Tampa Stadium (Capacity 74,270)
Playing Surface: Grass
Stadium Address: North Dale Mabry, Tampa, Florida 33607
Colours: Florida Orange, White and Red
Summer Training Camp: One Buccaneer Place, Tampa,
  Flordia 33607

TAMPA BAY BUCCANEERS 1985 SCHEDULE

PRE-SEASON

Aug.	10	PITTSBURGH	8:00
Aug.	17	ATLANTA	8:00
Aug.	24	at New Orleans	7:00
Aug.	31	WASHINGTON	8:00

REGULAR SEASON

Sep.	8	at Chicago	12:00
Sep.	15	MINNESOTA	4:00
Sep.	22	at New Orleans	12:00
Sep.	29	at Detroit	1:00
Oct.	6	CHICAGO	1:00
Oct.	13	LOS ANGELES RAMS	1:00
Oct.	20	at Miami	4:00
Oct.	27	NEW ENGLAND	1:00
Nov.	3	at New York Giants	1:00
Nov.	10	ST. LOUIS	1:00
Nov.	17	at New York Jets	1:00
Nov.	24	DETROIT	1:00
Dec.	1	at Green Bay	12:00
Dec.	8	at Minnesota	3:00
Dec.	15	INDIANAPOLIS	1:00
Dec.	22	GREEN BAY	1:00

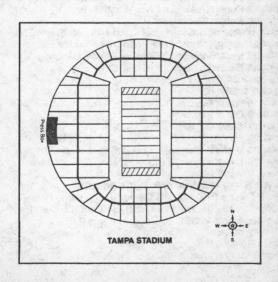

Press Box

TAMPA STADIUM

TAMPA BAY BUCCANEERS
END OF SEASON DEPTH CHART

OFFENSE

WR — 89 Kevin House, 81 Dwayne Dixon, Zack Thomas
OLT — 74 Gene Sanders, 79 Ken Kaplan, 70 Kelly Thomas
OLG — 72 Steve Courson, 77 Glenn Bujnoch, 60 Randy Grimes
C — 60 Randy Grimes, 50 Steve Wilson, 79 Ken Kaplan
ORG — 62 Sean Farrell, 77 Glenn Bujnoch, 60 Randy Grimes
ORT — 73 Ron Heller, 70 Kelly Thomas, 79 Ken Kaplan
TE — 88 Jimmie Giles, 82 Jerry Bell, 86 Jay Carroll,
       85 Mark Witte
WR — 87 Gerald Carter, 83 Theo Bell, Zack Thomas
QB — 17 Steve DeBerg, 14 Jack Thompson
RB — 46 Adger Armstrong, 25 Scott Dierking,
       38 George Peoples
RB — 32 James Wilder, 20 Michael Morton, 29 Leon Bright

DEFENSE

DLE — 78 John Cannon, 71 Byron Braggs
NT — 76 Dave Logan, 67 Karl Morgan
DRE — 63 Lee Roy Selmon, 78 John Cannon
LOLB — 57 Keith Browner, 59 Robert Thompson
LILB — 58 Jeff Davis, 55 Danny Spradlin, 54 Richard Wood
RILB — 52 Scot Brantley, 55 Danny Spradlin, 54 Richard Wood
ROLB — 53 Hugh Green, 51 Chris Washington,
        59 Robert Thompson
LCB — 23 Jeremiah Castille, 21 John Holt, 41 Norris Thomas
RCB — 21 John Holt, 27 Fred Acorn, 24 Maurice Harvey
LS — 33 Mark Cotney, 43 Beasley Reece, 31 Craig Curry
RS — 43 Beasley Reece, 31 Craig Curry

SPECIAL TEAMS

P — 5 Frank Garcia
K — 2 Obed Ariri
H — 17 Steve DeBerg
PR — 29 Leon Bright, 21 John Holt, 83 Theo Bell
KR — 20 Michael Morton, 29 Leon Bright, Zack Thomas
LSN — 79 Ken Kaplan, 50 Steve Wilson, 73 Ron Heller

ALSO WITH THE TAMPA BAY BUCCANEERS
26 James Owens (RB), 28 Mel Carver (RB), Andre Tyler (WR),
7 Jeff Komlo (QB), 16 Blair Kiel (QB), 34 Cedric Brown (S),
40 Mike Washington (CB), 56 Cecil Johnson (LB)

TAMPA BAY BUCCANEERS

INDIVIDUAL RUSHERS

	Att	Yards	Avg	Long	TD
Wilder, James	407	1544	3.8	37	13
DeBerg, Steve	28	59	2.1	14	2
Carver, Mel	11	44	4.0	12	0
Thompson, Jack	5	35	7.0	13	0
Armstrong, Adger	10	34	3.4	9	2
Morton, Michael	16	27	1.7	8	0
Carter, Gerald	1	16	16.0	16	0
Dierking, Scott	3	14	4.7	9	0
Peoples, George	1	2	2.0	2	0
Owens, James	1	1	1.0	1	0

INDIVIDUAL PASSING

	Att	Comp	Pct Comp	Yds	Avg Gain	TD	Pct TD	Long	Int	Pct Int	Rating Points
DeBerg, Steve	509	308	60.5	3554	6.98	19	3.7	55	18	3.5	79.3
Thompson, Jack	52	25	48.1	337	6.48	2	3.8	t74	5	9.6	42.4
Garcia, Frank	1	0	0.0	0	0.00	0	0.0	0	0	0.0	39.6
Wilder, James	1	1	100.0	16	16.00	1	100.0	t16	0	0.0	158.3

INDIVIDUAL RECEIVERS

	No	Yards	Avg	Long	TD
Wilder, James	85	685	8.1	50	0
House, Kevin	76	1005	13.2	55	5
Carter, Gerald	60	816	13.6	t74	5
Bell, Jerry	29	397	13.7	27	4
Giles, Jimmie	24	310	12.9	38	2
Bell, Theo	22	350	15.9	29	0
Armstrong, Adger	22	180	8.2	18	3
Dixon, Dwayne	5	69	13.8	21	0
Carroll, Jay	5	50	10.0	17	1
Carver, Mel	3	27	9.0	12	0
Owens, James	2	13	6.5	9	1
Dierking, Scott	1	5	5.0	t5	1

INDIVIDUAL INTERCEPTORS

	No	Yards	Avg	Long	TD
Cotney, Mark	5	123	24.6	29	0
Brantley, Scot	3	55	18.3	38	0
Castille, Jeremiah	3	38	12.7	30	0
Logan, Dave	1	27	27.0	t27	1
Holt, John	1	25	25.0	25	0
Acorn, Fred	1	14	14.0	14	0
Brown, Cedric	1	14	14.0	14	0
Reece, Beasley	1	12	12.0	12	0

	No	Yards	Avg	Long	TD
Cannon, John	1	0	0.0	0	0
Davis, Jeff	1	0	0.0	0	0

INDIVIDUAL KICKOFF RETURNERS

	No	Yards	Avg	Long	TD
Morton, Michael	38	835	22.0	43	0
Thomas, Zack, Den.-T.B.	18	351	19.5	33	0
Bright, Leon	16	303	18.9	33	0
Owens, James	8	168	21.0	36	0
Wood, Richard	5	43	8.6	16	0
Spradlin, Danny	1	5	5.0	5	0

INDIVIDUAL PUNTERS

	No	Yards	Long	Avg	Total Punts	TB	Blk	Opp Ret	Ret Yds	In 20	Net Avg
Garcia, Frank	68	2849	60	41.9	68	9	0	36	310	12	34.7

INDIVIDUAL PUNT RETURNERS

	No	FC	Yards	Avg	Long	TD
Bright, Leon	23	1	173	7.5	21	0
Thomas, Zack, Den.-T.B.	21	3	125	6.0	15	0
Holt, John	6	3	17	2.8	8	0
Bell, Theo	4	1	10	2.5	8	0

INDIVIDUAL SCORERS
KICKERS

	XP	XPA	FG	FGA	PTS
Ariri, Obed	38	40	19	26	95

NON-KICKERS

	TD	TDR	TDP	TDM	PTS
Wilder, James	13	13	0	0	78
Armstrong, Adger	5	2	3	0	30
Carter, Gerald	5	0	5	0	30
House, Kevin	5	0	5	0	30
Bell, Jerry	4	0	4	0	24
DeBerg, Steve	2	2	0	0	12
Giles, Jimmie	2	0	2	0	12
Carroll, Jay	1	0	1	0	6
Dierking, Scott	1	0	1	0	6
Logan, Dave	1	0	0	1	6
Owens, James	1	0	1	0	6

WASHINGTON REDSKINS
NFC Eastern Division

Address: Redskin Park, PO Box 17247, Dulles International
   Airport, Washington, DC 20041
Telephone: (703) 471 9100

CLUB OFFICIALS
Chairman of the Board and Chief Operating Executive:
   Jack Kent Cooke
Executive Vice President: John Kent Cooke
Senior Vice President: Gerard T. Gabrys
General Manager: Bobby Beathard
Assistant General Managers: Bobby Mitchell, Charles Casserly
Head Coach: Joe Gibbs
Assistant Coaches: Don Breaux, Joe Bugel, Bill Hickman,
   Larry Peccatiello, Richie Petitbon, Jerry Rhome, Dan Riley,
   Wayne Sevier, Warren Simmons, Charley Taylor,
   LaVern Torgeson
Director of Pro Scouting: Kirk Mee
Talent Scouts: Billy Devaney, George Saimes
Director Public Relations: Charles M. Taylor
Assistant Public Relations Directors: Ronn Levine,
   John C. Konoza
Ticket Manager: Sue Barton
Head Trainer: Lamar 'Bubba' Tyer
Assistant Trainers: Joe Kuczo, Keoki Kamau
Director of Stadium Operations: Dale Morris
Equipment Manager: Jay Brunetti

Stadium: Robert F. Kennedy Stadium (Capacity 55,431)
Playing Surface: Grass (PAT)
Stadium Address: East Capitol Street, Washington DC 20003
Colours: Burgundy and Gold
Summer Training Camp: Dickinson College, Carlisle,
   Pennsylvania 17013

WASHINGTON REDSKINS 1985 SCHEDULE

PRE-SEASON

Aug.	10	at Atlanta	8:00
Aug.	17	at Los Angeles Raiders	1:00
Aug.	24	NEW ENGLAND	8:00
Aug.	31	at Tampa Bay	8:00

REGULAR SEASON

Sep.	9	at Dallas	8:00
Sep.	15	HOUSTON	1:00
Sep.	22	PHILADELPHIA	1:00
Sep.	29	at Chicago	12:00
Oct.	7	ST. LOUIS	9:00
Oct.	13	DETROIT	1:00
Oct.	20	at New York Giants	1:00
Oct.	27	at Cleveland	1:00
Nov.	3	at Atlanta	1:00
Nov.	10	DALLAS	4:00
Nov.	18	NEW YORK GIANTS	9:00
Nov.	24	at Pittsburgh	1:00
Dec.	1	SAN FRANCISCO	4:00
Dec.	8	at Philadelphia	1:00
Dec.	15	CINCINNATI	1:00
Dec.	21	at St. Louis	3:00

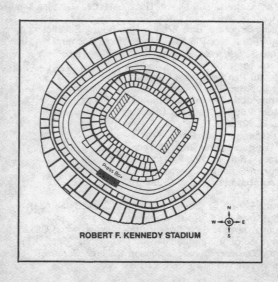

ROBERT F. KENNEDY STADIUM

WASHINGTON REDSKINS
END OF SEASON DEPTH CHART

OFFENSE

WR — 89 Calvin Muhammad, 87 Charlie Brown, 84 Rich Mauti
OLT — 66 Joe Jacoby, 68 Russ Grimm
OLG — 68 Russ Grimm, 61 Ken Huff
C — 76 Rick Donnalley, 68 Russ Grimm
ORG — 61 Ken Huff, 73 Mark May, 63 Bruce Kimball
ORT — 73 Mark May, 74 George Starke, 70 Morris Towns
TE — 88 Rick Walker, 86 Clint Didier
TE — 85 Don Warren
WR — 81 Art Monk, 83 Mark McGrath, 21 Mike Nelms
QB — 7 Joe Theismann, 17 Jim Hart, 10 Jay Schroeder
RB — 44 John Riggins, 25 Joe Washington, 35 Keith Griffin,
       39 Otis Wonsley, 40 Rick Kane

DEFENSE

DLE — 71 Charles Mann, 78 Tony McGee, 67 Tom Beasley
DLT — 65 Dave Butz, 69 Perry Brooks
DRT — 77 Darryl Grant, 69 Perry Brooks
DRE — 72 Dexter Manley, 67 Tom Beasley
LLB — 55 Mel Kaufman, 51 Monte Coleman
MLB — 52 Neil Olkewicz, 50 Larry Kubin, 54 Peter Cronan
RLB — 57 Rich Milot, 51 Monte Coleman, 56 Trey Junkin
LCB — 28 Darrell Green, 24 Anthony Washington,
       26 Ricky Smith
RCB — 32 Vernon Dean, 24 Anthony Washington,
       26 Ricky Smith
SS — 48 Ken Coffey, 22 Curtis Jordan
FS — 22 Curtis Jordan, 29 Mark Murphy, 27 Greg Williams

SPECIAL TEAMS

P — 5 Jeff Hayes, 7 Joe Theismann
K — 3 Mark Moseley, 5 Jeff Hayes
H — 7 Joe Theismann, 5 Jeff Hayes
PR — 21 Mike Nelms, 28 Darrell Green, 84 Rich Mauti
KR — 21 Mike Nelms, 35 Keith Griffin, 83 Mark McGrath
LSN — 77 Darryl Grant, 56 Trey Junkin, 10 Jay Schroeder

ALSO WITH THE WASHINGTON REDSKINS
12 Babe Laufenberg (QB), 30 Jeff Moore (RB),
89 Alvin Garrett (WR), 53 Jeff Bostic (C), Steve Hamilton (DE),
79 Todd Liebenstein (DE), 75 Bob Slater (DE),
23 Tony Peters (S), 82 Anthony Jones (TE), Mike Williams (TE)

WASHINGTON REDSKINS

INDIVIDUAL RUSHERS

	Att	Yards	Avg	Long	TD
Riggins, John	327	1239	3.8	24	14
Griffin, Keith	97	408	4.2	31	0
Theismann, Joe	62	314	5.1	27	1
Washington, Joe	56	192	3.4	12	1
Kane, Rick	17	43	2.5	10	0
Wonsley, Otis	18	38	2.1	7	4
Monk, Art	2	18	9.0	18	0
Hayes, Jeff	2	13	6.5	24	0
Moore, Jeff	3	13	4.3	5	0
Walker, Rick	1	2	2.0	2	0
Hart, Jim	3	−6	−2.0	−2	0

INDIVIDUAL PASSING

	Att	Comp	Pct Comp	Yds	Avg Gain	TD	Pct TD	Long	Int	Pct Int	Rating Points
Theismann, Joe	477	283	59.3	3391	7.11	24	5.0	t80	13	2.7	86.6
Hart, Jim	7	3	42.9	26	3.71	0	0.0	13	0	0.0	53.3
Washington, Joe	1	0	0.0	0	0.00	0	0.0	0	0	0.0	39.6

INDIVIDUAL RECEIVERS

	No	Yards	Avg	Long	TD
Monk, Art	106	1372	12.9	72	7
Muhammad, Calvin	42	729	17.4	t80	4
Didier, Clint	30	350	11.7	44	5
Brown, Charlie	18	200	11.1	36	3
Warren, Don	18	192	10.7	26	0
Moore, Jeff	17	115	6.8	18	2
Washington, Joe	13	74	5.7	12	0
McGrath, Mark	10	118	11.8	24	1
Seay, Virgil	9	111	12.3	19	1
Griffin, Keith	8	43	5.4	8	0
Riggins, John	7	43	6.1	11	0
Walker, Rick	5	52	10.4	19	1
Kane, Rick	1	7	7.0	7	0
Jones, Anthony	1	6	6.0	6	0
Garrett, Alvin	1	5	5.0	5	0

INDIVIDUAL INTERCEPTORS

	No	Yards	Avg	Long	TD
Dean, Vernon	7	114	16.3	t36	2
Green, Darrell	5	91	18.2	50	1
Milot, Rich	3	42	14.0	27	0
Jordan, Curtis	2	18	9.0	16	0
Coleman, Monte	1	49	49.0	t49	1
Smith, Ricky, N.E.-Wash.	1	37	37.0	37	0
Washington, Anthony	1	25	25.0	25	0

	No	Yards	Avg	Long	TD
Coffey, Ken	1	15	15.0	15	0

INDIVIDUAL KICKOFF RETURNERS

	No	Yards	Avg	Long	TD
Nelms, Mike	42	860	20.5	36	0
Griffin, Keith	9	164	18.2	31	0
Kane, Rick	3	43	14.3	31	0
Smith, Jimmy	2	38	19.0	22	0
Smith, Ricky, N.E.-Wash.	1	22	22.0	22	0
Mauti, Rich	1	16	16.0	16	0

INDIVIDUAL PUNTERS

	No	Yards	Long	Avg	Total Punts	TB	Blk	Opp Ret	Ret Yds	In 20	Net Avg
Hayes, Jeff	72	2834	59	39.4	73	5	1	38	187	11	34.9

INDIVIDUAL PUNT RETURNERS

	No	FC	Yards	Avg	Long	TD
Nelms, Mike	49	1	428	8.7	46	0
Green, Darrell	2	0	13	6.5	13	0
Williams, Greg	1	0	0	0.0	0	0
Mauti, Rich	1	1	2	2.0	2	0
Coffey, Ken	1	0	6	6.0	6	0
Coleman, Monte	0	0	27	—	27	0

INDIVIDUAL SCORERS

KICKERS	XP	XPA	FG	FGA	PTS
Moseley, Mark	48	51	24	31	120

NON-KICKERS	TD	TDR	TDP	TDM	PTS
Riggins, John	14	14	0	0	84
Monk, Art	7	0	7	0	42
Didier, Clint	5	0	5	0	30
Muhammad, Calvin	4	0	4	0	24
Wonsley, Otis	4	4	0	0	24
Brown, Charlie	3	0	3	0	18
Dean, Vernon	2	0	0	2	12
Moore, Jeff	2	0	2	0	12
Coleman, Monte	1	0	0	1	6
Grant, Darryl	1	0	0	1	6
Green, Darrell	1	0	0	1	6
Jacoby, Joe	1	0	0	1	6
Jordan, Curtis	1	0	0	1	6
McGrath, Mark	1	0	1	0	6
Seay, Virgil	1	0	1	0	6
Theismann, Joe	1	1	0	0	6
Walker, Rick	1	0	1	0	6
Washington, Joe	1	1	0	0	6

ACTIVE COACHES' CAREER RECORDS

Coach	Team(s)	Yrs	W	L	T	Pct.	W	L	T	Pct.	W	L	T	Pct.
				Regular Season				Postseason				Career		
Joe Gibbs	WASH.	4	41	16	0	.719	6	2	0	.750	47	18	0	.723
Don Shula	Balt., MIA.	22	227	82	6	.730	15	12	0	.556	242	94	6	.716
Tom Flores	RAIDERS	6	58	31	0	.652	8	2	0	.800	66	33	0	.667
Tom Landry	DALL.	25	223	126	6	.637	20	15	0	.571	243	141	6	.631
Chuck Knox	Rams, Buff., SEA.	12	112	62	1	.643	7	9	0	.438	119	71	1	.626
Chuck Noll	PITT.	16	142	88	1	.617	15	7	0	.682	157	95	1	.623
Bud Grant	MINN.	17	151	87	5	.632	10	12	0	.455	161	99	5	.617
Don Coryell	St. Lou., S.D.	12	102	68	1	.599	3	6	0	.333	105	74	1	.586
Bill Walsh	S.F.	6	49	40	0	.551	7	1	0	.875	56	41	0	.577
Dan Reeves	DEN	4	34	23	0	.596	0	2	0	.000	34	25	0	.576
John Robinson	RAMS	2	19	13	0	.594	1	2	0	.333	20	15	0	.571
O.A. "Bum" Phillips	Hou., N.O.	10	78	69	0	.531	4	3	0	.571	82	72	0	.532
Leeman Bennett	Atl., T.B.	6	46	41	0	.529	1	3	0	.250	47	44	0	.516
Mike Ditka	CHI.	3	21	20	0	.512	1	1	0	.500	22	21	0	.512
Forrest Gregg	Cle., Cinn., G.B.	8	58	56	0	.509	2	2	0	.500	60	58	0	.508
Raymond Berry	N. ENG.	1	4	4	0	.500	0	0	0	.000	4	4	0	.500
M. Schottenheimer	CLEV.	1	4	4	0	.500	0	0	0	.000	4	4	0	.500
Sam Wyche	CINN.	1	8	8	0	.500	0	0	0	.000	8	8	0	.500
Jim Hanifan	St. LOU.	5	34	38	1	.473	0	1	0	.000	34	39	1	.466
John Mackovic	K.C.	2	14	18	0	.438	0	0	0	.000	14	18	0	.438
Joe Walton	N.Y.J.	2	14	18	0	.438	0	0	0	.000	14	18	0	.438
Bill Parcells	N.Y.G.	2	12	19	1	.391	1	1	0	.500	13	20	1	.397
Dan Henning	ATL.	2	11	21	0	.344	0	0	0	.000	11	21	0	.344
Kay Stephenson	BUFF.	2	10	22	0	.313	0	0	0	.000	10	22	0	.313
Marion Campbell	Atl., PHIL.	4	17	39	1	.307	0	0	0	.000	17	39	1	.307
Hugh Campbell	HOU.	1	3	13	0	.188	0	0	0	.000	3	13	0	.188
Rod Dowhower	IND.	0	0	0	0	.000	0	0	0	.000	0	0	0	.000
Darryl Rogers	DET.	0	0	0	0	.000	0	0	0	.000	0	0	0	.000

Current team in capitals

AMERICAN FOOTBALL CONFERENCE

INDIVIDUAL PLAYER
STATISTICS

AFC — INDIVIDUAL RUSHERS

	Att	Yards	Avg	Long	TD
Jackson, Earnest, S.D.	296	1179	4.0	t32	8
Allen, Marcus, Raiders	275	1168	4.2	t52	13
Winder, Sammy, Den.	296	1153	3.9	24	4
Bell, Greg, Buff.	262	1100	4.2	t85	7
McNeil, Freeman, Jets	229	1070	4.7	53	5
Pollard, Frank, Pitt.	213	851	4.0	52	6
James, Craig, N.E.	160	790	4.9	73	1
Moriarty, Larry, Hou.	189	785	4.2	t51	6
McMillan, Randy, Ind.	163	705	4.3	t31	5
Heard, Herman, K.C.	165	684	4.1	t69	4
Green, Boyce, Clev.	202	673	3.3	29	0
Kinnebrew, Larry, Cin.	154	623	4.0	23	9
Abercrombie, Walter, Pitt.	145	610	4.2	31	1
Bennett, Woody, Mia.	144	606	4.2	23	7
Nathan, Tony, Mia.	118	558	4.7	22	1
Tatupu, Mosi, N.E.	133	553	4.2	t20	4
Collins, Anthony, N.E.	138	550	4.0	21	5
Hector, Johnny, Jets	124	531	4.3	64	1
Dickey, Curtis, Ind.	131	523	4.0	30	3
Pruitt, Mike, Clev.	163	506	3.1	14	6
Carter, Joe, Mia.	100	495	5.0	35	1
Alexander, Charles, Cin.	132	479	3.6	22	2
Byner, Earnest, Clev.	72	426	5.9	54	2
Erenberg, Rich, Pitt.	115	405	3.5	t31	2
Brooks, James, Cin.	103	396	3.8	33	2
Jennings, Stanford, Cin.	79	379	4.8	t20	2
Hawkins, Frank, Raiders	108	376	3.5	17	3
Willhite, Gerald, Den.	77	371	4.8	52	2
Brown, Theotis, K.C.	97	337	3.5	25	4
Hughes, David, Sea.	94	327	3.5	14	1
Lane, Eric, Sea.	80	299	3.7	t40	4
Middleton, Frank, Ind.	92	275	3.0	20	1
Edwards, Stan, Hou.	60	267	4.5	20	1
King, Kenny, Raiders	67	254	3.8	18	0
Elway, John, Den.	56	237	4.2	21	1
McGee, Buford, S.D.	67	226	3.4	30	4
Jackson, Billy, K.C.	50	225	4.5	16	1
Doornink, Dan, Sea.	57	215	3.8	25	0
Moon, Warren, Hou.	58	211	3.6	31	1
Parros, Rick, Den.	46	208	4.5	25	2
Johnson, Pete, S.D.-Mia.	87	205	2.4	9	12
Morris, Randall, Sea.	58	189	3.3	16	0
Krieg, Dave, Sea.	46	186	4.0	t37	3
Neal, Speedy, Buff.	49	175	3.6	10	1
Harris, Franco, Sea.	68	170	2.5	16	0

	Att	Yards	Avg	Long	TD
Lacy, Kenneth, K.C.	46	165	3.6	t24	2
Eason, Tony, N.E.	40	154	3.9	t25	5
Dixon, Zachary, Sea.	52	149	2.9	17	2
Pagel, Mike, Ind.	26	149	5.7	23	1
Barber, Marion, Jets	31	148	4.8	18	2
Schlichter, Art, Ind.	19	145	7.6	22	1
Minter, Cedric, Jets	34	136	4.0	14	1
Paige, Tony, Jets	35	130	3.7	24	7
Moore, Alvin, Ind.	38	127	3.3	18	2
James, Lionel, S.D.	25	115	4.6	20	0
Wonsley, George, Ind.	37	111	3.0	13	0
Blackledge, Todd, K.C.	18	102	5.7	26	1
Ferguson, Joe, Buff.	19	102	5.4	20	0
Ryan, Pat, Jets	23	92	4.0	16	0
Corley, Anthony, Pitt.	18	89	4.9	23	0
Veals, Elton, Pitt.	31	87	2.8	9	0
Moore, Booker, Buff.	24	84	3.5	21	0
Kofler, Matt, Buff.	10	80	8.0	19	0
Schonert, Turk, Cin.	13	77	5.9	17	1
Luck, Oliver, Hou.	10	75	7.5	18	1
Franklin, Andra, Mia.	20	74	3.7	12	0
Wilson, Stanley, Cin.	17	74	4.4	9	0
Lipps, Louis, Pitt.	3	71	23.7	t36	1
Anderson, Ken, Cin.	11	64	5.8	14	0
Esiason, Boomer, Cin.	19	63	3.3	9	2
White, Charles, Clev.	24	62	2.6	8	0
Bryant, Cullen, Sea.	20	58	2.9	8	0
Wilson, Marc, Raiders	30	56	1.9	t14	1
Muncie, Chuck, S.D.	14	51	3.6	11	0
Williams, Van, Buff.	18	51	2.8	7	0
Harper, Bruce, Jets	10	48	4.8	16	1
Thomas, Jewerl, S.D.	14	43	3.1	9	2
Lang, Gene, Den.	8	42	5.3	15	2
Malone, Mark, Pitt.	25	42	1.7	t13	3
Warner, Curt, Sea.	10	40	4.0	9	0
Clayton, Mark, Mia.	3	35	11.7	30	0
O'Brien, Ken, Jets	16	29	1.8	7	0
Brewer, Chris, Den.	10	28	2.8	8	0
Brookins, Mitchell, Buff.	2	27	13.5	16	0
Kubiak, Gary, Den.	9	27	3.0	17	1
Dufek, Joe, Buff.	9	22	2.4	13	1
Joyner, Willie, Hou.	14	22	1.6	9	0
Walls, Herkie, Hou.	4	20	5.0	20	0
Paige, Stephon, K.C.	3	19	6.3	9	0
Gillespie, Fernandars, Pitt.	7	18	2.6	9	0
Davis, Johnny, Clev.	3	15	5.0	8	1
Plunkett, Jim, Raiders	16	14	0.9	9	1

	Att	Yards	Avg	Long	TD
Woodley, David, Pitt.	11	14	1.3	7	0
Grogan, Steve, N.E.	7	12	1.7	1	0
Gunter, Michael, K.C.	15	12	0.8	4	0
Holt, Harry, Clev.	1	12	12.0	12	0
Morris, Wayne, S.D.	5	12	2.4	5	1
Farley, John, Cin.	7	11	1.6	5	0
Luther, Ed, S.D.	4	11	2.8	7	0
Largent, Steve, Sea.	2	10	5.0	6	0
Collinsworth, Cris, Cin.	1	7	7.0	7	0
Humm, David, Raiders	2	7	3.5	9	0
Myles, Jesse, Den.	5	7	1.4	2	0
Davis, Bruce, Clev.	1	6	6.0	6	0
Hunter, Tony, Buff.	1	6	6.0	6	0
Verser, David, Cin.	2	5	2.5	3	0
Young, Charle, Sea.	1	5	5.0	5	0
Dennison, Glenn, Jets	1	4	4.0	4	0
McDonald, Paul, Clev.	22	4	0.2	10	1
Willis, Chester, Raiders	5	4	0.8	2	0
Jensen, Derrick, Raiders	3	3	1.0	2	1
Johnson, Butch, Den.	1	3	3.0	3	0
Martin, Mike, Cin.	1	3	3.0	3	0
McCall, Joe, Raiders	1	3	3.0	3	0
Moore, Nat, Mia.	1	3	3.0	3	0
Riddick, Robb, Buff.	3	3	1.0	6	0
Montgomery, Cleotha, Raiders	1	1	1.0	1	0
Ricks, Lawrence, K.C.	2	1	0.5	1	0
Walker, Wesley, Jets	1	1	1.0	1	0
Arnold, Jim, K.C.	1	0	0.0	0	0
Colquitt, Craig, Pitt.	1	0	0.0	0	0
Mullins, Eric, Hou.	1	0	0.0	0	0
Pruitt, Greg, Raiders	8	0	0.0	3	0
Spencer, Todd, Pitt.	1	0	0.0	0	0
Stark, Rohn, Ind.	2	0	0.0	0	0
Cooper, Joe, Hou.	1	−2	−2.0	−2	0
Harris, M.L., Cin.	1	−2	−2.0	−2	0
Osiecki, Sandy, K.C.	1	−2	−2.0	−2	0
Capers, Wayne, Pitt.	1	−3	−3.0	−3	0
Zorn, Jim, Sea.	7	−3	−0.4	7	0
Avellini, Bob, Chi.-Jets	3	−5	−1.7	0	0
Campbell, Scott, Pitt.	3	−5	−1.7	0	0
Strock, Don, Mia.	2	−5	−2.5	0	0
Franklin, Byron, Buff.	1	−7	−7.0	−7	0
Marino, Dan, Mia.	28	−7	−0.3	10	0
Carson, Carlos, K.C.	1	−8	−8.0	−8	0
Kenney, Bill, K.C.	9	−8	−0.9	1	0
Walker, Dwight, Clev.	1	−8	−8.0	−8	0
Smith, Phil, Ind.	2	−10	−5.0	−3	0

	Att	Yards	Avg	Long	TD
Fryar, Irving, N.E.	2	−11	−5.5	0	0
Starring, Stephen, N.E.	2	−16	−8.0	0	0
Fouts, Dan, S.D.	12	−29	−2.4	3	0

t = touchdown
Leader based on most yards gained

AFC — TEAM RUSHING

	Att	Yards	Avg	Long	TD
Jets	504	2189	4.3	64	17
Cincinnati	540	2179	4.0	33	18
Pittsburgh	574	2179	3.8	52	13
Denver	508	2076	4.1	52	12
New England	482	2032	4.2	73	15
Indianapolis	510	2025	4.0	t31	13
Miami	484	1918	4.0	35	18
Raiders	516	1886	3.7	t52	19
Cleveland	489	1696	3.5	54	10
Houston	433	1656	3.8	t51	13
San Diego	456	1654	3.6	t32	18
Seattle	495	1645	3.3	t40	10
Buffalo	398	1643	4.1	t85	9
Kansas City	408	1527	3.7	t69	12
Conference Total	6797	26305	—	t85	197
Conference Average	485.5	1878.9	3.9	—	14.1

AFC — INDIVIDUAL PASSING

QUALIFIERS

	Att	Comp	Pct Comp	Yds	Avg Gain	TD	Pct TD	Long	Int	Pct Int	Rating Points
Marino, Dan, Mia.	564	362	64.2	5084	9.01	48	8.5	t80	17	3.0	108.9
Eason, Tony, N.E.	431	259	60.1	3228	7.49	23	5.3	t76	8	1.9	93.4
Fouts, Dan, S.D.	507	317	62.5	3740	7.38	19	3.7	t61	17	3.4	83.4
Krieg, Dave, Sea.	480	276	57.5	3671	7.65	32	6.7	t80	24	5.0	83.3
Anderson, Ken, Cin.	275	175	63.6	2107	7.66	10	3.6	t80	12	4.4	81.0
Kenney, Bill, K.C.	282	151	53.5	2098	7.44	15	5.3	t65	10	3.5	80.7
Moon, Warren, Hou.	450	259	57.6	3338	7.42	12	2.7	76	14	3.1	76.9
Elway, John, Den.	380	214	56.3	2598	6.84	18	4.7	73	15	3.9	76.8
Malone, Mark, Pitt.	272	147	54.0	2137	7.86	16	5.9	t61	17	6.3	73.4
Ryan, Pat, Jets	285	156	54.7	1939	6.80	14	4.9	t44	14	4.9	72.0
Wilson, Marc, Raiders	282	153	54.3	2151	7.63	15	5.3	92	17	6.0	71.7
McDonald, Paul, Clev.	493	271	55.0	3472	7.04	14	2.8	64	23	4.7	67.3
Ferguson, Joe, Buff.	344	191	55.5	1991	5.79	12	3.5	t68	17	4.9	63.5
Blackledge, Todd, K.C.	294	147	50.0	1707	5.81	6	2.0	t46	11	3.7	59.2

NON-QUALIFIERS

	Att	Comp	Pct Comp	Yds	Avg Gain	TD	Pct TD	Long	Int	Pct Int	Rating Points
Luck, Oliver, Hou.	36	22	61.1	256	7.11	2	5.6	37	1	2.8	89.6
Kubiak, Gary, Den.	75	44	58.7	440	5.87	4	5.3	41	1	1.3	87.6
Luther, Ed, S.D.	151	83	55.0	1163	7.70	5	3.3	t88	3	2.0	82.7
Woodley, David, Pitt.	156	85	54.5	1273	8.16	8	5.1	180	7	4.5	79.9
Schonert, Turk, Cin.	117	78	66.7	945	8.08	4	3.4	t57	7	6.0	77.8
O'Brien, Ken, Jets	203	116	57.1	1402	6.91	6	3.0	49	7	3.4	74.0
Pagel, Mike, Ind.	212	114	53.8	1426	6.73	8	3.8	t54	8	3.8	71.8
Campbell, Scott, Pitt.	15	8	53.3	109	7.27	1	6.7	t25	1	6.7	71.3
Plunkett, Jim, Raiders	198	108	54.5	1473	7.44	6	3.0	t73	10	5.1	67.6
Esiason, Boomer, Cin.	102	51	50.0	530	5.20	3	2.9	36	3	2.9	62.9
Dufek, Joe, Buff.	150	74	49.3	829	5.53	4	2.7	t64	8	5.3	52.9
Avellini, Bob, Chi.-Jets.	53	30	56.6	288	5.43	0	0.0	50	3	5.7	48.3
Grogan, Steve, N.E.	68	32	47.1	444	6.53	3	4.4	t65	6	8.8	46.4
Schlichter, Art, Ind.	140	62	44.3	702	5.01	3	2.1	54	7	5.0	46.2
Herrmann, Mark, Ind.	56	29	51.8	352	6.29	1	1.8	t74	6	10.7	37.8
Kofler, Matt, Buff.	93	33	35.5	432	4.65	2	2.2	t70	5	5.4	35.8
Osiecki, Sandy, K.C.	17	7	41.2	64	3.76	0	0.0	19	1	5.9	27.6
Stankavage, Scott, Den.	18	4	22.2	58	3.22	0	0.0	16	1	5.6	17.4
Zorn, Jim, Sea.	17	7	41.2	80	4.71	0	0.0	21	2	11.8	16.4
(Less than 10 attempts)											
Allen, Marcus, Raiders	4	1	25.0	38	9.50	0	0.0	38	0	0.0	66.7
Clayton, Mark, Mia.	1	0	0.0	0	0.00	0	0.0	0	1	100.0	0.0
Cox, Steve, Clev.	1	1	100.0	16	16.00	0	0.0	16	0	0.0	118.8
Dickey, Curtis, Ind.	1	1	100.0	63	63.00	1	100.0	t63	0	0.0	158.3
Flick, Tom, Clev.	1	1	100.0	2	2.00	0	0.0	2	0	0.0	79.2
Holohan, Pete, S.D.	2	1	50.0	25	12.50	1	50.0	t25	0	0.0	135.4
Humm, David, Raiders	7	4	57.1	56	8.00	0	0.0	21	1	14.3	43.5
James, Lionel, S.D.	2	0	0.0	0	0.00	0	0.0	0	1	50.0	0.0
Jensen, Jim, Mia.	1	1	100.0	35	35.00	1	100.0	t35	0	0.0	158.3
Kerrigan, Mike, N.E.	1	1	100.0	13	13.00	0	0.0	13	0	0.0	118.8
McInally, Pat, Cin.	2	2	100.0	77	38.50	0	0.0	43	0	0.0	118.8
Moore, Alvin, Ind.	1	0	0.0	0	0.00	0	0.0	0	0	0.0	39.6

	Att	Comp	Pct Comp	Yds	Avg Gain	TD	Pct TD	Long	Int	Pct Int	Rating Points
Moriarty, Larry, Hou.............	1	1	100.0	16	16.00	0	0.0	16	0	0.0	118.8
Morris, Randall, Sea...........	0	0	—	0	—	0	—	0	0	—	0.0
Mosley, Mike, Buff.	1	0	0.0	0	0.00	0	0.0	0	0	0.0	39.6
Stark, Rohn, Ind.	1	0	0.0	0	0.00	0	0.0	0	1	100.0	0.0
Strock, Don, Mia..................	6	4	66.7	27	4.50	0	0.0	12	0	0.0	76.4
Willhite, Gerald, Den............	2	1	50.0	20	10.00	0	0.0	20	0	0.0	85.4

t = Touchdown

AFC — TEAM PASSING

	Att	Comp	Pct Comp	Gross Yards	Tkd	Yds Lost	Net Yards	Avg Yds Att	Avg Yds Comp	TD	Pct TD	Long	Int	Pct Int
Miami...............	572	367	64.2	5146	14	128	5018	9.00	14.02	49	8.6	t80	18	3.1
San Diego........	662	401	60.6	4928	36	285	4643	7.44	12.29	25	3.8	t88	21	3.2
Kansas City......	593	305	51.4	3869	33	301	3568	6.52	12.69	21	3.5	t65	22	3.7
Seattle.............	497	283	56.9	3751	42	328	3423	7.55	13.25	32	6.4	t80	26	5.2
Raiders	491	266	54.2	3718	54	360	3358	7.57	13.98	21	4.3	92	28	5.7
Cincinnati.........	496	306	61.7	3659	45	358	3301	7.38	11.96	17	3.4	t80	22	4.4
Pittsburgh	443	240	54.2	3519	35	278	3241	7.94	14.66	25	5.6	t80	25	5.6
New England	500	292	58.4	3685	66	454	3231	7.37	12.62	26	5.2	t76	14	2.8
Houston	487	282	57.9	3610	49	382	3228	7.41	12.80	14	2.9	76	15	3.1
Cleveland.........	495	273	55.2	3490	55	358	3132	7.05	12.78	14	2.8	64	23	4.6
Jets.................	488	272	55.7	3341	52	382	2959	6.85	12.28	20	4.1	49	21	4.3
Denver	475	263	55.4	3116	35	257	2859	6.56	11.85	22	4.6	73	17	3.6
Buffalo	588	298	50.7	3252	60	554	2698	5.53	10.91	18	3.1	t70	30	5.1
Indianapolis	411	206	50.1	2543	58	436	2107	6.19	12.34	13	3.2	t74	22	5.4
Conf. Total.......	7198	4054	—	51627	634	4861	46766	—	—	317	—	t88	304	—
Conf. Average..	514.1	289.6	56.3	3687.6	45.3	347.2	3340.4	7.17	12.73	22.6	4.4	—	21.7	4.2

AFC — INDIVIDUAL RECEIVERS

	No	Yards	Avg	Long	TD
Newsome, Ozzie, Clev.	89	1001	11.2	52	5
Stallworth, John, Pitt.	80	1395	17.4	51	11
Christensen, Todd, Raiders	80	1007	12.6	38	7
Largent, Steve, Sea.	74	1164	15.7	65	12
Clayton, Mark, Mia.	73	1389	19.0	t65	18
Duper, Mark, Mia.	71	1306	18.4	t80	8
Watson, Steve, Den.	69	1170	17.0	73	7
Smith, Tim, Hou.	69	1141	16.5	t75	4
Franklin, Byron, Buff.	69	862	12.5	t64	4
Shuler, Mickey, Jets	68	782	11.5	49	6
Ramsey, Derrick, N.E.	66	792	12.0	34	7
Collinsworth, Cris, Cin.	64	989	15.5	t57	6
Allen, Marcus, Raiders	64	758	11.8	92	5
Marshall, Henry, K.C.	62	912	14.7	37	4
Joiner, Charlie, S.D.	61	793	13.0	41	6
Nathan, Tony, Mia.	61	579	9.5	26	2
Carson, Carlos, K.C.	57	1078	18.9	57	4
Holohan, Pete, S.D.	56	734	13.1	51	1
Winslow, Kellen, S.D.	55	663	12.1	33	2
Chandler, Wes, S.D.	52	708	13.6	t63	6
Harris, M. L., Cin.	48	759	15.8	t80	2
Starring, Stephen, N.E.	46	657	14.3	t65	4
Lipps, Louis, Pitt.	45	860	19.1	t80	9
Barnwell, Malcolm, Raiders	45	851	18.9	t51	2
Winder, Sammy, Den.	44	288	6.5	21	2
Butler, Raymond, Ind.	43	664	15.4	t74	6
Moore, Nat, Mia.	43	573	13.3	t37	6
Johnson, Butch, Den.	42	587	14.0	49	6
Walker, Wesley, Jets	41	623	15.2	t44	7
Williams, Jamie, Hou.	41	545	13.3	32	3
Sievers, Eric, S.D.	41	438	10.7	32	3
Dressel, Chris, Hou.	40	378	9.5	42	2
Porter, Tracy, Ind.	39	590	15.1	t63	2
Dawson, Lin, N.E.	39	427	10.9	27	4
Jackson, Earnest, S.D.	39	222	5.7	21	1
Morgan, Stanley, N.E.	38	709	18.7	t76	5
Erenberg, Rich, Pitt.	38	358	9.4	25	1
Brown, Theotis, K.C.	38	236	6.2	17	0
Turner, Daryl, Sea.	35	715	20.4	t80	10
Brennan, Brian, Clev.	35	455	13.0	52	3
Jennings, Stanford, Cin.	35	346	9.9	43	3
Johnson, Dan, Mia.	34	426	12.5	42	3
Bell, Greg, Buff.	34	277	8.1	37	1
Brooks, James, Cin.	34	268	7.9	t27	2
Young, Charle, Sea.	33	337	10.2	31	1

	No	Yards	Avg	Long	TD
Hunter, Tony, Buff.	33	331	10.0	30	2
Moore, Booker, Buff.	33	172	5.2	14	0
Jones, Lam, Jets	32	470	14.7	37	1
Doornink, Dan, Sea.	31	365	11.8	32	2
Moriarty, Larry, Hou.	31	206	6.6	24	1
Paige, Stephon, K.C.	30	541	18.0	t65	4
Dennard, Preston, Buff.	30	417	13.9	t68	7
Alexander, Charles, Cin.	29	203	7.0	22	0
Hardy, Bruce, Mia.	28	257	9.2	19	5
Scott, Willie, K.C.	28	253	9.0	27	3
Branch, Cliff, Raiders	27	401	14.9	47	0
Willhite, Gerald, Den.	27	298	11.0	63	0
Duckworth, Bobby, S.D.	25	715	28.6	t88	4
McNeil, Freeman, Jets	25	294	11.8	32	1
Heard, Herman, K.C.	25	223	8.9	17	0
Riddick, Robb, Buff.	23	276	12.0	38	0
James, Lionel, S.D.	23	206	9.0	31	0
Williams, Dokie, Raiders	22	509	23.1	t75	4
Feacher, Ricky, Clev.	22	382	17.4	64	1
Holston, Michael, Hou.	22	287	13.0	28	1
Bouza, Matt, Ind.	22	270	12.3	22	0
James, Craig, N.E.	22	159	7.2	16	0
Hughes, David, Sea.	22	121	5.5	25	1
Dawkins, Julius, Buff.	21	295	14.0	t37	2
Adams, Willis, Clev.	21	261	12.4	24	0
Holman, Rodney, Cin.	21	239	11.4	27	1
Pollard, Frank, Pitt.	21	186	8.9	18	0
Holt, Harry, Clev.	20	261	13.1	36	0
Kreider, Steve, Cin.	20	243	12.2	27	1
Hector, Johnny, Jets	20	182	9.1	26	0
Edwards, Stan, Hou.	20	151	7.6	20	0
Gaffney, Derrick, Jets	19	285	15.0	29	0
Bryant, Steve, Hou.	19	278	14.6	28	0
Jones, Cedric, N.E.	19	244	12.8	22	2
McMillan, Randy, Ind.	19	201	10.6	44	0
Kinnebrew, Larry, Cin.	19	159	8.4	22	1
Brookins, Mitchell, Buff.	18	318	17.7	t70	1
Walls, Herkie, Hou.	18	291	16.2	76	1
Cefalo, Jimmy, Mia.	18	185	10.3	t25	2
Thompson, Weegie, Pitt.	17	291	17.1	59	3
Johns, Paul, Sea.	17	207	12.2	32	1
Sawyer, John, Den.	17	122	7.2	25	0
Bendross, Jesse, S.D.	16	213	13.3	29	0
Tatupu, Mosi, N.E.	16	159	9.9	24	0
Dennison, Glenn, Jets	16	141	8.8	20	1
Kay, Clarence, Den.	16	136	8.5	21	3
Abercrombie, Walter, Pitt.	16	135	8.4	59	0

	No	Yards	Avg	Long	TD
Collins, Anthony, N.E.	16	100	6.3	19	0
Middleton, Frank, Ind.	15	112	7.5	16	1
Jackson, Billy, K.C.	15	101	6.7	11	1
Humphery, Bobby, Jets	14	206	14.7	t44	1
Young, Dave, Ind.	14	164	11.7	28	2
Dickey, Curtis, Ind.	14	135	9.6	33	0
King, Kenny, Raiders	14	99	7.1	15	0
Walker, Byron, Sea.	13	236	18.2	41	1
Jensen, Jim, Mia.	13	139	10.7	20	2
Lacy, Kenneth, K.C.	13	87	6.7	20	2
Rose, Joe, Mia.	12	195	16.3	t34	2
Curtis, Issac, Cin.	12	135	11.3	22	0
Green, Boyce, Clev.	12	124	10.3	t44	1
Sherwin, Tim, Ind.	11	169	15.4	26	0
Fryar, Irving, N.E.	11	164	14.9	26	1
Martin, Mike, Cin.	11	164	14.9	42	0
Henry, Bernard, Ind.	11	139	12.6	t19	2
Byner, Earnest, Clev.	11	118	10.7	26	0
Wright, James, Den.	11	118	10.7	21	1
Lane, Eric, Sea.	11	101	9.2	t55	1
Arnold, Walt, Wash.-K.C.	11	95	8.6	15	1
Egloff, Ron, S.D.	11	92	8.4	17	0
Hancock, Anthony, K.C.	10	217	21.7	t46	1
Walker, Dwight, Clev.	10	122	12.2	25	0
Minter, Cedric, Jets	10	109	10.9	t39	1
Barber, Marion, Jets	10	79	7.9	17	0
McCloskey, Mike, Hou.	9	152	16.9	51	1
Sampson, Clinton, Den.	9	123	13.7	25	1
McGee, Buford, S.D.	9	76	8.4	43	2
Neal, Speedy, Buff.	9	76	8.4	18	0
Morris, Randall, Sea.	9	61	6.8	18	0
Moore, Alvin, Ind.	9	52	5.8	12	0
Wonsley, George, Ind.	9	47	5.2	17	0
Alexander, Ray, Den.	8	132	16.5	41	1
Weathers, Clarence, N.E.	8	115	14.4	29	2
Tice, Mike, Sea.	8	90	11.3	30	3
Castor, Chris, Sea.	8	89	11.1	21	0
Smith, J. T., K.C.	8	69	8.6	16	0
Barnett, Buster, Buff.	8	67	8.4	18	0
Carter, Joe, Mia.	8	53	6.6	15	0
Hawthorne, Greg, N.E.	7	127	18.1	26	0
Davis, Bruce, Clev.	7	119	17.0	t43	2
Skansi, Paul, Sea.	7	85	12.1	27	0
Capers, Wayne, Pitt.	7	81	11.6	19	0
Hawkins, Frank, Raiders	7	51	7.3	15	0
Brammer, Mark, Buff.	7	49	7.0	12	0
Beckman, Ed, K.C.	7	44	6.3	9	1

	No	Yards	Avg	Long	TD
Verser, David, Cin.	6	113	18.8	28	0
Mullins, Eric, Hou.	6	85	14.2	25	1
Bennett, Woody, Mia.	6	44	7.3	20	1
Paige, Tony, Jets	6	31	5.2	10	1
Parros, Rick, Den.	6	25	4.2	9	0
Metzelaars, Pete, Sea.	5	80	16.0	25	0
Harper, Bruce, Jets	5	71	14.2	28	0
Kolodziejski, Chris, Pitt.	5	59	11.8	22	0
Williams, Van, Buff.	5	46	9.2	32	1
Pruitt, Mike, Clev.	5	29	5.8	9	0
White, Charles, Clev.	5	29	5.8	17	0
Morris, Wayne, S.D.	5	20	4.0	9	0
Roaches, Carl, Hou.	4	69	17.3	24	0
Cunningham, Bennie, Pitt.	4	64	16.0	29	1
Mosley, Mike, Buff.	4	38	9.5	17	0
Muncie, Chuck, S.D.	4	38	9.5	20	0
Robinson, Bo, N.E.	4	32	8.0	17	1
Casper, Dave, Raiders	4	29	7.3	13	2
White, Craig, Buff.	4	28	7.0	11	0
Lang, Gene, Den.	4	24	6.0	t9	1
Summers, Don, Den.	3	32	10.7	16	0
Klever, Rocky, Jets	3	29	9.7	13	1
Bryant, Cullen, Sea.	3	20	6.7	11	0
Nelson, Darrell, Pitt.	2	31	15.5	19	0
Sohn, Kurt, Jets	2	28	14.0	16	0
Sweeney, Calvin, Pitt.	2	25	12.5	16	0
Myles, Jesse, Den.	2	22	11.0	12	0
Scales, Dwight, Sea.	2	22	11.0	11	0
Brewer, Chris, Den.	2	20	10.0	16	0
Wilson, Stanley, Cin.	2	15	7.5	11	0
Kern, Don, Cin.	2	14	7.0	9	0
Pruitt, Greg, Raiders	2	12	6.0	8	0
Farley, John, Cin.	2	11	5.5	10	0
Johnson, Pete, S.D.	2	7	3.5	7	0
Dixon, Zachary, Sea.	2	6	3.0	6	0
Young, Glen, Clev.	1	47	47.0	47	0
Pratt, Bob, Sea.	1	30	30.0	30	0
Kubiak, Gary, Den.	1	20	20.0	20	0
Bolden, Rickey, Clev.	1	19	19.0	19	0
Warner, Curt, Sea.	1	19	19.0	19	0
Stracka, Tim, Clev.	1	15	15.0	15	0
Little, David, K.C.	1	13	13.0	13	0
Gillespie, Fernandars, Pitt.	1	12	12.0	12	0
Bruckner, Nick, Jets	1	11	11.0	11	0
Gissinger, Andy, S.D.	1	3	3.0	3	0
Harris, Franco, Sea.	1	3	3.0	3	0
Logan, Dave, Den.	1	3	3.0	3	0

	No	Yards	Avg	Long	Td
Jensen, Derrick, Raiders	1	1	1.0	t1	1
Munoz, Anthony, Cin.	1	1	1.0	t1	1
Fouts, Dan, S.D.	1	0	0.0	0	0
McDonald, Paul, Clev.	1	−4	−4.0	−4	0
Studdard, Dave, Den.	1	−4	−4.0	−4	0

t = touchdown
Leader based on most passes caught

AFC — TOP 25 RECEIVERS BY YARDS

	Yards	No	Avg	Long	TD
Stallworth, John, Pitt.	1395	80	17.4	51	11
Clayton, Mark, Mia.	1389	73	19.0	t65	18
Duper, Mark, Mia.	1306	71	18.4	t80	8
Watson, Steve, Den.	1170	69	17.0	73	7
Largent, Steve, Sea.	1164	74	15.7	65	12
Smith, Tim, Hou.	1141	69	16.5	t75	4
Carson, Carlos, K.C.	1078	57	18.9	57	4
Christensen, Todd, Raiders	1007	80	12.6	38	7
Newsome, Ozzie, Clev.	1001	89	11.2	52	5
Collinsworth, Cris, Cin.	989	64	15.5	t57	6
Marshall, Henry, K.C.	912	62	14.7	37	4
Franklin, Byron, Buff.	862	69	12.5	t64	4
Lipps, Louis, Pitt.	860	45	19.1	t80	9
Barnwell, Malcolm, Raiders	851	45	18.9	t51	2
Joiner, Charlie, S.D.	793	61	13.0	41	6
Ramsey, Derrick, N.E.	792	66	12.0	34	7
Shuler, Mickey, Jets	782	68	11.5	49	6
Harris, M. L., Cin.	759	48	15.8	t80	2
Allen, Marcus, Raiders	758	64	11.8	92	5
Holohan, Pete, S.D.	734	56	13.1	51	1
Duckworth, Bobby, S.D.	715	25	28.6	t88	4
Turner, Daryl, Sea.	715	35	20.4	t80	10
Morgan, Stanley, N.E.	709	38	18.7	t76	5
Chandler, Wes, S.D.	708	52	13.6	t63	6
Butler, Raymond, Ind.	664	43	15.4	t74	6

AFC — INDIVIDUAL INTERCEPTORS

	No	Yards	Avg	Long	TD
Easley, Ken, Sea.	10	126	12.6	t58	2
Brown, Dave, Sea.	8	179	22.4	t90	2
Cherry, Deron, K.C.	7	140	20.0	67	0
Shell, Donnie, Pitt.	7	61	8.7	t52	1
Haynes, Mike, Raiders	6	220	36.7	t97	1
Blackwood, Glenn, Mia.	6	169	28.2	50	0
Washington, Sam, Pitt.	6	138	23.0	t69	2
Ross, Kevin, K.C.	6	124	20.7	t71	1
Foley, Steve, Den.	6	97	16.2	t40	1
Harden, Mike, Den.	6	79	13.2	t45	1
Harris, John, Sea.	6	79	13.2	29	0
Daniel, Eugene, Ind.	6	25	4.2	18	0
Romes, Charles, Buff.	5	130	26.0	55	0
Gross, Al, Clev.	5	103	20.6	47	0
Woodruff, Dwayne, Pitt.	5	56	11.2	t42	1
Dixon, Hanford, Clev.	5	31	6.2	18	0
Byrd, Gill, S.D.	4	157	39.3	t99	2
Simpson, Keith, Sea.	4	138	34.5	t76	2
Judson, William, Mia.	4	121	30.3	t60	1
Breeden, Louis, Cin.	4	96	24.0	70	0
Jackson, Terry, Sea.	4	78	19.5	t62	1
Wilson, Steve, Den.	4	59	14.8	22	0
Lewis, Albert, K.C.	4	57	14.3	31	0
Tullis, Willie, Hou.	4	48	12.0	22	0
McElroy, Vann, Raiders	4	42	10.5	31	0
Jackson, Robert, Cin.	4	32	8.0	t28	1
Kemp, Bobby, Cin.	4	27	6.8	14	0
Carter, Russell, Jets	4	26	6.5	19	0
Clayborn, Ray, N.E.	3	102	34.0	85	0
Hinkle, Bryan, Pitt.	3	77	25.7	43	0
Randle, Tate, Ind.	3	66	22.0	54	0
Taylor, Terry, Sea.	3	63	21.0	37	0
Lowe, Woodrow, S.D.	3	61	20.3	t32	1
Williams, Eric, Pitt.	3	49	16.3	44	0
Horton, Ray, Cin.	3	48	16.0	t48	1
Freeman, Steve, Buff.	3	45	15.0	45	0
McNeal, Don, Mia.	3	41	13.7	30	1
Smith, Billy Ray, S.D.	3	41	13.7	21	0
Blackwood, Lyle, Mia.	3	29	9.7	15	0
Lankford, Paul, Mia.	3	25	8.3	22	0
Hartwig, Carter, Hou.	3	23	7.7	19	0
Lippett, Ronnie, N.E.	3	23	7.7	13	0
Krauss, Barry, Ind.	3	20	6.7	18	0
Smith, Dennis, Den.	3	13	4.3	10	0
Carpenter, Brian, Wash.-Buff.	3	11	3.7	11	0
Burroughs, Jim, Ind.	3	9	3.0	6	0

	No	Yards	Avg	Long	TD
Mecklenburg, Karl, Den.	2	105	52.5	63	0
Robbins, Randy, Den.	2	62	31.0	t62	1
Radecic, Scott, K.C.	2	54	27.0	35	1
Ray, Darrol, Jets	2	54	27.0	28	0
King, Linden, S.D.	2	52	26.0	37	0
Simmons, John, Cin.	2	43	21.5	t43	1
Turner, John, S.D.	2	43	21.5	43	0
Marion, Fred, N.E.	2	39	19.5	26	0
McAlister, Ken, K.C.	2	33	16.5	22	0
Williams, Reggie, Cin.	2	33	16.5	33	0
Martin, Rod, Raiders	2	31	15.5	17	1
Young, Andre, S.D.	2	31	15.5	31	0
Busick, Steve, Den.	2	21	10.5	16	0
Burruss, Lloyd, K.C.	2	16	8.0	16	0
Lynn, Johnny, Jets	2	16	8.0	16	0
James, Roland, N.E.	2	14	7.0	14	0
Griffin, Ray, Cin.	2	13	6.5	13	0
Schroy, Ken, Jets	2	13	6.5	13	0
Daniels, Calvin, K.C.	2	11	5.5	11	0
Davis, Mike, Raiders	2	11	5.5	11	0
Cousineau, Tom, Clev.	2	9	4.5	9	0
Merriweather, Mike, Pitt.	2	9	4.5	8	0
Buttle, Greg, Jets	2	5	2.5	5	0
Gibson, Ernest, N.E.	2	4	2.0	4	0
Johnson, Eddie, Clev.	2	3	1.5	3	0
Sanford, Rick, N.E.	2	2	1.0	2	0
Woods, Rick, Pitt.	2	0	0.0	0	0
Hill, Greg, K.C.	2	−1	−0.5	0	0
Williams, Lee, S.D.	1	66	66.0	t66	1
Kafentzis, Mark, Ind.	1	59	59.0	t59	1
Griffin, James, Cin.	1	57	57.0	t57	1
Brown, Bud, Mia.	1	53	53.0	53	0
Rogers, Don, Clev.	1	39	39.0	39	0
Fox, Tim, S.D.	1	36	36.0	36	0
Brown, Chris, Pitt.	1	31	31.0	31	0
Woodard, Ken, Den.	1	27	27.0	t27	1
Brown, Steve, Hou.	1	26	26.0	26	0
Kozlowski, Mike, Mia.	1	26	26.0	26	0
Minnifield, Frank, Clev.	1	26	26.0	26	0
Mullen, Davlin, Jets	1	25	25.0	25	0
Smerlas, Fred, Buff.	1	25	25.0	25	0
Dombroski, Paul, N.E.	1	23	23.0	23	0
Jackson, Roger, Den.	1	23	23.0	23	0
Eason, Bo, Hou.	1	20	20.0	20	0
Gaines, Greg, Sea.	1	18	18.0	18	0
Perry, Rod, Clev.	1	17	17.0	17	0
Jackson, Charles, K.C.	1	16	16.0	16	0
Barnes, Jeff, Raiders	1	15	15.0	15	0

	No	Yards	Avg	Long	TD
Cameron, Glenn, Cin.	1	15	15.0	15	0
Kush, Rod, Buff.	1	15	15.0	15	0
Scholtz, Bruce, Sea.	1	15	15.0	15	0
Blanton, Jerry, K.C.	1	14	14.0	14	0
Ryan, Jim, Den.	1	13	13.0	13	0
Springs, Kirk, Jets	1	13	13.0	13	0
Cole, Robin, Pitt.	1	12	12.0	12	0
Gregor, Bob, S.D.	1	12	12.0	12	0
Lyday, Allen, Hou.	1	12	12.0	12	0
Van Pelt, Brad, Raiders	1	9	9.0	9	0
Banks, Chip, Clev.	1	8	8.0	8	0
Davis, James, Raiders	1	8	8.0	8	0
Glasgow, Nesby, Ind.	1	8	8.0	8	0
Duhe, A.J., Mia.	1	7	7.0	7	0
Smith, Lucious, Buff.	1	7	7.0	7	0
Sowell, Robert, Mia.	1	7	7.0	7	0
Comeaux, Darren, Den.	1	5	5.0	5	0
Lilly, Tony, Den.	1	5	5.0	5	0
Turner, Jim, Cin.	1	4	4.0	4	0
Blackmon, Don, N.E.	1	3	3.0	3	0
Davis, Preston, Ind.	1	3	3.0	3	0
Hayes, Lester, Raiders	1	3	3.0	3	0
Allen, Patrick, Hou.	1	2	2.0	2	0
Brazile, Robert, Hou.	1	2	2.0	2	0
Abraham, Robert, Hou.	1	1	1.0	1	0
Bryant, Jeff, Sea.	1	1	1.0	1	0
Kremer, Ken, K.C.	1	1	1.0	1	0
Wright, Louis, Den.	1	1	1.0	1	0

t = touchdown
Leader based on most interceptions

AFC — TEAM INTERCEPTIONS

	Att	Yards	Avg	Long	TD
Seattle	38	697	18.3	t90	7
Denver	31	510	16.5	63	4
Pittsburgh	31	433	14.0	t69	4
Kansas City	30	465	15.5	t71	2
Cincinnati	25	368	14.7	70	4
Miami	24	478	19.9	t86	2
Raiders	20	339	17.0	t97	2
Cleveland	20	236	11.8	47	0
San Diego	19	499	26.3	t99	4
Indianapolis	18	190	10.6	t59	1
New England	17	210	12.4	85	0
Buffalo	16	233	14.6	55	0
Jets	15	152	10.1	28	0
Houston	13	139	10.7	26	0
Conference Total	317	4949	—	t99	30
Conference Average	22.6	353.5	15.6	—	2.1

AFC — INDIVIDUAL PUNTERS

	No	Yards	Long	Avg	Total Punts	TB	Blk	Opp Ret	Ret Yds	In 20	Net Avg
Arnold, Jim, K.C...........	98	4397	63	44.9	98	13	0	60	461	22	37.5
Roby, Reggie, Mia.	51	2281	69	44.7	51	10	0	17	138	15	38.1
Stark, Rohn, Ind...........	98	4383	72	44.7	98	7	0	62	600	21	37.2
Cox, Steve, Clev.	74	3213	69	43.4	76	8	2	43	489	16	33.7
Prestridge, Luke, N.E...	44	1884	89	42.8	44	5	0	21	228	8	35.4
McInally, Pat, Cin........	67	2832	61	42.3	67	8	0	38	310	19	35.3
Camarillo, Rich, N.E. ...	48	2020	61	42.1	48	7	0	24	214	12	34.7
Buford, Maury, S.D.	66	2773	60	42.0	66	3	0	43	399	11	35.1
Kidd, John, Buff.	88	3696	63	42.0	90	8	2	52	597	16	32.7
Guy, Ray, Raiders	91	3809	63	41.9	91	12	0	34	345	25	35.4
Colquitt; Craig, Pitt.	70	2883	62	41.2	70	5	0	37	351	21	34.7
Norman, Chris, Den. ...	96	3850	83	40.1	96	6	0	44	335	16	35.4
Ramsey, Chuck, Jets ...	74	2935	64	39.7	75	8	1	37	242	19	33.8
James, John, Hou.	88	3482	55	39.6	88	5	0	60	618	20	31.4
West, Jeff, Sea.	95	3567	60	37.5	95	10	0	32	205	24	33.3

Leader based on gross average, minimum 40 punts

AFC — TEAM PUNTING

	Total Punts	Yards	Long	Avg	TB	Blk	Opp Ret	Ret Yds	In 20	Net Avg
Kansas City...............	98	4397	63	44.9	13	0	60	461	22	37.5
Miami........................	51	2281	69	44.7	10	0	17	138	15	38.1
Indianapolis	98	4383	72	44.7	7	0	62	600	21	37.2
New England	92	3904	89	42.4	12	0	45	442	20	35.0
Cleveland..................	76	3213	69	42.3	8	2	43	489	16	33.7
Cincinnati.................	67	2832	61	42.3	8	0	38	310	19	35.3
San Diego.................	66	2773	60	42.0	3	0	43	399	11	35.1
Raiders	91	3809	63	41.9	12	0	34	345	25	35.4
Pittsburgh	70	2883	62	41.2	5	0	37	351	21	34.7
Buffalo	90	3696	63	41.1	8	2	52	597	16	32.7
Denver	96	3850	83	40.1	6	0	44	335	16	35.4
Houston	88	3482	55	39.6	5	0	60	618	20	31.4
Jets.........................	75	2935	64	39.1	8	1	37	242	19	33.8
Seattle	95	3567	60	37.5	10	0	32	205	24	33.3
Conference Total	1153	48005	89	—	115	5	604	5532	265	—
Conference Average .	82.4	3428.9	—	41.6	8.2	0.4	43.1	395.1	18.9	34.8

AFC — INDIVIDUAL PUNT RETURNERS

	No	FC	Yards	Avg	Long	TD
Martin, Mike, Cin.	24	5	376	15.7	55	0
Lipps, Louis, Pitt.	53	2	656	12.4	t76	1
Willhite, Gerald, Den.	20	9	200	10.0	35	0
Fryar, Irving, N.E.	36	10	347	9.6	55	0
Wilson, Don, Buff.	33	8	297	9.0	t65	1
Pruitt, Greg, Raiders	53	16	473	8.9	38	0
Springs, Kirk, Jets	28	10	247	8.8	33	0
Smith, J.T., K.C.	39	14	332	8.5	27	0
Walker, Fulton, Mia.	21	14	169	8.0	33	0
Brennan, Brian, Clev.	25	10	199	8.0	19	0
James, Lionel, S.D.	30	9	208	6.9	t58	1
Anderson, Larry, Ind.	27	7	182	6.7	19	0
Roaches, Carl, Hou.	26	8	152	5.8	18	0
(Non-Qualifiers)						
Skansi, Paul, Sea.	16	2	145	9.1	16	0
Easley, Ken, Sea.	16	5	194	12.1	42	0
Montgomery, Cleotha, Raiders...	14	1	194	13.9	t69	1
Simmons, John, Cin.	12	6	98	8.2	30	0
Johns, Paul, Sea.	11	4	140	12.7	t47	1
Starring, Stephen, N.E.	10	1	73	7.3	16	0
Clayton, Mark, Mia.	8	2	79	9.9	22	0
Glasgow, Nesby, Ind.	7	2	79	11.3	35	0
Woods, Rick, Pitt.	6	0	40	6.7	14	0
Walker, Dwight, Clev.	6	3	50	8.3	13	0
Bird, Steve, St.L.-S.D.	6	0	60	10.0	17	0
Heflin, Vince, Mia.	6	1	76	12.7	37	0
Kozlowski, Mike, Mia.	4	4	41	10.3	20	0
Minter, Cedric, Jets	4	2	44	11.0	18	0
Hancock, Anthony, K.C.	3	1	14	4.7	7	0
Bouza, Matt, Ind.	3	3	17	5.7	11	0
Horton, Ray, Cin.	2	0	-1	-0.5	1	0
Bruckner, Nick, Jets	2	0	25	12.5	20	0
Clayton, Harvey, Pitt.	1	0	0	0.0	0	0
Henderson, Reuben, S.D.	1	2	0	0.0	0	0
Long, Terry, Pitt.	1	0	0	0.0	0	0
Padjen, Gary, Ind.	1	0	0	0.0	0	0
Smith, Lucious, Buff.-S.D.	1	0	0	0.0	0	0
Wilson, Steve, Den.	1	0	0	0.0	0	0
Gibson, Ernest, N.E.	1	0	3	3.0	3	0
Dixon, Zachary, Sea.	1	0	5	5.0	5	0
Weathers, Clarence, N.E.	1	0	7	7.0	7	0
Mullen, Davlin, Jets	1	0	8	8.0	8	0
Blackwood, Glenn, Mia.	0	4	0	—	0	0
Blackwood, Lyle, Mia.	0	2	0	—	0	0
Chandler, Wes, S.D.	0	1	0	—	0	0

	No	FC	Yards	Avg	Long	TD
James, Roland, N.E.	0	2	0	—	0	0
Sanford, Rick, N.E.	0	2	0	—	0	0

t = touchdown
Leader based on average return, minimum 20 returns

AFC — TEAM PUNT RETURNS

	Att	FC	Yards	Avg	Long	TD
Raiders	67	17	667	10.0	t69	1
Pittsburgh	61	2	696	11.4	t76	1
New England	48	15	430	9.0	55	0
Seattle	44	11	484	11.0	t47	1
Kansas City	42	15	346	8.2	27	0
Denver	41	12	318	7.8	35	0
Cleveland	40	13	322	8.1	19	0
Miami	39	27	365	9.4	37	0
Cincinnati	38	11	473	12.4	55	0
Indianapolis	38	12	278	7.3	35	0
Jets	35	12	324	9.3	33	0
Buffalo	33	8	297	9.0	t65	1
San Diego	33	12	212	6.4	t58	1
Houston	26	8	152	5.8	18	0
Conference Total	585	175	5364	—	t76	5
Conference Average	41.8	12.5	383.1	9.2	—	0.4

AFC — INDIVIDUAL KICKOFF RETURNERS

	No	Yards	Avg	Long	TD
Humphery, Bobby, Jets	22	675	30.7	t97	1
Williams, Dokie, Raiders	24	621	25.9	62	0
Anderson, Larry, Ind.	22	525	23.9	69	0
Springs, Kirk, Jets	23	521	22.7	73	0
Roaches, Carl, Hou.	30	679	22.6	49	0
James, Lionel, S.D.	43	959	22.3	55	0
Collins, Anthony, N.E.	25	544	21.8	46	0
Montgomery, Cleotha, Raiders	26	555	21.3	42	0
Walker, Fulton, Mia.	29	617	21.3	41	0
Williams, Van, Buff.	39	820	21.0	65	0
Jennings, Stanford, Cin.	22	452	20.5	46	0
Erenberg, Rich, Pitt.	28	575	20.5	47	0
Smith, Phil, Ind.	32	651	20.3	t96	1
Paige, Stephon, K.C.	27	544	20.1	45	0
Williams, Jon, N.E.	23	461	20.0	29	0
Byner, Earnest, Clev.	22	415	18.9	28	0
Dixon, Zachary, Sea.	25	446	17.8	36	0
Wilson, Don, Buff.	34	576	16.9	36	0
(Non-Qualifiers)					
Lang, Gene, Den.	19	404	21.3	38	0
Smith, J.T., K.C.	19	391	20.6	39	0
Martin, Mike, Cin.	19	386	20.3	44	0
Spencer, Todd, Pitt.	18	373	20.7	40	0
Davis, Bruce, Clev.	18	369	20.5	40	0
Hughes, David, Sea.	17	348	20.5	38	0
Walls, Herkie, Hou.	15	289	19.3	29	0
McGee, Buford, S.D.	14	315	22.5	35	0
Allen, Patrick, Hou.	11	210	19.1	23	0
Bird, Steve, St. L.-S.D.	11	205	18.6	28	0
Minter, Cedric, Jets	10	224	22.4	52	0
Heflin, Vince, Mia.	9	130	14.4	26	0
Morris, Randall, Sea.	8	153	19.1	34	0
Brown, Preston, Clev.	8	136	17.0	27	0
Brooks, James, Cin.	7	144	20.6	37	0
Farley, John, Cin.	6	93	15.5	32	0
Young, Glen, Clev.	5	134	26.8	36	0
Fryar, Irving, N.E.	5	95	19.0	22	0
Williams, Richard, Atl.-Hou.	5	84	16.8	21	0
Ricks, Lawrence, K.C.	5	83	16.6	21	0
White, Charles, Clev.	5	80	16.0	23	0
Kafentzis, Mark, Ind.	5	69	13.8	22	0
Willhite, Gerald, Den.	4	109	27.3	40	0
Wonsley, George, Ind.	4	52	13.0	20	0
Veals, Elton, Pitt.	4	40	10.0	18	0
Joyner, Willie, Hou.	3	57	19.0	24	0

	No	Yards	Avg	Long	TD
Bryant, Cullen, Sea.	3	53	17.7	21	0
Verser, David, Cin.	3	46	15.3	23	0
Lee, Keith L., N.E.	3	43	14.3	17	0
Robinson, Bo, N.E.	3	38	12.7	14	0
Brown, Steve, Hou.	3	17	5.7	17	0
Pruitt, Greg, Raiders	3	16	5.3	13	0
Paige, Tony, Jets	3	7	2.3	7	0
Mullen, Davlin, Jets	2	34	17.0	23	0
Hancock, Anthony, K.C.	2	32	16.0	17	0
Dennison, Rick, Den.	2	27	13.5	16	0
Kozlowski, Mike, Mia.	2	23	11.5	12	0
Egloff, Ron, S.D.	2	20	10.0	11	0
Moore, Alvin, Ind.	2	19	9.5	10	0
Clayton, Mark, Mia.	2	15	7.5	14	0
Jones, Cedric, N.E.	1	20	20.0	20	0
Bruckner, Nick, Jets	1	17	17.0	17	0
Thompson, Ted, Hou.	1	16	16.0	16	0
Bell, Greg, Buff.	1	15	15.0	15	0
Corley, Anthony, Pitt.	1	15	15.0	15	0
Simmons, John, Cin.	1	15	15.0	15	0
Hawthorne, Greg, N.E.	1	14	14.0	14	0
Hill, Eddie, Mia.	1	14	14.0	14	0
Willis, Chester, Raiders	1	13	13.0	13	0
Gillespie, Fernandars, Pitt.	1	12	12.0	12	0
Harris, M.L., Cin.	1	12	12.0	12	0
Nicolas, Scott, Clev.	1	12	12.0	12	0
Brown, Chris, Pitt.	1	11	11.0	11	0
Jensen, Derrick, Raiders	1	11	11.0	11	0
Middleton, Frank, Ind.	1	11	11.0	11	0
Contz, Bill, Clev.	1	10	10.0	10	0
Jackson, Earnest, S.D.	1	10	10.0	10	0
Davidson, Chy, Jets	1	9	9.0	9	0
Scott, Willie, K.C.	1	9	9.0	9	0
Tatupu, Mosi, N.E.	1	9	9.0	9	0
Harris, John, Sea.	1	7	7.0	7	0
Kinnebrew, Larry, Cin.	1	7	7.0	7	0
David, Stan, Buff.	1	6	6.0	6	0
Gaffney, Derrick, Jets	1	6	6.0	6	0
Banker, Ted, Jets	1	5	5.0	5	0
White, Craig, Buff.	1	5	5.0	5	0
Harden, Mike, Den.	1	4	4.0	4	0
Carson, Carlos, K.C.	1	2	2.0	2	0
Hathaway, Steve, Ind.	1	2	2.0	2	0
Sherwin, Tim, Ind.	1	2	2.0	2	0
Smith, Aaron, Den.	1	2	2.0	2	0
Holt, Harry, Clev.	1	1	1.0	1	0
Catano, Mark, Pitt.	1	0	0.0	0	0

	No	Yards	Avg	Long	TD
Cherry, Deron, K.C.	1	0	0.0	0	0
Duhe, A.J., Mia.	1	0	0.0	0	0
Gofourth, Derrel, S.D.	1	0	0.0	0	0
McKinney, Odis, Raiders	1	0	0.0	0	0
Radachowsky, George, Ind.	1	0	0.0	0	0
Shuler, Mickey, Jets	1	0	0.0	0	0
Williams, Gary, Cin.	1	0	0.0	0	0
Williams, Jamie, Hou.	1	0	0.0	0	0

t = touchdown
Leader based on average return, minimum 20 returns

AFC — TEAM KICKOFF RETURNS

	No	Yards	Avg	Long	TD
Jets	65	1498	23.0	t97	1
Buffalo	76	1422	18.7	65	0
Houston	69	1352	19.6	49	0
Indianapolis	69	1331	19.3	t96	1
San Diego	63	1319	20.9	55	0
New England	63	1246	19.8	46	0
Raiders	56	1216	21.7	62	0
Cleveland	61	1157	19.0	40	0
Cincinnati	61	1155	18.9	46	0
Kansas City	56	1061	18.9	45	0
Pittsburgh	54	1026	19.0	47	0
Seattle	54	1007	18.6	38	0
Denver	45	897	19.9	40	0
Miami	44	799	18.2	41	0
Conference Total	836	16486	—	t97	2
Conference Average	59.7	1177.5	19.7	—	0.1

AFC — INDIVIDUAL SCORERS

KICKERS	XP	XPA	FG	FGA	PTS
Anderson, Gary, Pitt.	45	45	24	32	117
Johnson, Norm, Sea.	50	51	20	24	110
Franklin, Tony, N.E.	42	42	22	28	108
Lowery, Nick, K.C.	35	35	23	33	104
Breech, Jim, Cin.	37	37	22	31	103
Karlis, Rich, Den.	38	41	21	28	101
Bahr, Chris, Raiders	40	42	20	27	100
Bahr, Matt, Clev.	25	25	24	32	97
von Schamann, Uwe, Mia.	66	70	9	19	93
Benirschke, Rolf, S.D.	41	41	17	26	92
Leahy, Pat, Jets.....................	38	39	17	24	89
Allegre, Raul, Ind.	14	14	11	18	47
Cooper, Joe, Hou.	13	13	11	13	46
Danelo, Joe, Buff.	17	17	8	16	41
Kempf, Florian, Hou.	14	14	4	6	26
Nelson, Chuck, Buff.	14	14	3	5	23
Biasucci, Dean, Ind.	13	14	3	5	22
Ricardo, Benny, S.D.	5	6	3	3	14
Cox, Steve, Clev.	0	0	1	3	3

NON-KICKERS	TD	TDR	TDP	TDM	PTS
Allen, Marcus, Raiders.............	18	13	5	0	108
Clayton, Mark, Mia..................	18	0	18	0	108
Johnson, Pete, S.D.-Mia.	12	12	0	0	72
Largent, Steve, Sea.	12	0	12	0	72
Lipps, Louis, Pitt......................	11	1	9	1	66
Stallworth, John, Pitt...............	11	0	11	0	66
Kinnebrew, Larry, Cin.	10	9	1	0	60
Turner, Daryl, Sea.	10	0	10	0	60
Jackson, Earnest, S.D.	9	8	1	0	54
Bell, Greg, Buff.......................	8	7	1	0	48
Bennett, Woody, Mia.	8	7	1	0	48
Duper, Mark, Mia....................	8	0	8	0	48
Paige, Tony, Jets....................	8	7	1	0	48
Christensen, Todd, Raiders.....	7	0	7	0	42
Dennard, Preston, Buff.	7	0	7	0	42
Moriarty, Larry, Hou...............	7	6	1	0	42
Ramsey, Derrick, N.E.	7	0	7	0	42
Walker, Wesley, Jets	7	0	7	0	42
Watson, Steve, Den.	7	0	7	0	42
Butler, Raymond, Ind.	6	0	6	0	36
Chandler, Wes, S.D.	6	0	6	0	36
Collinsworth, Cris, Cin.	6	0	6	0	36
Johnson, Butch, Den.	6	0	6	0	36

	TD	TDR	TDP	TDM	PTS
Joiner, Charlie, S.D.	6	0	6	0	36
McGee, Buford, S.D................	6	4	2	0	36
McNeil, Freeman, Jets............	6	5	1	0	36
Moore, Nat, Mia.....................	6	0	6	0	36
Pollard, Frank, Pitt.................	6	6	0	0	36
Pruitt, Mike, Clev....................	6	6	0	0	36
Shuler, Mickey, Jets	6	0	6	0	36
Winder, Sammy, Den.............	6	4	2	0	36
Collins, Anthony, N.E.............	5	5	0	0	30
Eason, Tony, N.E....................	5	5	0	0	30
Hardy, Bruce, Mia...................	5	0	5	0	30
Jennings, Stanford, Cin.	5	2	3	0	30
Lane, Eric, Sea......................	5	4	1	0	30
McMillan, Randy, Ind.	5	5	0	0	30
Morgan, Stanley, N.E.............	5	0	5	0	30
Newsome, Ozzie, Clev............	5	0	5	0	30
Brooks, James, Cin................	4	2	2	0	24
Brown, Theotis, K.C...............	4	4	0	0	24
Carson, Carlos, K.C.	4	0	4	0	24
Dawson, Lin, N.E....................	4	0	4	0	24
Duckworth, Bobby, S.D..........	4	0	4	0	24
Franklin, Byron, Buff..............	4	0	4	0	24
Heard, Herman, K.C.	4	4	0	0	24
Lacy, Kenneth, K.C................	4	2	2	0	24
Marshall, Henry, K.C..............	4	0	4	0	24
Paige, Stephon, K.C.	4	0	4	0	24
Smith, Tim, Hou.....................	4	0	4	0	24
Starring, Stephen, N.E...........	4	0	4	0	24
Tatupu, Mosi, N.E..................	4	4	0	0	24
Williams, Dokie, Raiders	4	0	4	0	24
Brennan, Brian, Clev.	3	0	3	0	18
Byner, Earnest, Clev..............	3	2	0	1	18
Dickey, Curtis, Ind.	3	3	0	0	18
Erenberg, Rich, Pitt.	3	2	1	0	18
Hawkins, Frank, Raiders.........	3	3	0	0	18
Johnson, Dan, Mia.................	3	0	3	0	18
Jones, Cedric, N.E.................	3	0	2	1	18
Kay, Clarence, Den................	3	0	3	0	18
Krieg, Dave, Sea....................	3	3	0	0	18
Lang, Gene, Den.	3	2	1	0	18
Malone, Mark, Pitt.	3	3	0	0	18
Nathan, Tony, Mia.	3	1	2	0	18
Scott, Willie, K.C...................	3	0	3	0	18
Sievers, Eric, S.D.	3	0	3	0	18
Thompson, Weegie, Pitt..........	3	0	3	0	18
Tice, Mike, Sea......................	3	0	3	0	18
Williams, Jamie, Hou.	3	0	3	0	18

	TD	TDR	TDP	TDM	PTS
Martin, Rod, Raiders...............	2	0	0	2	*14
Alexander, Charles, Cin.	2	2	0	0	12
Barber, Marion, Jets	2	2	0	0	12
Barnwell, Malcolm, Raiders.....	2	0	2	0	12
Brown, Dave, Sea.	2	0	0	2	12
Byrd, Gill, S.D.....................	2	0	0	2	12
Casper, Dave, Raiders............	2	0	2	0	12
Cefalo, Jimmy, Mia.	2	0	2	0	12
Davis, Bruce, Clev.	2	0	2	0	12
Dawkins, Julius, Buff.	2	0	2	0	12
Dixon, Zachary, Sea.	2	2	0	0	12
Doornink, Dan, Sea.	2	0	2	0	12
Dressel, Chris, Hou................	2	0	2	0	12
Easley, Ken, Sea.	2	0	0	2	12
Esiason, Boomer, Cin.	2	2	0	0	12
Foley, Steve, Den.	2	0	0	2	12
Harris, M.L., Cin.	2	0	2	0	12
Henry, Bernard, Ind.	2	0	2	0	12
Hughes, David, Sea................	2	1	1	0	12
Humphery, Bobby, Jets...........	2	0	1	1	12
Hunter, Tony, Buff.	2	0	2	0	12
Jackson, Billy, K.C.................	2	1	1	0	12
Jensen, Derrick, Raiders........	2	1	1	0	12
Jensen, Jim, Mia.	2	0	2	0	12
Johns, Paul, Sea.	2	0	1	1	12
Middleton, Frank, Ind.............	2	1	1	0	12
Minter, Cedric, Jets	2	1	1	0	12
Moore, Alvin, Ind.	2	2	0	0	12
Parros, Rick, Den.	2	2	0	0	12
Porter, Tracy, Ind...................	2	0	2	0	12
Rose, Joe, Mia......................	2	0	2	0	12
Simpson, Keith, Sea.	2	0	0	2	12
Thomas, Jewerl, S.D..............	2	2	0	0	12
Washington, Sam, Pitt.	2	0	0	2	12
Weathers, Clarence, N.E.	2	0	2	0	12
Willhite, Gerald, Den.............	2	2	0	0	12
Winslow, Kellen, S.D.............	2	0	2	0	12
Woodruff, Dwayne, Pitt.	2	0	0	2	12
Young, Dave, Ind...................	2	0	2	0	12
Abercrombie, Walter, Pitt.	1	1	0	0	6
Alexander, Ray, Den..............	1	0	1	0	6
Arnold, Walt, Wash.-K.C.	1	0	1	0	6
Baumhower, Bob, Mia.............	1	0	0	1	6
Beckman, Ed, K.C.................	1	0	1	0	6
Blackledge, Todd, K.C.	1	1	0	0	6
Bostic, Keith, Hou.................	1	0	0	1	6
Brookins, Mitchell, Buff...........	1	0	1	0	6

	TD	TDR	TDP	TDM	PTS
Buttle, Greg, Jets.....................	1	0	0	1	6
Carter, Joe, Mia......................	1	1	0	0	6
Cunningham, Bennie, Pitt.	1	0	1	0	6
David, Stan, Buff.	1	0	0	1	6
Davis, Johnny, Clev.	1	1	0	0	6
Dennison, Glenn, Jets.............	1	0	1	0	6
Dufek, Joe, Buff......................	1	1	0	0	6
Edwards, Stan, Hou................	1	1	0	0	6
Elway, John, Den....................	1	1	0	0	6
Feacher, Ricky, Clev..............	1	0	1	0	6
Fryar, Irving, N.E.	1	0	1	0	6
Gastineau, Mark, Jets.............	1	0	0	1	6
Green, Boyce, Clev................	1	0	1	0	6
Griffin, James, Cin.................	1	0	0	1	6
Hancock, Anthony, K.C...........	1	0	1	0	6
Harden, Mike, Den.................	1	0	0	1	6
Harper, Bruce, Jets.................	1	1	0	0	6
Haynes, Mike, Raiders............	1	0	0	1	6
Hector, Johnny, Jets..............	1	1	0	0	6
Hinkle, Bryan, Pitt..................	1	0	0	1	6
Holman, Rodney, Cin..............	1	0	1	0	6
Holohan, Pete, S.D.................	1	0	1	0	6
Holston, Michael, Hou.............	1	0	1	0	6
Horton, Ray, Cin.....................	1	0	0	1	6
Jackson, Robert, Cin.	1	0	0	1	6
Jackson, Terry, Sea................	1	0	0	1	6
James, Craig, N.E.	1	1	0	0	6
James, Lionel, S.D.	1	0	0	1	6
Jones, Lam, Jets	1	0	1	0	6
Jones, Rulon, Den.	1	0	0	1	6
Judson, William, Mia...............	1	0	0	1	6
Kafentzis, Mark, Ind................	1	0	0	1	6
Keating, Chris, Buff.	1	0	0	1	6
Klever, Rocky, Jets.................	1	0	1	0	6
Kreider, Steve, Cin.	1	0	1	0	6
Kubiak, Gary, Den.	1	1	0	0	6
Lowe, Woodrow, S.D.	1	0	0	1	6
Luck, Oliver, Hou....................	1	1	0	0	6
McCloskey, Mike, Hou.	1	0	1	0	6
McDonald, Paul, Clev.	1	1	0	0	6
McNeal, Don, Mia.	1	0	0	1	6
Montgomery, Cleotha, Raiders	1	0	0	1	6
Moon, Warren, Hou.	1	1	0	0	6
Morris, Wayne, S.D.................	1	1	0	0	6
Mullins, Eric, Hou.	1	0	1	0	6
Munoz, Anthony, Cin.	1	0	1	0	6
Nash, Joe, Sea.......................	1	0	0	1	6

	TD	TDR	TDP	TDM	PTS
Neal, Speedy, Buff.	1	1	0	0	6
Pagel, Mike, Ind.	1	1	0	0	6
Plunkett, Jim, Raiders	1	1	0	0	6
Radecic, Scott, K.C.	1	0	0	1	6
Robbins, Randy, Den.	1	0	0	1	6
Robinson, Bo, N.E.	1	0	1	0	6
Ross, Kevin, K.C.	1	0	0	1	6
Sampson, Clinton, Den.	1	0	1	0	6
Sanford, Lucius, Buff.	1	0	0	1	6
Schlichter, Art, Ind.	1	1	0	0	6
Schonert, Turk, Cin.	1	1	0	0	6
Shell, Donnie, Pitt.	1	0	0	1	6
Simmons, John, Cin.	1	0	0	1	6
Smith, Dennis, Den.	1	0	0	1	6
Smith, Phil, Ind.	1	0	0	1	6
Walker, Byron, Sea.	1	0	1	0	6
Walls, Herkie, Hou.	1	0	1	0	6
Williams, Lee, S.D.	1	0	0	1	6
Williams, Van, Buff.	1	0	1	0	6
Wilson, Don, Buff.	1	0	0	1	6
Wilson, Marc, Raiders	1	1	0	0	6
Woodard, Ken, Den.	1	0	0	1	6
Wright, James, Den.	1	0	1	0	6
Wright, Louis, Den.	1	0	0	1	6
Young, Charle, Sea.	1	0	1	0	6
Bryant, Jeff, Sea.	0	0	0	0	*2
Humiston, Mike, Ind.	0	0	0	0	*2
James, Roland, N.E.	0	0	0	0	*2
Ryan, Pat, Jets	0	0	0	0	§1

§ Scored extra point
* Safety (also 1 each: Cin., Raiders, Jets)

AFC — TEAM SCORING

	TD	TDR	TDP	TDM	XP	XPA	FG	FGA	SAF	PTS
Miami	70	18	49	3	66	70	9	19	0	513
Seattle	51	10	32	9	50	51	20	24	1	418
San Diego	48	18	25	5	46	47	20	29	0	394
Pittsburgh	45	13	25	7	45	45	24	32	0	387
Raiders	44	19	21	4	40	44	20	27	2	368
New England	42	15	26	1	42	42	22	28	1	362
Denver	42	12	22	8	38	42	21	28	0	353
Cincinnati	39	18	17	4	37	39	22	31	1	339
Jets	40	17	20	3	39	40	17	24	1	332
Kansas City	35	12	21	2	35	35	23	33	0	314
Buffalo	31	9	18	4	31	31	11	21	0	250
Cleveland	25	10	14	1	25	25	25	35	0	250
Houston	28	13	14	1	27	28	15	19	0	240
Indianapolis	28	13	13	2	27	28	14	23	1	239
Conf. Total	568	197	317	54	548	567	263	373	7	4759
Conf. Average	40.6	14.1	22.6	3.9	39.1	40.5	18.8	26.6	0.5	339.9

AFC — Team-by-Team Summary

AFC Offense	Buff.	Cin.	Clev.	Den.	Hou.
Rushes	398	540	489	508	433
Net Yds. Gained	1643	2179	1696	2076	1656
Avg. Gain	4.1	4.0	3.5	4.1	3.8
Avg. Yds. per Game	102.7	136.2	106.0	129.8	103.5
Passes Attempted	588	496	495	475	487
Completed	298	306	273	263	282
% Completed	50.7	61.7	55.2	55.4	57.9
Total Yds. Gained	3252	3659	3490	3116	3610
Times Sacked	60	45	55	35	49
Yds. Lost	554	358	358	257	382
Net Yds. Gained	2698	3301	3132	2859	3228
Avg. Yds. per Game	168.6	206.3	195.8	178.7	201.8
Net Yds. per Pass Play	4.16	6.10	5.69	5.61	6.02
Yds. Gained per Comp.	10.91	11.96	12.78	11.85	12.80
Combined Net Yds. Gained	4341	5480	4828	4935	4884
% Total Yds. Rushing	37.8	39.8	35.1	42.1	33.9
% Total Yds. Passing	62.2	60.2	64.9	57.9	66.1
Avg. Yds. per Game	271.3	342.5	301.8	308.4	305.3
Had Intercepted	30	22	23	17	15
Yds. Opp. Returned	416	364	518	189	214
Ret. by Opp. for TD	4	2	3	0	2
Punts	90	67	76	96	88
Yds. Punted	3696	2832	3213	3850	3482
Avg. Yds. per Punt	41.1	42.3	42.3	40.1	39.6
Punt Returns	33	38	40	41	26
Yds. Returned	297	473	322	318	152
Avg. Yds. per Return	9.0	12.4	8.1	7.8	5.8
Returned for TD	1	0	0	0	0
Kickoff Returns	76	61	61	45	69
Yds. Returned	1422	1155	1157	897	1352
Avg. Yds. per Return	18.7	18.9	19.0	19.9	19.6
Returned for TD	0	0	0	0	0
Total Points Scored	250	339	250	353	240
Total TDs	31	39	25	42	28
TDs Rushing	9	18	10	12	13
TDs Passing	18	17	14	22	14
TDs on Ret. and Rec.	4	4	1	8	1
Extra Points	31	37	25	38	27
Safeties	0	1	0	0	0
Field Goals Made	11	22	25	21	15
Field Goals Attempted	21	31	35	28	19
% Successful	52.4	71.0	71.4	75.0	78.9

Ind.	K.C.	Raid.	Mia.	N.E.	N.Y.J.	Pitt.	S.D.	Sea
510	408	516	484	482	504	574	456	495
2025	1527	1886	1918	2032	2189	2179	1654	1645
4.0	3.7	3.7	4.0	4.2	4.3	3.8	3.6	3.3
126.6	95.4	117.9	119.9	127.0	136.8	136.2	103.4	102.8
411	593	491	572	500	488	443	662	497
206	305	266	367	292	272	240	401	283
50.1	51.4	54.2	64.2	58.4	55.7	54.2	60.6	56.9
2543	3869	3718	5146	3685	3341	3519	4928	3751
58	33	54	14	66	52	35	36	42
436	301	360	128	454	382	278	285	328
2107	3568	3358	5018	3231	2959	3241	4643	3423
131.7	223.0	209.9	313.6	201.9	184.9	202.6	290.2	213.9
4.49	5.70	6.16	8.56	5.71	5.48	6.78	6.65	6.35
12.34	12.69	13.98	14.02	12.62	12.28	14.66	12.29	13.25
4132	5095	5244	6936	5263	5148	5420	6297	5068
49.0	30.0	36.0	27.7	38.6	42.5	40.2	26.3	32.5
51.0	70.0	64.0	72.3	61.4	57.5	59.8	73.7	67.5
258.3	318.4	327.8	433.5	328.9	321.8	338.8	393.6	316.8
22	22	28	18	14	21	25	21	26
423	683	300	377	237	207	371	180	333
2	7	2	1	3	0	1	0	3
98	98	91	51	92	75	70	66	95
4383	4397	3809	2281	3904	2935	2883	2773	3567
44.7	44.9	41.9	44.7	42.4	39.1	41.2	42.0	37.5
38	42	67	39	48	35	61	33	44
278	346	667	365	430	324	696	212	484
7.3	8.2	10.0	9.4	9.0	9.3	11.4	6.4	11.0
0	0	1	0	0	0	1	1	1
69	56	56	44	63	65	54	63	54
1331	1061	1216	799	1246	1498	1026	1319	1007
19.3	18.9	21.7	18.2	19.8	23.0	19.0	20.9	18.6
1	0	0	0	0	1	0	0	0
239	314	368	513	362	332	387	394	418
28	35	44	70	42	40	45	48	51
13	12	19	18	15	17	13	18	10
13	21	21	49	26	20	25	25	32
2	2	4	3	1	3	7	5	9
27	35	40	66	42	39	45	46	50
1	0	2	0	1	1	0	0	1
14	23	20	9	22	17	24	20	20
23	33	27	19	28	24	32	29	24
60.9	69.7	74.1	47.4	78.6	70.8	75.0	69.0	83.3

AFC Defense	Buff.	Cin.	Clev.	Den.	Hou.
Rushes	531	477	494	435	596
Net Yds. Gained	2106	1868	1945	1664	2789
Avg. Gain	4.0	3.9	3.9	3.8	4.7
Avg. Yds. per Game	131.6	116.8	121.6	104.0	174.3
Passes Attempted	495	517	458	631	447
Completed	300	302	261	346	271
% Completed	60.6	58.4	57.0	54.8	60.6
Total Yds. Gained	3667	3689	3049	4453	3446
Times Sacked	26	40	43	57	32
Yds. Lost	191	298	353	430	267
Net Yds. Gained	3476	3391	2696	4023	3179
Avg. Yds. per Game	217.3	211.9	168.5	251.4	198.7
Net Yds. per Pass Play	6.67	6.09	5.38	5.85	6.64
Yds. Gained per Comp.	12.22	12.22	11.68	12.87	12.72
Combined Net Yds. Gained	5582	5259	4641	5687	5968
% Total Yds. Rushing	37.7	35.5	41.9	29.3	46.7
% Total Yds. Passing	62.3	64.5	58.1	70.7	53.3
Avg. Yds. per Game	348.9	328.7	290.1	355.4	373.0
Intercepted by	16	25	20	31	13
Yds. Returned by	233	368	236	510	139
Returned for TD	0	4	0	4	0
Punts	72	67	77	81	64
Yds. Punted	2812	2771	3123	3361	2702
Avg. Yds. per Punt	39.1	41.4	40.6	41.5	42.2
Punt Returns	52	38	43	44	60
Yds. Returned	597	310	489	335	618
Avg. Yds. per Return	11.5	8.2	11.4	7.6	10.3
Returned for TD	0	0	0	0	0
Kickoff Returns	44	69	52	55	51
Yds. Returned	958	1446	1159	1181	986
Avg. Yds. per Return	21.8	21.0	22.3	21.5	19.3
Returned for TD	0	1	0	0	0
Total Points Scored	454	339	297	241	437
Total TDs	56	39	30	26	53
TDs Rushing	19	21	10	10	27
TDs Passing	32	15	15	16	23
TDs on Ret. and Rec.	5	3	5	0	3
Extra Points	56	37	30	26	51
Safeties	1	1	0	1	1
Field Goals Made	20	22	29	19	22
Field Goals Attempted	28	27	33	33	30
% Successful	71.4	81.5	87.9	57.6	73.3

Ind.	K.C.	Raid.	Mia.	N.E.	N.Y.J.	Pitt.	S.D.	Sea
559	523	517	458	498	497	454	457	475
2007	1980	1892	2155	1886	2064	1617	1851	1789
3.6	3.8	3.7	4.7	3.8	4.2	3.6	4.1	3.8
125.4	123.8	118.3	134.7	117.9	129.0	101.1	115.7	111.8
515	586	508	551	513	511	515	531	521
298	332	254	310	283	312	299	323	265
57.9	56.7	50.0	56.3	55.2	61.1	58.1	60.8	50.9
3890	4009	3268	3604	3666	3862	3689	4303	3572
42	50	64	42	55	44	47	33	55
320	364	516	339	452	360	390	218	398
3570	3645	2752	3265	3214	3502	3299	4085	3174
223.1	227.8	172.0	204.1	200.9	218.9	206.2	255.3	198.4
6.41	5.73	4.81	5.51	5.66	6.31	5.87	7.24	5.51
13.05	12.08	12.87	11.63	12.95	12.38	12.34	13.32	13.48
5577	5625	4644	5420	5100	5566	4916	5936	4963
36.0	35.2	40.7	39.8	37.0	37.1	32.9	31.2	36.0
64.0	64.8	59.3	60.2	63.0	62.9	67.1	68.8	64.0
348.6	351.6	290.3	338.8	318.8	347.9	307.3	371.0	310.2
18	30	20	24	17	15	31	19	38
190	465	339	478	210	152	433	499	697
1	2	2	2	0	0	4	4	7
80	91	117	83	83	67	90	73	83
3363	3642	5071	3476	3347	2854	3818	2890	3345
42.0	40.0	43.3	41.9	40.3	42.6	42.4	39.6	40.3
62	60	34	17	45	37	37	43	32
600	461	345	138	442	242	351	399	205
9.7	7.7	10.1	8.1	9.8	6.5	9.5	9.3	6.4
0	0	0	0	1	0	1	0	1
42	64	61	66	73	48	61	72	67
849	1354	1063	1368	1373	1030	1338	1437	1116
20.2	21.2	17.4	20.7	18.8	21.5	21.9	20.0	16.7
0	0	0	0	0	0	1	0	0
414	324	278	298	352	364	310	413	282
50	38	33	39	42	41	35	51	34
16	10	12	16	11	16	12	23	11
31	19	19	22	25	24	19	27	18
3	9	2	1	6	1	4	1	5
47	37	29	37	37	40	34	50	34
2	1	0	0	0	0	0	0	1
21	19	17	9	21	26	22	19	14
23	27	21	17	31	37	28	25	22
91.3	70.4	81.0	52.9	67.7	70.3	78.6	76.0	63.6

NATIONAL FOOTBALL CONFERENCE

INDIVIDUAL PLAYER
STATISTICS

NFC — INDIVIDUAL RUSHERS

	Att	Yards	Avg	Long	TD
Dickerson, Eric, Rams	379	2105	5.6	66	14
Payton, Walter, Chi.	381	1684	4.4	t72	11
• Wilder, James, T.B.	407	1544	3.8	37	13
← Riggs, Gerald, Atl.	353	1486	4.2	57	13
Tyler, Wendell, S.F.	246	1262	5.1	40	7
Riggins, John, Wash.	327	1239	3.8	24	14
← Dorsett, Tony, Dall.	302	1189	3.9	t31	6
Anderson, Ottis, St.L.	289	1174	4.1	24	6
Rogers, George, N.O.	239	914	3.8	28	2
Carpenter, Rob, Giants	250	795	3.2	22	7
Montgomery, Wilbert, Phil.	201	789	3.9	27	2
Anderson, Alfred, Minn.	201	773	3.8	23	2
Sims, Billy, Det.	130	687	5.3	81	5
Craig, Roger, S.F.	155	649	4.2	28	7
Gajan, Hokie, N.O.	102	615	6.0	t62	5
Ellis, Gerry, G.B.	123	581	4.7	50	4
Ivery, Eddie Lee, G.B.	99	552	5.6	49	6
Jones, James, Det.	137	532	3.9	34	3
← Morris, Joe, Giants	133	510	3.8	28	4
Campbell, Earl, Hou.-N.O.	146	468	3.2	22	4
Brown, Ted, Minn.	98	442	4.5	19	3
Mitchell, Stump, St.L.	81	434	5.4	39	9
Suhey, Matt, Chi.	124	424	3.4	21	4
Griffin, Keith, Wash.	97	408	4.2	31	0
Nelson, Darrin, Minn.	80	406	5.1	39	3
Clark, Jessie, G.B.	87	375	4.3	t43	4
Jenkins, Ken, Det.	78	358	4.6	t25	1
Crutchfield, Dwayne, Rams	73	337	4.6	36	1
Theismann, Joe, Wash.	62	314	5.1	27	1
Cain, Lynn, Atl.	77	276	3.6	t31	3
McMahon, Jim, Chi.	39	276	7.1	30	2
Newsome, Tim, Dall.	66	268	4.1	30	5
Oliver, Hubert, Phil.	72	263	3.7	17	0
Wilson, Wayne, N.O.	74	261	3.5	36	1
Redden, Barry, Rams	45	247	5.5	35	0
Danielson, Gary, Det.	41	218	5.3	40	3
Springs, Ron, Dall.	68	197	2.9	16	1
Harmon, Derrick, S.F.	39	192	4.9	19	1
Washington, Joe, Wash.	56	192	3.4	12	1
Ferrell, Earl, St.L.	41	190	4.6	25	1
Thomas, Calvin, Chi.	40	186	4.7	37	1
Lomax, Neil, St.L.	35	184	5.3	20	3
Crouse, Ray, G.B.	53	169	3.2	14	0
Ring, Bill, S.F.	38	162	4.3	34	3
Simms, Phil, Giants	42	162	3.9	21	0

	Att	Yards	Avg	Long	TD
Kemp, Jeff, Rams	34	153	4.5	23	1
Huckleby, Harlan, G.B.	35	145	4.1	23	0
Haddix, Michael, Phil.	48	130	2.7	21	1
Lisch, Rusty, Chi.	18	121	6.7	31	0
Montana, Joe, S.F.	39	118	3.0	15	2
Todd, Richard, N.O.	28	111	4.0	15	0
Anthony, Tyrone, N.O.	20	105	5.3	19	1
Moroski, Mike, Atl.	21	98	4.7	17	0
Galbreath, Tony, Giants	22	97	4.4	11	0
Rodgers, Del, G.B.	25	94	3.8	15	0
Woolfolk, Butch, Giants	40	92	2.3	17	1
Bussey, Dexter, Det.	32	91	2.8	18	0
Love, Randy, St.L.	25	90	3.6	13	1
Fuller, Steve, Chi.	15	89	5.9	26	1
Williams, Mike, Phil.	33	83	2.5	8	0
Lofton, James, G.B.	10	82	8.2	26	0
Gentry, Dennis, Chi.	21	79	3.8	28	1
Solomon, Freddie, S.F.	6	72	12.0	47	1
Jordan, Donald, Chi.	11	70	6.4	29	0
DeBerg, Steve, T.B.	28	59	2.1	14	2
Rice, Allen, Minn.	14	58	4.1	16	1
D'Addio, Dave, Det.	7	46	6.6	14	0
Jones, Mike, Minn.	4	45	11.3	36	0
Carver, Mel, T.B.	11	44	4.0	12	0
Kane, Rick, Wash.	17	43	2.5	10	0
Manning, Archie, Minn.	11	42	3.8	16	0
Hardy, Andre, Phil.	14	41	2.9	10	0
Hutchison, Anthony, Chi.	14	39	2.8	6	1
Archer, David, Atl.	6	38	6.3	12	0
Wonsley, Otis, Wash.	18	38	2.1	7	4
Thompson, Jack, T.B.	5	35	7.0	13	0
Armstrong, Adger, T.B.	10	34	3.4	9	2
Bartkowski, Steve, Atl.	15	34	2.3	8	0
Witkowski, John, Det.	7	33	4.7	10	0
Wilson, Wade, Minn.	9	30	3.3	12	0
Morton, Michael, T.B.	16	27	1.7	8	0
Nichols, Mark, Det.	3	27	9.0	13	0
Brown, Ron, Rams	2	25	12.5	16	0
Waddy, Billy, Minn.	3	24	8.0	11	0
White, Danny, Dall.	6	21	3.5	8	0
Harrell, Willard, St.L.	9	20	2.2	7	1
Hogeboom, Gary, Dall.	15	19	1.3	11	0
Pisarcik, Joe, Phil.	7	19	2.7	16	2
Jaworski, Ron, Phil.	5	18	3.6	10	1
Monk, Art, Wash.	2	18	9.0	18	0
Hodge, Floyd, Atl.	2	17	8.5	9	0
Carter, Gerald, T.B.	1	16	16.0	16	0

	Att	Yards	Avg	Long	TD
Stamps, Sylvester, Atl.	3	15	5.0	8	0
Dierking, Scott, T.B.	3	14	4.7	9	0
Martin, Robbie, Det.	1	14	14.0	14	0
Cooper, Earl, S.F.	3	13	4.3	7	0
Hayes, Jeff, Wash.	2	13	6.5	24	0
Jones, James, Dall.	8	13	1.6	6	0
Monroe, Carl, S.F.	3	13	4.3	7	0
Moore, Jeff, Wash.	3	13	4.3	5	0
Chadwick, Jeff, Det.	1	12	12.0	t12	1
McKinnon, Dennis, Chi.	2	12	6.0	21	0
Coleman, Greg, Minn.	2	11	5.5	13	0
Lewis, Leo, Minn.	2	11	5.5	6	0
Wright, Randy, G.B.	8	11	1.4	5	0
Kramer, Tommy, Minn.	15	9	0.6	14	0
Machurek, Mike, Det.	1	9	9.0	9	0
Benson, Cliff, Atl.	3	8	2.7	6	0
Johnson, Billy, Atl.	3	8	2.7	11	0
Wilson, Tim, N.O.	2	8	4.0	5	0
Austin, Cliff, Atl.	4	7	1.8	3	0
Hill, Tony, Dall.	1	7	7.0	7	0
Pridemore, Tom, Atl.	1	7	7.0	7	0
Dickey, Lynn, G.B.	18	6	0.3	9	3
Harrington, Perry, St.L.	3	6	2.0	5	0
Donley, Doug, Dall.	2	5	2.5	6	0
Goodlow, Eugene, N.O.	1	5	5.0	5	0
McIvor, Rick, St.L.	3	5	1.7	6	0
Jordan, Steve, Minn.	1	4	4.0	t4	1
Hipple, Eric, Det.	2	3	1.5	2	0
Nelson, David, Minn.	1	3	3.0	3	0
Campbell, Rich, G.B.	2	2	1.0	5	0
Cephous, Frank, Giants	3	2	0.7	2	0
Guman, Mike, Rams	1	2	2.0	2	0
Manuel, Lionel, Giants	3	2	0.7	11	0
Peoples, George, T.B.	1	2	2.0	2	0
Walker, Rick, Wash.	1	2	2.0	2	0
West, Ed, G.B.	1	2	2.0	t2	1
Landry, Greg, Chi.	2	1	0.5	t1	1
Owens, James, T.B.	1	1	1.0	1	0
Baschnagel, Brian, Chi.	1	0	0.0	0	0
Ferragamo, Vince, Rams	4	0	0.0	2	0
Finzer, David, Chi.	2	0	0.0	5	0
Giacomarro, Ralph, Atl.	1	0	0.0	0	0
Stabler, Ken, N.O.	1	−1	−1.0	−1	0
Moorehead, Emery, Chi.	1	−2	−2.0	−2	0
Duckett, Kenny, N.O.	1	−3	−3.0	−3	0
Ellard, Henry, Rams	3	−5	−1.7	5	0
Marsh, Doug, St. L.	1	−5	−5.0	−5	0

	Att	Yards	Avg	Long	TD
Quick, Mike, Phil.	1	−5	−5.0	−5	0
Runager, Max, S.F.	1	−5	−5.0	−5	0
Smith, Waddell, Dall.	1	−5	−5.0	−5	0
Black, Mike, Det.	3	−6	−2.0	4	0
Hart, Jim, Wash.	3	−6	−2.0	−2	0
Thompson, Leonard, Det.	3	−7	−2.3	4	0
Wilson, Dave, N.O.	3	−7	−2.3	−2	0
Green, Roy, St.L.	1	−10	−10.0	−10	0
Cavanaugh, Matt, S.F.	4	−11	−2.8	−1	0
Collins, Dwight, Minn.	3	−14	−4.7	1	0
Hansen, Brian, N.O.	2	−27	−13.5	−12	0

t = touchdown
Leader based on most yards gained

NFC — TEAM RUSHING

	Att	Yards	Avg	Long	TD
Chicago	674	2974	4.4	t72	22
Rams	541	2864	5.3	66	16
San Francisco	534	2465	4.6	47	21
Washington	588	2274	3.9	31	20
New Orleans	523	2171	4.2	t62	9
St. Louis	488	2088	4.3	39	21
Green Bay	461	2019	4.4	50	18
Detroit	446	2017	4.5	81	13
Atlanta	489	1994	4.1	57	16
Minnesota	444	1844	4.2	39	10
Tampa Bay	483	1776	3.7	37	17
Dallas	469	1714	3.7	t31	12
Giants	493	1660	3.4	28	12
Philadelphia	381	1338	3.5	27	6
Conference Total	7014	29198	—	81	213
Conference Average	501.0	2085.6	4.2	—	15.2

NFC — INDIVIDUAL PASSING

QUALIFIERS

	Att	Comp	Pct Comp	Yds	Avg Gain	TD	Pct TD	Long	Int	Pct Int	Rating Points
Montana, Joe, S.F.	432	279	64.6	3630	8.40	28	6.5	t80	10	2.3	102.9
Lomax, Neil, St.L.	560	345	61.6	4614	8.24	28	5.0	t83	16	2.9	92.5
Bartkowski, Steve, Atl.	269	181	67.3	2158	8.02	11	4.1	61	10	3.7	89.7
Theismann, Joe, Wash.	477	283	59.3	3391	7.11	24	5.0	t80	13	2.7	86.6
Dickey, Lynn, G.B.	401	237	59.1	3195	7.97	25	6.2	179	19	4.7	85.6
Danielson, Gary, Det.	410	252	61.5	3076	7.50	17	4.1	t77	15	3.7	83.1
DeBerg, Steve, T.B.	509	308	60.5	3554	6.98	19	3.7	55	18	3.5	79.3
Kemp, Jeff, Rams	284	143	50.4	2021	7.12	13	4.6	t63	7	2.5	78.7
Simms, Phil, Giants	533	286	53.7	4044	7.59	22	4.1	t65	18	3.4	78.1
Jaworski, Ron, Phil.	427	234	54.8	2754	6.45	16	3.7	t90	14	3.3	73.5
White, Danny, Dall.	233	126	54.1	1580	6.78	11	4.7	t66	11	4.7	71.5
Kramer, Tommy, Minn.	236	124	52.5	1678	7.11	9	3.8	t70	10	4.2	70.6
Hogeboom, Gary, Dall.	367	195	53.1	2366	6.45	7	1.9	t68	14	3.8	63.7
Todd, Richard, N.O.	312	161	51.6	2178	6.98	11	3.5	74	19	6.1	60.6

NON-QUALIFIERS

	Att	Comp	Pct Comp	Yds	Avg Gain	TD	Pct TD	Long	Int	Pct Int	Rating Points
Fuller, Steve, Chi.	78	53	67.9	595	7.63	3	3.8	31	0	0.0	103.3
Cavanaugh, Matt, S.F.	61	33	54.1	449	7.36	4	6.6	t51	0	0.0	99.7
McMahon, Jim, Chi.	143	85	59.4	1146	8.01	8	5.6	t61	2	1.4	97.8
Archer, David, Atl.	18	11	61.1	181	10.06	1	5.6	34	1	5.6	90.3
Wilson, Dave, N.O.	93	51	54.8	647	6.96	7	7.5	t54	4	4.3	83.9
Pisarcik, Joe, Phil.	176	96	54.5	1036	5.89	3	1.7	40	3	1.7	70.6
Landry, Greg, Chi.	20	11	55.0	199	9.95	1	5.0	t55	3	15.0	66.5
Manning, Archie, Minn.	94	52	55.3	545	5.80	2	2.1	56	3	3.2	66.1
Hipple, Eric, Det.	38	16	42.1	246	6.47	1	2.6	40	1	2.6	62.0
Witkowski, John, Det.	34	13	38.2	210	6.18	0	0.0	39	0	0.0	59.7
Moroski, Mike, Atl.	191	102	53.4	1207	6.32	2	1.0	t48	9	4.7	56.8
Wilson, Wade, Minn.	195	102	52.3	1019	5.23	5	2.6	38	11	5.6	52.5
Campbell, Rich, G.B.	38	16	42.1	218	5.74	3	7.9	t43	5	13.2	47.8
Thompson, Jack, T.B.	52	25	48.1	337	6.48	2	3.8	t74	5	9.6	42.4
Stabler, Ken, N.O.	70	33	47.1	339	4.84	2	2.9	29	5	7.1	41.3
Lisch, Rusty, Chi.	85	43	50.6	413	4.86	0	0.0	23	6	7.1	35.1
Wright, Randy, G.B.	62	27	43.5	310	5.00	2	3.2	56	6	9.7	30.4
Ferragamo, Vince, Rams	66	29	43.9	317	4.80	2	3.0	68	8	12.1	29.2
Machurek, Mike, Det.	43	14	32.6	193	4.49	0	0.0	48	6	14.0	8.3
(Less than 10 attempts)											
Anderson, Alfred, Minn.	7	3	42.9	95	13.57	2	28.6	t43	1	14.3	89.9
Baschnagel, Brian, Chi.	2	1	50.0	7	3.50	0	0.0	7	0	0.0	58.3
Clark, Dwight, S.F.	1	0	0.0	0	0.00	0	0.0	0	0	0.0	39.6
Coleman, Greg, Minn.	1	0	0.0	0	0.00	0	0.0	0	0	0.0	39.6
Dickerson, Eric, Rams	1	0	0.0	0	0.00	0	0.0	0	1	100.0	0.0
Dils, Steve, Minn.-Rams	7	4	57.1	44	6.29	1	14.3	t14	1	14.3	75.9
Dorsett, Tony, Dall.	1	0	0.0	0	0.00	0	0.0	0	1	100.0	0.0
Ellis, Gerry, G.B.	4	1	25.0	17	4.25	0	0.0	17	0	0.0	44.8
Gajan, Hokie, N.O.	1	1	100.0	34	34.00	1	100.0	t34	0	0.0	158.3
Galbreath, Tony, Giants	1	1	100.0	13	13.00	0	0.0	13	0	0.0	118.8
Garcia, Frank, T.B.	1	0	0.0	0	0.00	0	0.0	0	0	0.0	39.6
Harmon, Derrick, S.F.	2	0	0.0	0	0.00	0	0.0	0	0	0.0	39.6
Hart, Jim, Wash.	7	3	42.9	26	3.71	0	0.0	13	0	0.0	53.3

	Att	Comp	Pct Comp	Yds	Avg Gain	TD	Pct TD	Long	Int	Pct Int	Rating Points
Jenkins, Ken, Det.	1	0	0.0	0	0.00	0	0.0	0	0	0.0	39.6
Jones, James, Det.	5	3	60.0	62	12.40	1	20.0	27	0	0.0	143.3
May, Dean, Phil.	1	1	100.0	33	33.00	0	0.0	33	0	0.0	118.8
McIvor, Rick, St.L.	4	0	0.0	0	0.00	0	0.0	0	0	0.0	39.6
Mitchell, Stump, St.L.	1	1	100.0	20	20.00	0	0.0	20	0	0.0	118.8
Montgomery, Wilbert, Phil. ...	2	0	0.0	0	0.00	0	0.0	0	0	0.0	39.6
Payton, Walter, Chi..............	8	3	37.5	47	5.88	2	25.0	42	1	12.5	57.8
Perrin, Benny, St.L.	1	1	100.0	0	0.0	0	0.0	0	0	0.0	79.2
Renfro, Mike, Dall.	2	1	50.0	49	24.50	1	50.0	t49	0	0.0	135.4
Rutledge, Jeff, Giants	1	1	100.0	9	9.00	0	0.0	9	0	0.0	104.2
Scribner, Bucky, G.B.	1	0	0.0	0	0.00	0	0.0	0	0	0.0	39.6
Springs, Ron, Dall.	1	0	0.0	0	0.00	0	0.0	0	0	0.0	39.6
Suhey, Matt, Chi.................	1	0	0.0	0	0.00	0	0.0	0	0	0.0	39.6
Washington, Joe, Wash.	1	0	0.0	0	0.00	0	0.0	0	0	0.0	39.6
Wilder, James, T.B.	1	1	100.0	16	16.00	1	100.0	t16	0	0.0	158.3

t = Touchdown

NFC — TEAM PASSING

	Att	Comp	Pct Comp	Gross Yards	Tkd	Yds Lost	Net Yards	Avg Yds Att	Avg Yds Comp	TD	Pct TD	Long	Int	Pct Int
St. Louis	566	347	61.3	4634	49	377	4257	8.19	13.35	28	4.9	t83	16	2.8
San Francisco..	496	312	62.9	4079	27	178	3901	8.22	13.07	32	6.5	t80	10	2.0
Giants	535	288	53.8	4066	55	434	3632	7.60	14.12	22	4.1	t65	18	3.4
Dallas..............	604	322	53.3	3995	48	389	3606	6.61	12.41	19	3.1	t68	26	4.3
Tampa Bay	563	334	59.3	3907	45	362	3545	6.94	11.70	22	3.9	t74	23	4.1
Green Bay........	506	281	55.5	3740	42	310	3430	7.39	13.31	30	5.9	t79	30	5.9
Philadelphia.....	606	331	54.6	3823	60	463	3360	6.31	11.55	19	3.1	t90	17	2.8
Detroit.............	531	298	56.1	3787	61	486	3301	7.13	12.71	19	3.6	t77	22	4.1
Washington......	485	286	59.0	3417	48	341	3076	7.05	11.95	24	4.9	t80	13	2.7
Atlanta	478	294	61.5	3546	67	496	3050	7.42	12.06	14	2.9	61	20	4.2
Minnesota	533	281	52.7	3337	64	465	2872	6.26	11.88	18	3.4	t70	25	4.7
New Orleans	476	246	51.7	3198	45	361	2837	6.72	13.00	21	4.4	74	28	5.9
Chicago	390	226	57.9	2695	36	232	2463	6.91	11.92	14	3.6	t61	15	3.8
Rams	358	176	49.2	2382	32	240	2142	6.65	13.53	16	4.5	68	17	4.7
Conf. Total	7127	4022	—	50606	679	5134	45472	—	—	298	—	t90	280	—
Conf. Average..	509.1	287.3	56.4	3614.7	48.5	366.7	3248.0	7.10	12.58	21.3	4.2	—	20.0	3.9

NFC — INDIVIDUAL RECEIVERS

	No	Yards	Avg	Long	TD
Monk, Art, Wash.	106	1372	12.9	72	7
Wilder, James, T.B.	85	685	8.1	50	0
Green, Roy, St. L.	78	1555	19.9	t83	12
Jones, James, Det.	77	662	8.6	39	5
House, Kevin, T.B.	76	1005	13.2	55	5
Craig, Roger, S.F.	71	675	9.5	t64	3
Anderson, Ottis, St. L.	70	611	8.7	57	2
Bailey, Stacey, Atl.	67	1138	17.0	61	6
Spagnola, John, Phil.	65	701	10.8	34	1
Lofton, James, G.B.	62	1361	22.0	t79	7
Quick, Mike, Phil.	61	1052	17.2	t90	9
Carter, Gerald, T.B.	60	816	13.6	t74	5
Cosbie, Doug, Dall.	60	789	13.2	36	4
Montgomery, Wilbert, Phil.	60	501	8.4	28	0
Hill, Tony, Dall.	58	864	14.9	t66	5
Clark, Dwight, S.F.	52	880	16.9	t80	6
Tilley, Pat, St. L.	52	758	14.6	42	5
Jackson, Alfred, Atl.	52	731	14.1	t50	2
Dorsett, Tony, Dall.	51	459	9.0	t68	1
Thompson, Leonard, Det.	50	773	15.5	t66	6
Johnson, Bob, Giants	48	795	16.6	45	7
Mowatt, Zeke, Giants	48	698	14.5	34	6
Lewis, Leo, Minn.	47	830	17.7	56	4
Springs, Ron, Dall.	46	454	9.9	t57	3
Brown, Ted, Minn.	46	349	7.6	35	3
Payton, Walter, Chi.	45	368	8.2	31	0
Coffman, Paul, G.B.	43	562	13.1	t44	9
Muhammad, Calvin, Wash.	42	729	17.4	t80	4
Suhey, Matt, Chi.	42	312	7.4	23	2
Riggs, Gerald, Atl.	42	277	6.6	21	0
Cooper, Earl, S.F.	41	459	11.2	26	4
Solomon, Freddie, S.F.	40	737	18.4	t64	10
Marsh, Doug, St. L.	39	608	15.6	47	5
Jones, Mike, Minn.	38	591	15.6	t70	1
Gray, Earnest, Giants	38	529	13.9	31	2
Jordan, Steve, Minn.	38	414	10.9	26	2
Chadwick, Jeff, Det.	37	540	14.6	46	2
Galbreath, Tony, Giants	37	357	9.6	37	0
Ellis, Gerry, G.B.	36	312	8.7	22	2
Renfro, Mike, Dall.	35	583	16.7	t60	2
Gajan, Hokie, N.O.	35	288	8.2	51	2
Nichols, Mark, Det.	34	744	21.9	t77	1
Ellard, Henry, Rams	34	622	18.3	t63	6
Gault, Willie, Chi.	34	587	17.3	t61	6
Cox, Arthur, Atl.	34	329	9.7	t23	3

	No	Yards	Avg	Long	TD
Manuel, Lionel, Giants......................	33	619	18.8	53	4
Harris, Duriel, Clev.-Dall.	33	521	15.8	43	2
Groth, Jeff, N.O...............................	33	487	14.8	31	0
Wilson, Wayne, N.O.........................	33	314	9.5	t34	3
Haddix, Michael, Phil......................	33	231	7.0	22	0
Donley, Doug, Dall.	32	473	14.8	t49	2
Oliver, Hubert, Phil.........................	32	142	4.4	21	0
Hill, David, Rams............................	31	300	9.7	26	1
Sims, Billy, Det.	31	239	7.7	20	0
Woodruff, Tony, Phil........................	30	484	16.1	38	3
Didier, Clint, Wash.	30	350	11.7	44	5
Young, Tyrone, N.O.	29	597	20.6	74	3
Moorehead, Emery, Chi....................	29	497	17.1	50	1
McKinnon, Dennis, Chi.....................	29	431	14.9	t32	3
Bell, Jerry, T.B.	29	397	13.7	27	4
Clark, Jessie, G.B.	29	234	8.1	20	2
Brenner, Hoby, N.O.........................	28	554	19.8	57	6
Tyler, Wendell, S.F..........................	28	230	8.2	t26	2
Nelson, Darrin, Minn.	27	162	6.0	17	1
Epps, Phillip, G.B.	26	435	16.7	56	3
Jackson, Kenny, Phil.	26	398	15.3	t83	1
Jefferson, John, G.B.	26	339	13.0	33	0
Mitchell, Stump, St. L......................	26	318	12.2	t44	2
Newsome, Tim, Dall.	26	263	10.1	29	0
Benson, Cliff, Atl.	26	244	9.4	30	0
Ferrell, Earl, St. L...........................	26	218	8.4	21	1
Carpenter, Rob, Giants.....................	26	209	8.0	19	1
Williams, Byron, Giants	24	471	19.6	t65	2
Johnson, Billy, Atl...........................	24	371	15.5	t45	3
Giles, Jimmie, T.B.	24	310	12.9	38	2
Hodge, Floyd, Atl............................	24	234	9.8	26	0
Brown, Ron, Rams	23	478	20.8	54	4
Francis, Russ, S.F...........................	23	285	12.4	32	2
Bell, Theo, T.B.	22	350	15.9	29	0
Goodlow, Eugene, N.O.....................	22	281	12.8	23	3
Armstrong, Adger, T.B......................	22	180	8.2	18	3
White, Sammy, Minn.	21	399	19.0	47	1
Scott, Lindsay, N.O.	21	278	13.2	37	1
Jenkins, Ken, Det.	21	246	11.7	68	0
Dickerson, Eric, Rams......................	21	139	6.6	19	0
Guman, Mike, Rams.........................	19	161	8.5	29	0
Ivery, Eddie Lee, G.B.	19	141	7.4	18	1
Nehemiah, Renaldo, S.F.	18	357	19.8	t59	2
Brown, Charlie, Wash.......................	18	200	11.1	36	3
Warren, Don, Wash..........................	18	192	10.7	26	0
Wilson, Mike, S.F............................	17	245	14.4	44	1
LaFleur, Greg, St. L.	17	198	11.6	23	0

	No	Yards	Avg	Long	TD
Moore, Jeff, Wash.	17	115	6.8	18	2
Anderson, Alfred, Minn.	17	102	6.0	t28	1
Lewis, David, Det.	16	236	14.8	58	3
Senser, Joe, Minn.	15	110	7.3	26	0
Hill, Drew, Rams	14	390	27.9	68	4
Rubick, Rob, Det.	14	188	13.4	29	1
Mularkey, Mike, Minn.	14	134	9.6	26	2
Harrell, Willard, St. L.	14	106	7.6	15	0
Washington, Joe, Wash.	13	74	5.7	12	0
Morris, Joe, Giants	12	124	10.3	26	0
Anthony, Tyrone, N.O.	12	113	9.4	32	0
Cain, Lynn, Atl.	12	87	7.3	18	0
Rogers, George, N.O.	12	76	6.3	15	0
Collins, Dwight, Minn.	11	143	13.0	t43	1
Monroe, Carl, S.F.	11	139	12.6	47	1
Pittman, Danny, St. L.	10	145	14.5	50	0
McGrath, Mark, Wash.	10	118	11.8	24	1
Seay, Virgil, Wash.	9	111	12.3	19	1
Dunsmore, Pat, Chi.	9	106	11.8	25	1
Kab, Vyto, Phil.	9	102	11.3	26	3
Crouse, Ray, G.B.	9	93	10.3	25	1
Saldi, Jay, Chi.	9	90	10.0	20	0
Grant, Otis, Rams.	9	64	7.1	15	0
Bussey, Dexter, Det.	9	63	7.0	19	0
Woolfolk, Butch, Giants	9	53	5.9	13	0
Thomas, Calvin, Chi.	9	39	4.3	9	0
McConkey, Phil, Giants	8	154	19.3	39	0
Miller, Junior, N.O.	8	81	10.1	22	1
Huckleby, Harlan, G.B.	8	65	8.1	13	0
Griffin, Keith, Wash.	8	43	5.4	8	0
Farmer, George, Rams	7	75	10.7	23	0
Frank, John, S.F.	7	60	8.6	21	1
Jones, James, Dall.	7	57	8.1	19	1
Williams, Mike, Phil.	7	47	6.7	15	0
Riggins, John, Wash.	7	43	6.1	11	0
Barber, Mike, Rams	7	42	6.0	11	0
Love, Randy, St. L.	7	33	4.7	16	1
Hoover, Mel, Phil.	6	143	23.8	44	2
Landrum, Mike, Atl.	6	66	11.0	30	0
Tice, John, N.O.	6	55	9.2	17	1
West, Ed, G.B.	6	54	9.0	t29	4
Baschnagel, Brian, Chi.	6	53	8.8	17	0
Dixon, Dwayne, T.B.	5	69	13.8	21	0
Mack, Cedric, St. L.	5	61	12.2	22	0
Rodgers, Del, G.B.	5	56	11.2	22	0
Walker, Rick, Wash.	5	52	10.4	19	1
Carroll, Jay, T.B.	5	50	10.0	17	1

	No	Yards	Avg	Long	TD
Rice, Allen, Minn.	4	59	14.8	24	1
McDonald, James, Rams	4	55	13.8	22	0
Hardy, Larry, N.O.	4	50	12.5	t28	1
Stamps, Sylvester, Atl.	4	48	12.0	31	0
Redden, Barry, Rams	4	39	9.8	6	0
Childs, Henry, G.B.	4	32	8.0	17	0
Gentry, Dennis, Chi.	4	29	7.3	13	0
Lewis, Gary, G.B.	4	29	7.3	15	0
Anderson, Brad, Chi.	3	77	25.7	t49	1
Mandley, Pete, Det.	3	38	12.7	19	0
Campbell, Earl, Hou.-N.O.	3	27	9.0	15	0
Carver, Mel, T.B.	3	27	9.0	12	0
Duckett, Kenny, N.O.	3	24	8.0	11	0
Goode, John, St. L.	3	23	7.7	10	0
McCall, Reese, Det.	3	15	5.0	7	0
Ring, Bill, S.F.	3	10	3.3	15	0
Mullady, Tom, Giants	2	35	17.5	22	0
Krenk, Mitch, Chi.	2	31	15.5	24	0
Cornwell, Fred, Dall.	2	23	11.5	13	1
Garrity, Gregg, Pitt.-Phil.	2	22	11.0	12	0
Hardy, Andre, Phil.	2	22	11.0	13	0
Cassidy, Ron, G.B.	2	16	8.0	10	0
Owens, James, T.B.	2	13	6.5	9	1
Crutchfield, Dwayne, Rams	2	11	5.5	7	1
McMahon, Jim, Chi.	1	42	42.0	42	0
Danielson, Gary, Det.	1	22	22.0	t22	1
Kramer, Tommy, Minn.	1	20	20.0	t20	1
LeCount, Terry, Minn.	1	14	14.0	14	0
Cameron, Jack, Chi.	1	13	13.0	13	0
Simms, Phil, Giants	1	13	13.0	13	0
D'Addio, Dave, Det.	1	12	12.0	12	0
Hasselbeck, Don, Minn.	1	10	10.0	10	0
Martin, Robbie, Det.	1	9	9.0	9	0
Taylor, Lenny, G.B.	1	8	8.0	8	0
Cabral, Brian, Chi.	1	7	7.0	7	0
Carmichael, Harold, Dall.	1	7	7.0	7	0
Curran, Willie, Atl.	1	7	7.0	7	0
Hutchison, Anthony, Chi.	1	7	7.0	7	0
Kane, Rick, Wash.	1	7	7.0	7	0
Matthews, Allama, Atl.	1	7	7.0	7	0
Smith, Waddell, Dall.	1	7	7.0	7	0
Tuttle, Perry, T.B.-Atl.	1	7	7.0	7	0
Faulkner, Chris, Rams	1	6	6.0	6	0
Jones, Anthony, Wash.	1	6	6.0	6	0
Jordan, Donald, Chi.	1	6	6.0	6	0
Phillips, Kirk, Dall.	1	6	6.0	6	0
Dierking, Scott, T.B.	1	5	5.0	t5	1

	No	Yards	Avg	Long	Td
Garrett, Alvin, Wash.	1	5	5.0	5	0
Mistler, John, Buff.-Giants	1	5	5.0	5	0
Belcher, Kevin, Giants......................	1	4	4.0	4	0
Moore, Blake, G.B............................	1	3	3.0	t3	1
Harmon, Derrick, S.F........................	1	2	2.0	2	0
Pozderac, Phil, Dall..........................	1	1	1.0	1	0

t = touchdown
Leader based on most passes caught

NFC — TOP 25 RECEIVERS BY YARDS

	Yards	No	Avg	Long	TD
Green, Roy, St. L...............................	1555	78	19.9	t83	12
Monk, Art, Wash.	1372	106	12.9	72	7
Lofton, James, G.B.	1361	62	22.0	t79	7
Bailey, Stacey, Atl.............................	1138	67	17.0	61	6
Quick, Mike, Phil...............................	1052	61	17.2	t90	9
House, Kevin, T.B..............................	1005	76	13.2	55	5
Clark, Dwight, S.F..............................	880	52	16.9	t80	6
Hill, Tony, Dall.	864	58	14.9	t66	5
Lewis, Leo, Minn................................	830	47	17.7	56	4
Carter, Gerald, T.B............................	816	60	13.6	t74	5
Johnson, Bob, Giants........................	795	48	16.6	45	7
Cosbie, Doug, Dall.	789	60	13.2	36	4
Thompson, Leonard, Det....................	773	50	15.5	t66	6
Tilley, Pat, St. L.	758	52	14.6	42	5
Nichols, Mark, Det.	744	34	21.9	t77	1
Solomon, Freddie, S.F.	737	40	18.4	t64	10
Jackson, Alfred, Atl...........................	731	52	14.1	t50	2
Muhammad, Calvin, Wash.	729	42	17.4	t80	4
Spagnola, John, Phil.	701	65	10.8	34	1
Mowatt, Zeke, Giants	698	48	14.5	34	6
Wilder, James, T.B.............................	685	85	8.1	50	0
Craig, Roger, S.F.	675	71	9.5	t64	3
Jones, James, Det.	662	77	8.6	39	5
Ellard, Henry, Rams..........................	662	34	18.3	t63	6
Manuel, Lionel, Giants	619	33	18.8	53	4

NFC — INDIVIDUAL INTERCEPTORS

	No	Yards	Avg	Long	TD
Flynn, Tom, G.B.	9	106	11.8	31	0
Lewis, Tim, G.B.	7	151	21.6	t99	1
Downs, Mike, Dall.	7	126	18.0	t27	1
Ellis, Ray, Phil.	7	119	17.0	31	0
Dean, Vernon, Wash.	7	114	16.3	t36	2
Haynes, Mark, Giants	7	90	12.9	22	0
Watkins, Bobby, Det.	6	0	0.0	0	0
Irvin, LeRoy, Rams	5	166	33.2	t81	2
Cotney, Mark, T.B.	5	123	24.6	29	0
Hopkins, Wes, Phil.	5	107	21.4	33	0
Fencik, Gary, Chi.	5	102	20.4	61	0
Green, Darrell, Wash.	5	91	18.2	50	1
Frazier, Leslie, Chi.	5	89	17.8	33	0
Thurman, Dennis, Dall.	5	81	16.2	43	1
Johnson, Kenny, Atl.	5	75	15.0	28	0
Washington, Lionel, St. L.	5	42	8.4	18	0
Turner, Keena, S.F.	4	51	12.8	21	0
Bell, Todd, Chi.	4	46	11.5	t36	1
Smith, Wayne, St. L.	4	35	8.8	23	0
Foules, Elbert, Phil.	4	27	6.8	20	0
Lott, Ronnie, S.F.	4	26	6.5	15	0
Perrin, Benny, St. L.	4	22	5.5	22	0
Waymer, Dave, N.O.	4	9	2.3	9	0
Green, Gary, Rams	3	88	29.3	60	0
Shell, Todd, S.F.	3	81	27.0	t53	1
Brantley, Scot, T.B.	3	55	18.3	38	0
Cromwell, Nolan, Rams	3	54	18.0	t33	1
Hicks, Dwight, S.F.	3	42	14.0	29	0
Milot, Rich, Wash.	3	42	14.0	27	0
Castille, Jeremiah, T.B.	3	38	12.7	30	0
Lee, Mark, G.B.	3	33	11.0	14	0
Clinkscale, Dextor, Dall.	3	32	10.7	23	0
Anderson, John, G.B.	3	24	8.0	22	0
Graham, William, Det.	3	22	7.3	15	0
Walls, Everson, Dall.	3	12	4.0	12	0
Bess, Rufus, Minn.	3	7	2.3	7	0
Williams, Perry, Giants	3	7	2.3	7	0
Fellows, Ron, Dall.	3	3	1.0	3	0
Hegman, Mike, Dall.	3	3	1.0	3	0
Winston, Dennis, N.O.	2	90	45.0	t47	2
Hall, Alvin, Det.	2	64	32.0	36	0
McLemore, Dana, S.F.	2	54	27.0	t54	1
Wattelet, Frank, N.O.	2	52	26.0	t35	1
Collins, Jim, Rams	2	43	21.5	40	0
Williamson, Carlton, S.F.	2	42	21.0	26	0

	No	Yards	Avg	Long	TD
Smith, Leonard, St. L.	2	31	15.5	t25	1
Kinard, Terry, Giants	2	29	14.5	29	0
Reasons, Gary, Giants	2	26	13.0	26	0
Butler, Bobby, Atl.	2	25	12.5	25	0
Johnson, Johnnie, Rams	2	21	10.5	21	0
Swain, John, Minn...........................	2	20	10.0	11	0
Jordan, Curtis, Wash.......................	2	18	9.0	16	0
Fahnhorst, Jim, S.F..........................	2	9	4.5	9	0
Richardson, Mike, Chi.	2	7	3.5	7	0
Edwards, Herman, Phil.....................	2	0	0.0	0	0
Griffin, Jeff, St. L............................	2	0	0.0	0	0
McNorton, Bruce, Det......................	2	0	0.0	0	0
Pridemore, Tom, Atl.	2	0	0.0	0	0
Wright, Eric, S.F.............................	2	0	0.0	0	0
Howard, Thomas, St. L.....................	2	−4	−2.0	1	0
Teal, Willie, Minn............................	1	53	53.0	t53	1
Coleman, Monte, Wash.	1	49	49.0	t49	1
Fuller, Jeff, S.F.	1	38	38.0	38	0
Smith, Ricky, N.E.-Wash.	1	37	37.0	37	0
Jackson, Jeff, Atl............................	1	35	35.0	t35	1
Harris, Al, Chi.................................	1	34	34.0	34	0
Lockhart, Eugene, Dall.	1	32	32.0	32	0
Newsome, Vince, Rams....................	1	31	31.0	31	0
Wilson, Brenard, Phil.......................	1	28	28.0	28	0
Logan, Dave, T.B.	1	27	27.0	t27	1
Holt, John, T.B.	1	25	25.0	25	0
Washington, Anthony, Wash.............	1	25	25.0	25	0
Browner, Joey, Minn........................	1	20	20.0	20	0
Studwell, Scott, Minn.......................	1	20	20.0	20	0
Heflin, Victor, St. L.	1	19	19.0	19	0
Junior, E.J., St. L.	1	18	18.0	18	0
Kovach, Jim, N.O.	1	16	16.0	16	0
Poe, Johnnie, N.O...........................	1	16	16.0	16	0
Coffey, Ken, Wash...........................	1	15	15.0	15	0
Acorn, Fred, T.B..............................	1	14	14.0	14	0
Brown, Cedric, T.B.	1	14	14.0	14	0
Hunt, Byron, Giants.........................	1	14	14.0	14	0
Jackson, Rickey, N.O.	1	14	14.0	14	0
Reece, Beasley, T.B.........................	1	12	12.0	12	0
Britt, James, Atl..............................	1	10	10.0	10	0
Clark, Bruce, N.O............................	1	9	9.0	9	0
Duerson, Dave, Chi.	1	9	9.0	9	0
Hood, Estus, G.B.	1	8	8.0	8	0
Cumby, George, G.B.	1	7	7.0	7	0
Currier, Bill, Giants.........................	1	7	7.0	7	0
Johnson, Bobby, N.O.	1	7	7.0	7	0
Carson, Harry, Giants......................	1	6	6.0	6	0

	No	Yards	Avg	Long	TD
Wilkes, Reggie, Phil.	1	6	6.0	6	0
Brown, Robert, G.B.	1	5	5.0	t5	0
Scott, Victory, Dall.	1	5	5.0	5	0
Headen, Andy, Giants	1	4	4.0	4	0
Murphy, Mark, G.B.	1	4	4.0	4	0
Singletary, Mike, Chi.	1	4	4.0	4	0
Bates, Bill, Dall.	1	3	3.0	3	0
Bunz, Dan, S.F.	1	2	2.0	2	0
Small, Gerald, Atl.	1	2	2.0	2	0
Fantetti, Ken, Det.	1	1	1.0	1	0
Cannon, John, T.B.	1	0	0.0	0	0
Clark, Mario, S.F.	1	0	0.0	0	0
Davis, Jeff, T.B.	1	0	0.0	0	0
Dickerson, Anthony, Dall.	1	0	0.0	0	0
Hannon, Tom, Minn.	1	0	0.0	0	0
Lee, Carl, Minn.	1	0	0.0	0	0
McLeod, Mike, G.B.	1	0	0.0	0	0
McNeill, Fred, Min.	1	0	0.0	0	0
Schmidt, Terry, Chi.	1	0	0.0	0	0
Gayle, Shaun, Chi.	1	−1	−1.0	−1	0
Taylor, Lawrence, Giants	1	−1	−1.0	−1	0
Owens, Mel, Rams	1	−4	−4.0	−4	0

t = touchdown
Leader based on most interceptions

NFC — TEAM INTERCEPTIONS

	Att	Yards	Avg	Long	TD
Dallas	28	297	10.6	43	2
Green Bay	27	338	12.5	t99	2
San Francisco	25	345	13.8	t54	2
Washington	21	391	18.6	50	4
Chicago	21	290	13.8	61	1
St. Louis	21	163	7.8	t25	1
Philadelphia	20	287	14.4	33	0
Giants	19	182	9.6	29	0
Tampa Bay	18	308	17.1	38	1
Rams	17	399	23.5	t81	3
Detroit	14	87	6.2	36	0
New Orleans	13	213	16.4	t47	3
Atlanta	12	147	12.3	t35	1
Minnesota	11	120	10.9	t53	1
Conference Total	267	3567	—	t99	21
Conference Average	19.1	254.8	13.4	—	1.5

NFC — INDIVIDUAL PUNTERS

	No	Yards	Long	Avg	Total Punts	TB	Blk	Opp Ret	Ret Yds	In 20	Net Avg
Hansen, Brian, N.O......	69	3020	66	43.8	70	7	1	47	550	9	33.3
Coleman, Greg, Minn...	82	3473	62	42.4	82	2	0	49	435	16	36.6
Scribner, Bucky, G.B. ..	85	3596	61	42.3	85	12	0	46	368	18	35.2
Horan, Mike, Phil.	92	3880	69	42.2	92	6	0	58	486	21	35.6
Giacomarro, Ralph, Atl.	68	2855	58	42.0	70	6	2	42	450	12	32.6
Garcia, Frank, T.B.	68	2849	60	41.9	68	9	0	36	310	12	34.7
Runager, Max, S.F.......	56	2341	59	41.8	57	12	1	26	176	18	33.8
Black, Mike, Det...........	76	3164	63	41.6	76	8	0	49	516	13	32.7
Finzer, David, Chi.........	83	3328	87	40.1	85	4	2	41	249	26	35.3
Jennings, Dave, Giants	90	3598	54	40.0	93	10	3	50	479	22	31.4
Hayes, Jeff, Wash.......	72	2834	59	39.4	73	5	1	38	187	11	34.9
Misko, John, Rams	74	2866	58	38.7	74	9	0	35	196	21	33.6
Birdsong, Carl, St.L.	67	2594	59	38.7	68	8	1	27	239	19	32.3
White, Danny, Dall.	82	3151	54	38.4	82	8	0	38	156	21	34.6
(Non-Qualifiers)											
Warren, John, Dall.	21	799	48	38.0	21	3	0	13	47	3	33.0
Miller, Jim, Dall.	5	173	41	34.6	5	0	0	4	27	1	29.2
Orosz, Tom, S.F...........	5	195	55	39.0	5	0	0	4	14	1	36.2
Haji-Sheikh, Ali, Giants	0	0	0	—	1	0	1	0	0	0	0.0

Leader based on gross average, minimum 40 punts

NFC — TEAM PUNTING

	Total Punts	Yards	Long	Avg	TB	Blk	Opp Ret	Ret Yds	In 20	Net Avg
New Orleans	70	3020	66	43.1	7	1	47	550	9	33.3
Minnesota	82	3473	62	42.4	2	0	49	435	16	36.6
Green Bay	85	3596	61	42.3	12	0	46	368	18	35.2
Philadelphia	92	3880	69	42.2	6	0	58	486	21	35.6
Tampa Bay	68	2849	60	41.9	9	0	36	310	12	34.7
Detroit	76	3164	63	41.6	8	0	49	516	13	32.7
San Francisco...........	62	2536	59	40.9	12	1	30	190	19	34.0
Atlanta	70	2855	58	40.8	6	2	42	450	12	32.6
Chicago	85	3328	87	39.2	4	2	41	249	26	35.3
Washington...............	73	2834	59	38.8	5	1	38	187	11	34.9
Rams	74	2866	58	38.7	9	0	35	196	21	33.6
Giants......................	94	3598	54	38.3	10	4	50	479	22	31.1
Dallas.......................	108	4123	54	38.2	11	0	55	230	25	34.0
St. Louis	68	2594	59	38.1	8	1	27	239	19	32.3
Conference Total	1107	44716	87	—	109	12	603	4885	244	—
Conference Average .	79.1	3194.0	—	40.4	7.8	0.9	43.1	348.9	17.4	34.0

NFC — INDIVIDUAL PUNT RETURNERS

	No	FC	Yards	Avg	Long	TD
Ellard, Henry, Rams	30	3	403	13.4	t83	2
McLemore, Dana, S.F.	45	11	521	11.6	t79	1
Mitchell, Stump, St.L.	38	3	333	8.8	39	0
Fields, Jitter, N.O.	27	6	236	8.7	61	0
Nelms, Mike, Wash.	49	1	428	8.7	46	0
Fisher, Jeff, Chi.	57	11	492	8.6	28	0
Martin, Robbie, Det.	25	8	210	8.4	23	0
Allen, Gary, Dall.	54	15	446	8.3	18	0
Nelson, Darrin, Minn.	23	9	180	7.8	21	0
Bright, Leon, T.B.	23	1	173	7.5	21	0
Epps, Phillip, G.B.	29	10	199	6.9	39	0
McConkey, Phil, Giants	46	15	306	6.7	31	0
Cooper, Evan, Phil.	40	19	250	6.3	16	0
Thomas, Zack, Den.-T.B.	21	3	125	6.0	15	0
(Non-Qualifiers)						
Flynn, Tom, G.B.	15	4	128	8.5	20	0
Johnson, Billy, Atl.	15	1	152	10.1	37	0
Johnson, Kenny, Atl.	10	1	79	7.9	14	0
Curran, Willie, Atl.	9	1	21	2.3	10	0
Harris, Duriel, Clev.-Dall.	9	0	73	8.1	13	0
Irvin, LeRoy, Rams	9	0	83	9.2	22	0
Seay, Virgil, Wash.-Atl.	8	1	10	1.3	7	0
Manuel, Lionel, Giants	8	3	62	7.8	22	0
Hall, Alvin, Det.	7	1	30	4.3	11	0
Holt, John, T.B.	6	3	17	2.8	8	0
Groth, Jeff, N.O.	6	12	32	5.3	9	0
McKinnon, Dennis, Chi.	5	0	62	12.4	18	0
Bell, Theo, T.B.	4	1	10	2.5	8	0
Pittman, Danny, St.L.	4	1	10	2.5	5	0
Hayes, Gary, G.B.	4	0	24	6.0	10	0
Lewis, Leo, Minn.	4	1	31	7.8	13	0
Mandley, Pete, Det.	2	2	0	0.0	0	0
Bess, Rufus, Minn.	2	0	9	4.5	7	0
Green, Darrell, Wash.	2	0	13	6.5	13	0
Waddy, Billy, Minn.	1	0	-3	-3.0	-3	0
Johnson, Demetrious, Det.	1	0	0	0.0	0	0
Kinard, Terry, Giants	1	0	0	0.0	0	0
Teal, Willie, Minn.	1	0	0	0.0	0	0
Williams, Greg, Wash.	1	0	0	0.0	0	0
Jenkins, Ken, Det.	1	0	1	1.0	1	0
Mauti, Rich, Wash.	1	1	2	2.0	2	0
Johnson, Johnnie, Rams	1	1	3	3.0	3	0
Duerson, Dave, Chi.	1	0	4	4.0	4	0
Coffey, Ken, Wash.	1	0	6	6.0	6	0
Green, Roy, St.L.	0	1	0	—	0	0

	No	FC	Yards	Avg	Long	TD
Murphy, Mark, G.B.	0	2	0	—	0	0
Coleman, Monte, Wash..............	0	0	27	—	27	0

t = touchdown
Leader based on average return, minimum 20 returns

NFC — TEAM PUNT RETURNS

	Att	FC	Yards	Avg	Long	TD
Chicago..................	63	11	558	8.9	28	0
Washington	55	2	474	8.6	46	0
Giants	55	18	368	6.7	31	0
Dallas.....................	54	15	446	8.3	18	0
Green Bay...............	48	16	351	7.3	39	0
St. Louis..................	47	5	399	8.5	39	0
San Francisco	45	11	521	11.6	t79	1
Atlanta....................	41	4	264	6.4	37	0
Rams......................	40	4	489	12.2	t83	2
Philadelphia.............	40	19	250	6.3	16	0
Detroit	36	11	241	6.7	23	0
Tampa Bay..............	34	5	207	6.1	21	0
New Orleans	33	18	268	8.1	61	0
Minnesota................	31	10	217	7.0	21	0
Conference Total.....	622	149	5053	—	t83	3
Conference Average	44.4	10.6	360.9	8.1	—	0.2

NFC — INDIVIDUAL KICKOFF RETURNERS

	No	Yards	Avg	Long	TD
Redden, Barry, Rams	23	530	23.0	40	0
Mitchell, Stump, St. L.	35	804	23.0	56	0
Nelson, Darrin, Minn.	39	891	22.8	47	0
Anthony, Tyrone, N.O.	22	490	22.3	64	0
Morton, Michael, T.B.	38	835	22.0	43	0
Rodgers, Del, G.B.	39	843	21.6	t97	1
Anderson, Alfred, Minn.	30	639	21.3	41	0
Hill, Drew, Rams	26	543	20.9	40	0
Monroe, Carl, S.F.	27	561	20.8	44	0
Nelms, Mike, Wash.	42	860	20.5	36	0
Allen, Gary, Dall.	33	666	20.2	34	0
McSwain, Chuck, Dall.	20	403	20.2	32	0
Hayes, Joe, Phil.	22	441	20.0	44	0
Duckett, Kenny, N.O.	29	580	20.0	39	0
McConkey, Phil, Giants	28	541	19.3	33	0
Cameron, Jack, Chi.	26	485	18.7	40	0
Mandley, Pete, Det.	22	390	17.7	32	0
(Non-Qualifiers)					
Stamps, Sylvester, Atl.	19	452	23.8	50	0
Hall, Alvin, Det.	19	385	20.3	46	0
Johnson, Kenny, Atl.	19	359	18.9	27	0
Fields, Jitter, N.O.	19	356	18.7	31	0
Jenkins, Ken, Det.	18	396	22.0	32	0
Thomas, Zack, Den.-T.B.	18	351	19.5	33	0
Cooper, Evan, Phil.	17	299	17.6	48	0
Bright, Leon, T.B.	16	303	18.9	33	0
Pittman, Danny, St. L.	14	319	22.8	43	0
Huckleby, Harlan, G.B.	14	261	18.6	54	0
Woolfolk, Butch, Giants	14	232	16.6	27	0
Harmon, Derrick, S.F.	13	357	27.5	51	0
Waters, Andre, Phil.	13	319	24.5	t89	1
Harrell, Willard, St. L.	13	231	17.8	28	0
Epps, Phillip, G.B.	12	232	19.3	47	0
Curran, Willie, Atl.	11	219	19.9	42	0
Gentry, Dennis, Chi.	11	209	19.0	33	0
Martin, Robbie, Det.	10	144	14.4	23	0
Cephous, Frank, Giants	9	178	19.8	30	0
Griffin, Keith, Wash.	9	164	18.2	31	0
Tate, Rodney, Atl.	9	148	16.4	31	0
Owens, James, T.B.	8	168	21.0	36	0
Fellows, Ron, Dall.	6	94	15.7	23	0
Morris, Joe, Giants:	6	69	11.5	14	0
Seay, Virgil, Wash.-Atl.	5	108	21.6	28	0
Jordan, Donald, Chi.	5	62	12.4	22	0
Wood, Richard, T.B.	5	43	8.6	16	0

	No	Yards	Avg	Long	TD
Duerson, Dave, Chi.	4	95	23.8	26	0
Austin, Cliff, Atl.	4	77	19.3	23	0
Meade, Mike, Det.	4	32	8.0	15	0
McLemore, Dana, S.F.	3	80	26.7	50	0
Waddy, Billy, Minn.	3	64	21.3	31	0
Bess, Rufus, Minn.	3	47	15.7	19	0
Kane, Rick, Wash.	3	43	14.3	31	0
Everett, Major, Phil.	3	40	13.3	18	0
Rice, Allen, Minn.	3	34	11.3	13	0
Pleasant, Mike, Rams	2	48	24.0	29	0
Johnson, Billy, Atl.	2	39	19.5	21	0
Smith, Jimmy, Wash.	2	38	19.0	22	0
Bell, Todd, Chi.	2	33	16.5	17	0
Irvin, LeRoy, Rams	2	33	16.5	22	0
Salonen, Brian, Dall.	2	30	15.0	22	0
Smith, Greg, Minn.	2	26	13.0	15	0
Ellis, Ray, Phil.	2	25	12.5	15	0
Ellard, Henry, Rams	2	24	12.0	12	0
Rouse, Curtis, Minn.	2	22	11.0	15	0
Turner, Maurice, Minn.	2	21	10.5	14	0
McLaughlin, Jim, Giants	2	18	9.0	11	0
Granger, Norm, Dall.	2	6	3.0	5	0
Daniel, Kenny, Giants	1	52	52.0	52	0
Guman, Mike, Rams	1	43	43.0	t43	1
Lewis, Leo, Minn.	1	31	31.0	31	0
Hill, Ken, Giants	1	27	27.0	27	0
Ring, Bill, S.F.	1	27	27.0	27	0
Wilson, Wayne, N.O.	1	23	23.0	23	0
Smith, Ricky, N.E.-Wash.	1	22	22.0	22	0
Crutchfield, Dwayne, Rams	1	20	20.0	20	0
Hardy, Andre, Phil.	1	20	20.0	20	0
Jones, Daryll, G.B.	1	19	19.0	19	0
Green, Roy, St. L.	1	18	18.0	18	0
Mauti, Rich, Wash.	1	16	16.0	16	0
Wilson, Tim, N.O.	1	16	16.0	16	0
Gaison, Blane, Atl.	1	15	15.0	15	0
Wilson, Mike, S.F.	1	14	14.0	14	0
Gault, Willie, Chi.	1	12	12.0	12	0
Strauthers, Thomas, Phil.	1	12	12.0	12	0
Prather, Guy, G.B.	1	7	7.0	7	0
Spradlin, Danny, T.B.	1	5	5.0	5	0
Matthews, Allama, Atl.	1	3	3.0	3	0
Sully, Ivory, Rams	1	3	3.0	3	0
Love, Randy, St.L.	1	1	1.0	1	0
Cooper, Earl, S.F.	1	0	0.0	0	0
D'Addio, Dave, Det.	1	0	0.0	0	0
Ferrell, Earl, St.L.	1	0	0.0	0	0

	No	Yards	Avg	Long	TD
Malancon, Rydell, Atl.........................	1	0	0.0	0	0
McIntyre, Guy, S.F.	1	0	0.0	0	0
Nelson, David, Minn.	1	0	0.0	0	0
Tyrrell, Tim, Atl................................	1	0	0.0	0	0

t = touchdown
Leader based on average return, minimum 20 returns

NFC — TEAM KICKOFF RETURNS

	No	Yards	Avg	Long	TD
Minnesota	86	1775	20.6	47	0
St. Louis..	74	1563	21.1	56	0
New Orleans	72	1465	20.3	64	0
Atlanta...	70	1367	19.5	50	0
Green Bay......................................	67	1362	20.3	t97	1
Tampa Bay.....................................	68	1354	19.9	43	0
Detroit	74	1347	18.2	46	0
Rams	58	1244	21.4	t43	1
Dallas..	63	1199	19.0	34	0
Washington	60	1174	19.6	36	0
Philadelphia	59	1156	19.6	t89	1
Giants	61	1117	18.3	52	0
San Francisco	47	1039	22.1	51	0
Chicago..	49	896	18.3	40	0
Conference Total..........................	908	18058	—	t97	3
Conference Average......................	64.9	1289.9	19.9	—	0.2

NFC — INDIVIDUAL SCORERS

KICKERS

	XP	XPA	FG	FGA	PTS
Wersching, Ray, S.F.	56	56	25	35	131
Moseley, Mark, Wash.	48	51	24	31	120
O'Donoghue, Neil, St.L.	48	51	23	35	117
McFadden, Paul, Phil.	26	27	30	37	116
Lansford, Mike, Rams	37	38	25	33	112
Septien, Rafael, Dall.	33	34	23	29	102
Thomas, Bob, Chi.	35	37	22	28	101
Ariri, Obed, T.B.	38	40	19	26	95
Andersen, Morten, N.O.	34	34	20	27	94
Luckhurst, Mick, Atl.	31	31	20	27	91
Murray, Ed, Det.	31	31	20	27	91
Stenerud, Jan, Minn.	30	31	20	23	90
Haji-Sheikh, Ali, Giants	32	35	17	33	83
Del Greco, Al, G.B.	34	34	9	12	61
Garcia, Eddie, G.B.	14	15	3	9	23

NON-KICKERS

	TD	TDR	TDP	TDM	PTS
Dickerson, Eric, Rams	14	14	0	0	84
Riggins, John, Wash.	14	14	0	0	84
Riggs, Gerald, Atl.	13	13	0	0	78
Wilder, James, T.B.	13	13	0	0	78
Green, Roy, St.L.	12	0	12	0	72
Mitchell, Stump, St.L.	11	9	2	0	66
Payton, Walter, Chi.	11	11	0	0	66
Solomon, Freddie, S.F.	11	1	10	0	66
Craig, Roger, S.F.	10	7	3	0	60
Coffman, Paul, G.B.	9	0	9	0	54
Quick, Mike, Phil.	9	0	9	0	54
Tyler, Wendell, S.F.	9	7	2	0	54
Anderson, Ottis, St.L.	8	6	2	0	48
Carpenter, Rob, Giants	8	7	1	0	48
Ellard, Henry, Rams	8	0	6	2	48
Jones, James, Det.	8	3	5	0	48
Dorsett, Tony, Dall.	7	6	1	0	42
Gajan, Hokie, N.O.	7	5	2	0	42
Ivery, Eddie Lee, G.B.	7	6	1	0	42
Johnson, Bob, Giants	7	0	7	0	42
Lofton, James, G.B.	7	0	7	0	42
Monk, Art, Wash.	7	0	7	0	42
Bailey, Stacey, Atl.	6	0	6	0	36
Brenner, Hoby, N.O.	6	0	6	0	36
Brown, Ted, Minn.	6	3	3	0	36
Clark, Dwight, S.F.	6	0	6	0	36

	TD	TDR	TDP	TDM	PTS
Clark, Jessie, G.B.	6	4	2	0	36
Ellis, Gerry, G.B.	6	4	2	0	36
Gault, Willie, Chi.	6	0	6	0	36
Mowatt, Zeke, Giants	6	0	6	0	36
Suhey, Matt, Chi.	6	4	2	0	36
Thompson, Leonard, Det.	6	0	6	0	36
Armstrong, Adger, T.B.	5	2	3	0	30
Carter, Gerald, T.B.	5	0	5	0	30
Didier, Clint, Wash.	5	0	5	0	30
Hill, Tony, Dall.	5	0	5	0	30
House, Kevin, T.B.	5	0	5	0	30
Marsh, Doug, St.L.	5	0	5	0	30
Newsome, Tim, Dall.	5	5	0	0	30
Sims, Billy, Det.	5	5	0	0	30
Tilley, Pat, St.L.	5	0	5	0	30
West, Ed, G.B.	5	1	4	0	30
Bell, Jerry, T.B.	4	0	4	0	24
Brown, Ron, Rams	4	0	4	0	24
Campbell, Earl, Hou.-N.O.	4	4	0	0	24
Cooper, Earl, S.F.	4	0	4	0	24
Cosbie, Doug, Dall.	4	0	4	0	24
Danielson, Gary, Det.	4	3	1	0	24
Hill, Drew, Rams	4	0	4	0	24
Lewis, Leo, Minn.	4	0	4	0	24
Manuel, Lionel, Giants	4	0	4	0	24
Morris, Joe, Giants	4	4	0	0	24
Muhammad, Calvin, Wash.	4	0	4	0	24
Nelson, Darrin, Minn.	4	3	1	0	24
Springs, Ron, Dall.	4	1	3	0	24
Wilson, Wayne, N.O.	4	1	3	0	24
Wonsley, Otis, Wash.	4	4	0	0	24
Anderson, Alfred, Minn.	3	2	1	0	18
Brown, Charlie, Wash.	3	0	3	0	18
Cain, Lynn, Atl.	3	3	0	0	18
Chadwick, Jeff, Det.	3	1	2	0	18
Cox, Arthur, Atl.	3	0	3	0	18
Dickey, Lynn, G.B.	3	3	0	0	18
Epps, Phillip, G.B.	3	0	3	0	18
Goodlow, Eugene, N.O.	3	0	3	0	18
Johnson, Billy, Atl.	3	0	3	0	18
Jordan, Steve, Minn.	3	1	2	0	18
Kab, Vyto, Phil.	3	0	3	0	18
Lewis, David, Det.	3	0	3	0	18
Lomax, Neil, St.L.	3	3	0	0	18
McKinnon, Dennis, Chi.	3	0	3	0	18
Ring, Bill, S.F.	3	3	0	0	18
Woodruff, Tony, Phil.	3	0	3	0	18

	TD	TDR	TDP	TDM	PTS
Young, Tyrone, N.O.	3	0	3	0	18
Crutchfield, Dwayne, Rams	2	1	1	0	12
DeBerg, Steve, T.B.	2	2	0	0	12
Dean, Vernon, Wash.	2	0	0	2	12
Donley, Doug, Dall.	2	0	2	0	12
Ferrell, Earl, St.L.	2	1	1	0	12
Francis, Russ, S.F.	2	0	2	0	12
Giles, Jimmie, T.B.	2	0	2	0	12
Gray, Earnest, Giants	2	0	2	0	12
Harris, Duriel, Clev.-Dall.	2	0	2	0	12
Hoover, Mel, Phil.	2	0	2	0	12
Irvin, LeRoy, Rams	2	0	0	2	12
Jackson, Alfred, Atl.	2	0	2	0	12
Love, Randy, St.L.	2	1	1	0	12
McLemore, Dana, S.F.	2	0	0	2	12
McMahon, Jim, Chi.	2	2	0	0	12
Montana, Joe, S.F.	2	2	0	0	12
Montgomery, Wilbert, Phil.	2	2	0	0	12
Moore, Jeff, Wash.	2	0	2	0	12
Mularkey, Mike, Minn.	2	0	2	0	12
Nehemiah, Renaldo, S.F.	2	0	2	0	12
Pisarcik, Joe, Phil.	2	2	0	0	12
Renfro, Mike, Dall.	2	0	2	0	12
Rice, Allen, Minn.	2	1	1	0	12
Rogers, George, N.O.	2	2	0	0	12
Wattelet, Frank, N.O.	2	0	0	2	12
Williams, Byron, Giants	2	0	2	0	12
Winston, Dennis, N.O.	2	0	0	2	12
Johnson, Gary, S.D.-S.F.	1	0	0	1	*8
Anderson, Brad, Chi.	1	0	1	0	6
Anthony, Tyrone, N.O.	1	1	0	0	6
Bell, Todd, Chi.	1	0	0	1	6
Brown, Robert, G.B.	1	0	0	1	6
Browner, Joey, Minn.	1	0	0	1	6
Carroll, Jay, T.B.	1	0	1	0	6
Coleman, Monte, Wash.	1	0	0	1	6
Collins, Dwight, Minn.	1	0	1	0	6
Cornwell, Fred, Dall.	1	0	1	0	6
Cromwell, Nolan, Rams	1	0	0	1	6
Crouse, Ray, G.B.	1	0	1	0	6
Dierking, Scott, T.B.	1	0	1	0	6
Downs, Mike, Dall.	1	0	0	1	6
Dunsmore, Pat, Chi.	1	0	1	0	6
Frank, John, S.F.	1	0	1	0	6
Fuller, Steve, Chi.	1	1	0	0	6
Gentry, Dennis, Chi.	1	1	0	0	6
Grant, Darryl, Wash.	1	0	0	1	6

	TD	TDR	TDP	TDM	PTS
Green, Darrell, Wash.	1	0	0	1	6
Guman, Mike, Rams	1	0	0	1	6
Haddix, Michael, Phil.	1	1	0	0	6
Hardy, Larry, N.O.	1	0	1	0	6
Harmon, Derrick, S.F.	1	1	0	0	6
Harrell, Willard, St.L.	1	1	0	0	6
Headen, Andy, Giants.............	1	0	0	1	6
Hill, David, Rams	1	0	1	0	6
Howard, Thomas, St.L.	1	0	0	1	6
Hutchison, Anthony, Chi.	1	1	0	0	6
Jackson, Jeff, Atl.	1	0	0	1	6
Jackson, Kenny, Phil.	1	0	1	0	6
Jacoby, Joe, Wash.	1	0	0	1	6
Jaworski, Ron, Phil.	1	1	0	0	6
Jeffcoat, Jim, Dall.	1	0	0	1	6
Jenkins, Ken, Det.	1	1	0	0	6
Jones, James, Dall.	1	0	1	0	6
Jones, Mike, Minn.	1	0	1	0	6
Jordan, Curtis, Wash.	1	0	0	1	6
Kemp, Jeff, Rams	1	1	0	0	6
Kramer, Tommy, Minn.	1	0	1	0	6
Kraynak, Rich, Phil.	1	0	0	1	6
Landry, Greg, Chi.	1	1	0	0	6
Lewis, Tim, G.B.	1	0	0	1	6
Logan, Dave, T.B.	1	0	0	1	6
Martin, Chris, Minn.	1	0	0	1	6
McConkey, Phil, Giants...........	1	0	0	1	6
McGrath, Mark, Wash.	1	0	1	0	6
Miller, Junior, N.O.	1	0	1	0	6
Monroe, Carl, S.F.	1	0	1	0	6
Moore, Blake, G.B.	1	0	1	0	6
Moorehead, Emery, Chi.	1	0	1	0	6
Nichols, Mark, Det.	1	0	1	0	6
Owens, James, T.B..................	1	0	1	0	6
Rodgers, Del, G.B.	1	0	0	1	6
Rubick, Rob, Det.	1	0	1	0	6
Scott, Lindsay, N.O.................	1	0	1	0	6
Seay, Virgil, Wash.	1	0	1	0	6
Shell, Todd, S.F......................	1	0	0	1	6
Smith, Leonard, St.L...............	1	0	0	1	6
Spagnola, John, Phil...............	1	0	1	0	6
Teal, Willie, Minn.	1	0	0	1	6
Theismann, Joe, Wash.	1	1	0	0	6
Thomas, Calvin, Chi.	1	1	0	0	6
Thurman, Dennis, Dall.	1	0	0	1	6
Tice, John, N.O.	1	0	1	0	6
Walker, Rick, Wash.	1	0	1	0	6

	TD	TDR	TDP	TDM	PTS
Washington, Joe, Wash.	1	1	0	0	6
Waters, Andre, Phil.................	1	0	0	1	6
White, Sammy, Minn...............	1	0	1	0	6
Wilson, Mike, S.F....................	1	0	1	0	6
Woolfolk, Butch, Giants	1	1	0	0	6
Bryan, Rick, Atl........................	0	0	0	0	*2
Case, Scott, Atl.......................	0	0	0	0	*2
Dutton, John, Dall.	0	0	0	0	*2
Sully, Ivory, Rams..................	0	0	0	0	*2
Vann, Norwood, Rams.............	0	0	0	0	*2

* Safety (also 1 each: Chi., Rams)

NFC — TEAM SCORING

	TD	TDR	TDP	TDM	XP	XPA	FG	FGA	SAF	PTS
San Francisco	57	21	32	4	56	57	25	35	1	475
Washington ..	51	20	24	7	48	51	24	31	0	426
St. Louis.......	51	21	28	2	48	51	23	35	0	423
Green Bay....	51	18	30	3	48	51	12	21	0	390
Rams............	38	16	16	6	37	38	25	33	3	346
Tampa Bay...	40	17	22	1	38	40	19	26	0	335
Chicago........	37	22	14	1	35	37	22	28	1	325
Dallas...........	34	12	19	3	33	34	23	29	1	308
Giants...........	36	12	22	2	32	36	17	33	0	299
New Orleans.	34	9	21	4	34	34	20	27	0	298
Detroit	32	13	19	0	31	31	20	27	0	283
Atlanta..........	31	16	14	1	31	31	20	27	2	281
Philadelphia..	27	6	19	2	26	27	30	37	0	278
Minnesota.....	31	10	18	3	30	31	20	23	0	276
Conf. Total.......	550	213	298	39	527	549	300	412	8	4743
Conf. Average .	39.3	15.2	21.3	2.8	37.6	39.2	21.4	29.4	0.6	338.8

P.A.F.A.—II

NFC — Team-by-Team Summary 1984

NFC Offense	Atl.	Chi.	Dall.	Det.	G.B.
Rushes	489	674	469	446	461
Net Yds. Gained	1994	2974	1714	2017	2019
Avg. Gain	4.1	4.4	3.7	4.5	4.4
Avg. Yds. per Game	124.6	185.9	107.1	126.1	126.2
Passes Attempted	478	390	604	531	506
Completed	294	226	322	298	281
% Completed	61.5	57.9	53.3	56.1	55.5
Total Yds. Gained	3546	2695	3995	3787	3740
Times Sacked	67	36	48	61	42
Yds. Lost	496	232	389	486	310
Net Yds. Gained	3050	2463	3606	3301	3430
Avg. Yds. per Game	190.6	153.9	225.4	206.3	214.4
Net Yds. per Pass Play	5.60	5.78	5.53	5.58	6.26
Yds. Gained per Comp.	12.06	11.92	12.41	12.71	13.31
Combined Net Yds. Gained	5044	5437	5320	5318	5449
% Total Yds. Rushing	39.5	54.7	32.2	37.9	37.1
% Total Yds. Passing	60.5	45.3	67.8	62.1	62.9
Avg. Yds. per Game	315.3	339.8	332.5	332.4	340.6
Had Intercepted	20	15	26	22	30
Yds. Opp. Returned	304	241	372	251	317
Ret. by Opp. for TD	2	3	4	1	2
Punts	70	85	108	76	85
Yds. Punted	2855	3328	4123	3164	3596
Avg. Yds. per Punt	40.8	39.2	38.2	41.6	42.3
Punt Returns	41	63	54	36	48
Yds. Returned	264	558	446	241	351
Avg. Yds. per Return	6.4	8.9	8.3	6.7	7.3
Returned for TD	0	0	0	0	0
Kickoff Returns	70	49	63	74	67
Yds. Returned	1367	896	1199	1347	1362
Avg. Yds. per Return	19.5	18.3	19.0	18.2	20.3
Returned for TD	0	0	0	0	1
Total Points Scored	281	325	308	283	390
Total TDs	31	37	34	32	51
TDs Rushing	16	22	12	13	18
TDs Passing	14	14	19	19	30
TDs on Ret. and Rec.	1	1	3	0	3
Extra Points	31	35	33	31	48
Safeties	2	1	1	0	0
Field Goals Made	20	22	23	20	12
Field Goals Attempted	27	28	29	27	21
% Successful	74.1	78.6	79.3	74.1	57.1

Rams	Minn.	N.O.	N.Y.G.	Phil.	St.L.	S.F.	T.B.	Wash.
541	444	523	493	381	488	534	483	588
2864	1844	2171	1660	1338	2088	2465	1776	2274
5.3	4.2	4.2	3.4	3.5	4.3	4.6	3.7	3.9
179.0	115.3	135.7	103.8	83.6	130.5	154.1	111.0	142.1
358	533	476	535	606	566	496	563	485
176	281	246	288	331	347	312	334	286
49.2	52.7	51.7	53.8	54.6	61.3	62.9	59.3	59.0
2382	3337	3198	4066	3823	4634	4079	3907	3417
32	64	45	55	60	49	27	45	48
240	465	361	343	463	377	178	362	341
2142	2872	2837	3632	3360	4257	3901	3545	3076
133.9	179.5	177.3	227.0	210.0	266.1	243.8	221.6	192.3
5.49	4.81	5.45	6.16	5.05	6.92	7.46	5.83	5.77
13.53	11.88	13.00	14.12	11.55	13.35	13.07	11.70	11.95
5006	4716	5008	5292	4698	6345	6366	5321	5350
57.2	39.1	43.4	31.4	28.5	32.9	38.7	33.4	42.5
42.8	60.9	56.6	68.6	71.5	67.1	61.3	66.6	57.5
312.9	294.8	313.0	330.8	293.6	396.6	397.9	332.6	334.4
17	25	28	18	17	16	10	23	13
240	344	420	222	211	219	155	249	159
2	2	3	1	1	0	0	0	0
74	82	70	94	92	68	62	68	73
2866	3473	3020	3598	3880	2594	2536	2849	2834
38.7	42.4	43.1	38.3	42.2	38.1	40.9	41.9	38.8
40	31	33	55	40	47	45	34	55
489	217	268	368	250	399	521	207	474
12.2	7.0	8.1	6.7	6.3	8.5	11.6	6.1	8.6
2	0	0	0	0	0	1	0	0
58	86	72	61	59	74	47	68	60
1244	1775	1465	1117	1156	1563	1039	1354	1174
21.4	20.6	20.3	18.3	19.6	21.1	22.1	19.9	19.6
1	0	0	0	1	0	0	0	0
346	276	298	299	278	423	475	335	426
38	31	34	36	27	51	57	40	51
16	10	9	12	6	21	21	17	20
16	18	21	22	19	28	32	22	24
6	3	4	2	2	2	4	1	7
37	30	34	32	26	48	56	38	48
3	0	0	0	0	0	1	0	0
25	20	20	17	30	23	25	19	24
33	23	27	33	37	35	35	26	31
75.8	87.0	74.1	51.5	81.1	65.7	71.4	73.1	77.4

NFC Defense	Atl.	Chi.	Dall.	Det.	G.B.
Rushes	538	378	510	519	245
Net Yds. Gained	2153	1377	2226	1808	2145
Avg. Gain	4.0	3.6	4.4	3.5	3.9
Avg. Yds. per Game	134.6	86.1	139.1	113.0	134.1
Passes Attempted	443	435	527	466	551
Completed	262	198	250	288	315
% Completed	59.1	45.5	47.4	61.8	57.2
Total Yds. Gained	3413	3069	3200	3782	3470
Times Sacked	38	72	57	37	44
Yds. Lost	287	583	390	271	324
Net Yds. Gained	3126	2486	2810	3511	3146
Avg. Yds. per Game	195.4	155.4	175.6	219.4	196.6
Net Yds. per Pass Play	6.50	4.90	4.81	6.98	5.29
Yds. Gained per Comp.	13.03	15.50	12.80	13.13	11.02
Combined Net Yds. Gained	5279	3863	5036	5319	5291
% Total Yds. Rushing	40.8	35.6	44.2	34.0	40.5
% Total Yds. Passing	59.2	64.4	55.8	66.0	59.5
Avg. Yds. per Game	329.9	241.4	314.8	332.4	330.7
Intercepted by	12	21	28	14	27
Yds. Returned by	147	290	297	87	338
Returned for TD	1	1	2	0	2
Punts	60	100	99	73	89
Yds. Punted	2497	4160	4236	2921	3643
Avg. Yds. per Punt	41.6	41.6	42.8	40.0	40.9
Punt Returns	42	41	55	49	46
Yds. Returned	450	249	230	516	368
Avg. Yds. per Return	10.7	6.1	4.2	10.5	8.0
Returned for TD	1	0	0	1	0
Kickoff Returns	48	68	65	60	73
Yds. Returned	1053	1443	1310	1250	1171
Avg. Yds. per Return	21.9	21.2	20.2	20.8	16.0
Returned for TD	0	1	0	0	0
Total Points Scored	382	248	308	408	309
Total TDs	48	29	36	48	34
TDs Rushing	16	10	8	17	14
TDs Passing	27	14	23	27	16
TDs on Ret. and Rec.	5	5	5	4	4
Extra Points	46	26	35	48	33
Safeties	0	0	0	0	0
Field Goals Made	16	16	19	24	24
Field Goals Attempted	30	22	28	29	31
% Successful	53.3	72.7	67.9	82.8	77.4

Rams	Minn.	N.O.	N.Y.G.	Phil.	St.L.	S.F.	T.B.	Wash.
449	547	549	474	556	442	432	511	390
1600	2573	2461	1818	2189	1923	1795	2233	1589
3.6	4.7	4.5	3.8	3.9	4.4	4.2	4.4	4.1
100.0	160.8	153.8	113.6	136.8	120.2	112.2	139.6	99.3
566	490	422	529	492	494	546	490	575
346	319	239	288	262	251	298	286	318
61.1	65.1	56.6	54.4	53.3	50.8	54.6	58.4	55.3
3964	3954	2873	3736	3506	3574	3744	3480	4301
43	25	55	48	60	55	51	32	66
298	175	420	361	456	403	363	239	529
3666	3779	2453	3375	3050	3171	3381	3241	3772
229.1	236.2	153.3	210.9	190.6	198.2	211.3	202.6	235.8
6.02	7.34	5.14	5.85	5.53	5.78	5.66	6.21	5.88
11.46	12.39	12.02	12.97	13.38	14.24	12.56	12.17	13.53
5266	6352	4914	5193	5239	5094	5176	5474	5361
30.4	40.5	50.1	35.0	41.8	37.8	34.7	40.8	29.6
69.6	59.5	49.9	65.0	58.2	62.2	65.3	59.2	70.4
329.1	397.0	307.1	324.6	327.4	318.4	323.5	342.1	335.1
17	11	13	19	20	21	25	18	21
399	120	213	182	287	163	345	308	391
3	1	3	0	0	1	2	1	4
71	68	84	92	89	81	80	68	78
2949	2777	3492	3677	3497	3157	3239	2787	3114
41.5	40.8	41.6	40.0	39.3	39.0	40.5	41.0	39.9
35	49	47	50	58	27	30	36	38
196	435	550	479	486	239	190	310	187
5.6	8.9	11.7	9.6	8.4	8.9	6.3	8.6	4.9
0	0	1	2	0	0	0	0	0
74	59	45	55	69	85	78	67	73
1288	1281	916	1088	1298	1549	1499	1336	1404
17.4	21.7	20.4	19.8	18.8	18.2	19.2	19.9	19.2
0	0	0	0	0	1	0	0	1
316	484	361	301	320	345	227	380	310
36	59	41	35	36	39	24	47	39
15	20	13	10	12	11	10	27	13
18	35	23	20	22	26	14	20	25
3	4	5	5	2	2	0	0	1
32	58	41	34	36	36	24	44	37
1	0	1	3	1	0	1	0	0
22	24	24	17	22	25	19	18	13
31	28	33	26	35	38	25	27	20
71.0	85.7	72.7	65.4	62.9	65.8	76.0	66.7	65.0

AFC, NFC AND NFL SUMMARY — 1984

	AFC Offense Total	AFC Offense Avg.	AFC Defense Total	AFC Defense Avg.
First Downs	4305	307.5	4426	316.1
Rushing	1508	107.7	1603	114.5
Passing	2464	176.0	2497	178.4
Penalty	333	23.8	326	23.3
Rushes	6797	485.5	6971	497.9
Net Yds. Gained	26,305	1878.9	27,613	1972.4
Avg. Gain	—	3.9	—	4.0
Avg. Yds. per Game	—	117.4	—	123.3
Passes Attempted	7198	514.1	7299	521.4
Completed	4054	289.6	4156	296.9
% Completed	—	56.3	—	56.9
Total Yds. Gained	51,627	3687.6	52,167	3726.2
Times Sacked	634	45.3	630	45.0
Yds. Lost	4861	347.2	4896	349.7
Net Yds. Gained	46,766	3340.4	47,271	3376.5
Avg. Yds. per Game	—	208.8	—	211.0
Net Yds. per Pass Play	—	5.97	—	5.96
Yds. Gained per Comp.	—	12.73	—	12.55
Combined Net Yds. Gained	73,071	5219.4	74,884	5348.9
% Total Yds. Rushing	—	36.00	—	36.87
% Total Yds. Passing	—	64.00	—	63.13
Avg. Yds. per Game	—	326.2	—	334.3
Ball Control Plays	14,629	1044.9	14,900	1064,3
Avg. Yds. per Play	—	5.0	—	5.0
Third Down Efficiency	—	38.6	—	38.8

NFC Offense Total	NFC Offense Avg.	NFC Defense Total	NFC Defense Avg.	NFL Total	NFL Avg.
4352	310.9	4231	302.2	8657	309.2
1715	122.5	1620	115.7	3223	115.1
2344	167.4	2311	165.1	4808	171.7
293	20.9	300	21.4	626	22.4
7014	501.0	6840	488.6	13,811	493.3
29,198	2085.6	27,890	1992.1	55,503	1982.3
—	4.2	—	4.1	—	4.0
—	130.3	—	124.5	—	123.9
7127	509.1	7026	501.9	14,325	511.6
4022	287.3	3920	280.0	8076	288.4
—	56.4	—	55.8	—	56.4
50,606	3614.7	50,066	3576.1	102,233	3651.2
679	48.5	683	48.8	1313	46.9
5134	366.7	5099	364.2	9995	357.0
45,472	3248.0	44,967	3211.9	92,238	3294.2
—	203.0	—	200.7	—	205.9
—	5.83	—	5.83	—	5.90
—	12.58	—	12.77	—	12.66
74,670	5333.6	72,857	5204.1	147,741	5276.5
—	39.10	—	38.28	—	37.57
—	60.90	—	61.72	—	62.43
—	333.3	—	325.3	—	329.8
14,820	1058.6	14,549	1039.2	29,449	1051.8
—	5.0	—	5.0	—	5.0
—	38.7	—	38.5	—	38.7

	AFC Offense Total	AFC Offense Avg.	AFC Defense Total	AFC Defense Avg.
Interceptions	304	21.7	317	22.6
Yds. Returned	4812	343.7	4949	353.5
Returned for TD	30	2.1	30	2.1
Punts	1153	82.4	1128	80.6
Yds. Punted	48,005	3428.9	46,575	3326.8
Avg. Yds. per Punt	—	41.6	—	41.3
Punt Returns	585	41.8	604	43.1
Yds. Returned	5364	383.1	5532	395.1
Avg. Yds. per Return	—	9.2	—	9.2
Returned for TD	5	0.4	3	0.2
Kickoff Returns	836	59.7	825	58.9
Yds. Returned	16,486	1177.6	16,658	1189.9
Avg. Yds. per Return	—	19.7	—	20.2
Returned for TD	2	0.1	2	0.1
Penalties	1431	102.2	1417	101.2
Yds. Penalized	12,005	857.5	11,835	845.4
Fumbles	457	32.6	441	31.5
Lost	215	15.4	216	15.4
Out of Bounds	32	2.3	29	2.1
Own Rec. for TD	2	0.1	1	0.1
Opp. Rec.	214	15.3	213	15.2
Opp. Rec. for TD	14	1.0	11	0.8
Total Points Scored	4759	339.9	4803	343.1
Total TDs	568	40.6	567	40.5
TDs Rushing	197	14.1	214	15.3
TDs Passing	317	22.6	305	21.8
TDs on Ret. and Rec.	54	3.9	48	3.4
Extra Points	548	39.1	545	38.9
Safeties	7	0.5	8	0.6
Field Goals Made	263	18.8	280	20.0
Field Goals Attempted	373	26.6	382	27.3
% Successful	—	70.5	—	73.3

NFC Offense Total	NFC Offense Avg.	NFC Defense Total	NFC Defense Avg.	NFL Total	NFL Avg.
280	20.0	267	19.1	584	20.9
3704	264.6	3567	254.8	8516	304.1
21	1.5	21	1.5	51	1.8
1107	79.1	1132	80.9	2260	80.7
44,716	3194.0	46,146	3296.1	92,721	3311.5
—	40.4	—	40.8	—	41.0
622	44.4	603	43.1	1207	43.1
5053	360.9	4885	348.9	10,417	372.0
—	8.1	—	8.1	—	8.6
3	0.2	5	0.4	8	0.3
908	64.9	919	65.6	1744	62.3
18,058	1289.9	17,886	1277.6	34,544	1233.7
—	19.9	—	19.5	—	19.8
3	0.2	3	0.2	5	0.2
1434	102.4	1448	103.4	2865	102.3
12,051	860.8	12,221	872.9	24,056	859.1
417	29.8	433	30.9	874	31.2
214	15.3	213	15.2	429	15.3
17	1.2	20	1.4	49	1.8
1	0.1	2	0.1	3	0.1
210	15.0	211	15.1	424	15.1
9	0.6	12	0.9	23	0.8
4743	338.8	4699	335.6	9502	339.4
550	39.3	551	39.4	1118	39.9
213	15.2	196	14.0	410	14.6
298	21.3	310	22.1	615	22.0
39	2.8	45	3.2	93	3.3
527	37.6	530	37.9	1075	38.4
8	0.6	7	0.5	15	0.5
300	21.4	283	20.2	563	20.1
412	29.4	403	28.8	785	28.0
—	72.8	—	70.2	—	71.7

CLUB LEADERS

	Offense	Defense
First Downs	Mia. 387	Chi. 216
Rushing	Chi. 164	Chi. 72
Passing	Mia. 243	Chi. 122
Penalty	N.O. 30	Mia. 12
Rushes	Chi. 674	Chi. 378
Net Yds. Gained	Chi. 2974	Chi. 1377
Avg. Gain	Rams 5.3	Det. 3.5
Passes Attempted	S.D. 662	N.O. 422
Completed	S.D. 401	Chi. 198
% Completed	Mia. 64.2	Chi. 45.5
Total Yds. Gained	Mia. 5146	N.O. 2873
Times Sacked	Mia. 14	Chi. 72
Yds. Lost	Mia. 128	Chi. 583
Net Yds. Gained	Mia. 5018	N.O. 2453
Net Yds. per Pass Play	Mia. 8.56	Raid. & Dal. 4.81
Yds. Gained per Comp.	Pitt. 14.66	G.B. 11.02
Combined Net Yds. Gained	Mia. 6936	Chi. 3863
% Total Yds. Rushing	Rams 57.2	Den. 29.3
% Total Yds. Passing	S.D. 73.7	N.O. 49.9
Ball Control Plays	S.D. 1154	Chi. 885
Avg. Yds. per Play	Mia. 6.5	Raiders 4.3
Avg. Time of Poss.	Chi. 35:08	—
Third Down Efficiency	Mia. 51.5	Chi. 26.4
Interceptions	—	Sea. 38
Yds. Returned	—	Sea. 697
Returned for TD	—	Sea. 7
Punts	Dall. 108	—
Yds. Punted	K.C. 4397	—
Avg. Yds. per Punt	K.C. 44.9	—
Punt Returns	Raiders 67	Mia. 17
Yds Returned	Pitt. 696	Mia. 138
Avg. Yds. per Return	Cin. 12.4	Dall. 4.2
Returned for TD	Rams 2	—
Kickoff Returns	Minn. 86	Ind. 42
Yds. Returned	Minn. 1775	Ind. 849
Avg. Yds. per Return	N.Y.J. 23.0	G.B. 16.0
Returned for TD	Five with 1	—
Total Points Scored	Mia. 513	S.F. 227
Total TDs	Mia. 70	S.F. 24
TDs Rushing	Chi. 22	Dall. 8
TD Passing	Mia. 49	Chi. & S.F. 14
TDs on Ret. and Rec.	Sea. 9	Three with 0
Extra Points	Mia. 66	S.F. 24
Safeties	Rams. 3	—
Field Goals Made	Phil. 30	Mia. 9
Field Goals Attempted	Phil. 37	Mia. 17
% Successful	Minn. 87.0	Mia. 52.9

CLUB RANKINGS BY YARDS

Team	Offense Total	Rush	Pass	Defense Total	Rush	Pass
Atlanta	19	15	20	15	21	7
Buffalo	27	26	25	23	19	19
Chicago	7	*1	26	*1	*1	2
Cincinnati	5	6t	13t	13	11	18
Cleveland	24	21	18	2	15	3
Dallas	11	20	6	7	24	5
Denver	22	10	23	25	5	27
Detroit	12	14	13t	17	8	21
Green Bay	6	13	9	16	20	8
Houston	23	23	17	27	28	11
Indianapolis	28	12	28	22	17	22
Kansas City	17	27	7	24	16	23
Los Angeles Raiders	15	17	12	3	13	4
Los Angeles Rams	21	2	27	14	3	24
Miami	*1	16	*1	19	22	14
Minnesota	25	18	22	28	27	26
New England	14	11	16	9	12	12
New Orleans	20	8	24	4	26	*1
New York Giants	13	22	5	11	9	16
New York Jets	16	5	21	21	18	20
Philadelphia	26	28	11	12	23	6
Pittsburgh	8	6t	15	5	4	15
St. Louis	3	9	3	8	14	9
San Diego	4	24	2	26	10	28
San Francisco	2	3	4	10	7	17
Seattle	18	25	10	6	6	10
Tampa Bay	10	19	8	20	25	13
Washington	9	4	19	18	2	25

t = Tie for position
* = League leader

SUPER BOWL RECORDS

RESULTS

GAME	DATE	WINNER	LOSER	SITE	ATTENDANCE
XIX	1-20-85	San Francisco (NFC) 38	Miami (AFC) 16	Stanford	84,059
XVIII	1-22-84	L.A. Raiders (AFC) 38	Washington (NFC) 9	Tampa	72,920
XVII	1-30-83	Washington (NFC) 27	Miami (AFC) 17	Pasadena	103,667
XVI	1-24-82	San Francisco (NFC) 26	Cincinnati (AFC) 21	Pontiac	81,270
XV	1-25-81	Oakland (AFC) 27	Philadelphia (NFC) 10	New Orleans	76,135
XIV	1-20-80	Pittsburgh (AFC) 31	Los Angeles (NFC) 19	Pasadena	103,985
XIII	1-21-79	Pittsburgh (AFC) 35	Dallas (NFC) 31	Miami	79,484
XII	1-15-78	Dallas (NFC) 27	Denver (AFC) 10	New Orleans	75,583
XI	1- 9-77	Oakland (AFC) 32	Minnesota (NFC) 14	Pasadena	103,438
X	1-18-76	Pittsburgh (AFC) 21	Dallas (NFC) 17	Miami	80,187
IX	1-12-75	Pittsburgh (AFC) 16	Minnesota (NFC) 6	New Orleans	80,997
VIII	1-13-74	Miami (AFC) 24	Minnesota (NFC) 7	Houston	71,882
VII	1-14-73	Miami (AFC) 14	Washington (NFC) 7	Los Angeles	90,182
VI	1-16-72	Dallas (NFC) 24	Miami (AFC) 3	New Orleans	81,023
V	1-17-71	Baltimore (AFC) 16	Dallas (NFC) 13	Miami	79,204
IV	1-11-70	Kansas City (AFL) 23	Minnesota (NFL) 7	New Orleans	80,562
III	1-12-69	N.Y. Jets (AFL) 16	Baltimore (NFL) 7	Miami	75,389
II	1-14-68	Green Bay (NFL) 33	Oakland (AFL) 14	Miami	75,546
I	1-15-67	Green Bay (NFL) 35	Kansas City (AFL) 10	Los Angeles	61,946

SUPER BOWL COMPOSITE STANDINGS

	W	L	Pct	Pts	OP
Pittsburgh Steelers	4	0	1.000	103	73
Green Bay Packers	2	0	1.000	68	24
San Francisco 49ers	2	0	1.000	64	37
New York Jets	1	0	1.000	16	7
Oakland/L.A. Raiders	3	1	.750	111	66
Baltimore Colts	1	1	.500	23	29
Kansas City Chiefs	1	1	.500	33	42
Dallas Cowboys	2	3	.400	112	85
Miami Dolphins	2	3	.400	74	103
Washington Redskins	1	2	.333	43	69
Cincinnati Bengals	0	1	.000	21	26
Denver Broncos	0	1	.000	10	27
Los Angeles Rams	0	1	.000	19	31
Philadelphia Eagles	0	1	.000	10	27
Minnesota Vikings	0	4	.000	34	95

SUPER BOWL RECORDS

1967: Super Bowl I
1968: Super Bowl II
1969: Super Bowl III
1970: Super Bowl IV
1971: Super Bowl V
1972: Super Bowl VI
1973: Super Bowl VII

1974: Super Bowl VIII
1975: Super Bowl IX
1976: Super Bowl X
1977: Super Bowl XI
1978: Super Bowl XII
1979: Super Bowl XIII
1980: Super Bowl XIV

1981: Super Bowl XV
1982: Super Bowl XVI
1983: Super Bowl XVII
1984: Super Bowl XVIII
1985: Super Bowl XIX

INDIVIDUAL RECORDS

SERVICE

Most Games
5   Marv Fleming, Green Bay, 1967-68; Miami, 1972-74
     Larry Cole, Dallas, 1971-72, 1976, 1978-79
     Cliff Harris, Dallas, 1971-72, 1976, 1978-79
     D.D. Lewis, Dallas, 1971-72, 1976, 1978-79
     Preston Pearson, Baltimore, 1969; Pittsburgh, 1975; Dallas, 1976, 1978-79
     Charlie Waters, Dallas, 1971-72, 1976, 1978-79
     Rayfield Wright, Dallas, 1971-72, 1976, 1978-79
4   By many players

Most Games, Coach
6   Don Shula, Baltimore, 1969; Miami, 1972-74, 1983, 1985
5   Tom Landry, Dallas, 1971-72, 1976, 1978-79
4   Bud Grant, Minnesota, 1970, 1974-75, 1977
     Chuck Noll, Pittsburgh, 1975-76, 1979-80

Most Games, Winning Team, Coach
4   Chuck Noll, Pittsburgh, 1975-76, 1979-80
2   Vince Lombardi, Green Bay, 1967-68
     Tom Landry, Dallas, 1972, 1978
     Don Shula, Miami, 1973-74
     Tom Flores, Oakland, 1981; L.A. Raiders, 1984

SCORING

POINTS
Most Points, Career
24   Franco Harris, Pittsburgh, 4 games (4-td)
20   Don Chandler, Green Bay, 2 games (8-pat, 4-fg)

Most Points, Game
18   Roger Craig, San Francisco vs. Miami, 1985 (3-td)
15   Don Chandler, Green Bay vs. Oakland, 1968 (3-pat, 4-fg)

TOUCHDOWNS
Most Touchdowns, Career
4   Franco Harris, Pittsburgh, 4 games (4-r)
3   John Stallworth, Pittsburgh, 4 games (3-p)
     Lynn Swann, Pittsburgh, 4 games (3-p)
     Cliff Branch, Oakland/L.A. Raiders, 3 games (3-p)

Most Touchdowns, Game
3   Roger Craig, San Francisco vs. Miami, 1985 (2-p, 1-r)
2   Max McGee, Green Bay vs. Kansas City, 1967 (2-p)
     Elijah Pitts, Green Bay vs. Kansas City, 1967 (2-r)
     Bill Miller, Oakland vs. Green Bay, 1968 (2-p)
     Larry Csonka, Miami vs. Minnesota, 1974 (2-r)
     Pete Banaszak, Oakland vs. Minnesota, 1977 (2-r)
     John Stallworth, Pittsburgh vs. Dallas, 1979 (2-p)
     Franco Harris, Pittsburgh vs. Los Angeles, 1980 (2-r)
     Cliff Branch, Oakland vs. Philadelphia, 1981 (2-p)
     Dan Ross, Cincinnati vs. San Francisco, 1982 (2-p)
     Marcus Allen, L.A. Raiders vs. Washington, 1984 (2-r)

FIELD GOALS
Field Goals, Attempted, Career
7   Roy Gerela, Pittsburgh, 3 games
6   Jim Turner, N.Y. Jets/Denver, 2 games

Most Field Goals, Attempted, Game
5   Jim Turner, N.Y. Jets vs. Baltimore, 1969
     Efren Herrera, Dallas vs. Denver, 1978

Most Field Goals, Career
5   Ray Wersching, San Francisco, 2 games (5 att)
4   Don Chandler, Green Bay, 2 games (4 att)
     Jim Turner, N.Y. Jets/Denver, 2 games (6 att)

Most Field Goals, Game
4   Don Chandler, Green Bay vs. Oakland, 1968
     Ray Wersching, San Francisco vs. Cincinnati, 1982

Longest Field Goal
48   Jan Stenerud, Kansas City vs. Minnesota, 1970

RUSHING

ATTEMPTS
Most Attempts, Career
101 Franco Harris, Pittsburgh, 4 games
64   John Riggins, Washington, 2 games
57   Larry Csonka, Miami, 3 games

Most Attempts, Game
38   John Riggins, Washington vs. Miami, 1983

YARDS GAINED
Most Yards Gained, Career
354 Franco Harris, Pittsburgh, 4 games
297 Larry Csonka, Miami, 3 games

Most Yards Gained, Game
191 Marcus Allen, L.A. Raiders vs. Washington, 1984

Longest Run from Scrimmage
74   Marcus Allen, L.A. Raiders vs. Washington, 1984

PASSING

ATTEMPTS
Most Passes Attempted, Career
98   Roger Staubach, Dallas, 4 games
89   Fran Tarkenton, Minnesota, 3 games

Most Passes Attempted, Game
50   Dan Marino, Miami vs. San Francisco, 1985

COMPLETIONS
Most Passes Completed, Career
61   Roger Staubach, Dallas, 4 games
49   Terry Bradshaw, Pittsburgh, 4 games

Most Passes Completed, Game
29   Dan Marino, Miami vs. San Francisco, 1985

Most Consecutive Completions, Game
8   Len Dawson, Kansas City vs. Green Bay, 1967
     Joe Theismann, Washington vs. Miami, 1983

YARDS GAINED
Most Yards Gained, Career
932   Terry Bradshaw, Pittsburgh, 4 games
734   Roger Staubach, Dallas, 4 games

Most Yards Gained, Game
331   Joe Montana, San Francisco vs. Miami, 1985

Longest Pass Completion
80   Jim Plunkett (to King), Oakland vs. Philadelphia, 1981 (TD)

TOUCHDOWNS
Most Touchdown Passes, Career
9   Terry Bradshaw, Pittsburgh, 4 games
8   Roger Staubach, Dallas, 4 games

Most Touchdown Passes, Game
4   Terry Bradshaw, Pittsburgh vs. Dallas, 1979

HAD INTERCEPTED
Lowest Percentage, Passes Had Intercepted, Career (40 attempts)
0.00 Joe Montana, San Francisco, 2 games (57-0)
0.00 Jim Plunkett, Oakland/L.A. Raiders, 2 games (46-0)
2.13 Bart Starr, Green Bay, 2 games (47-1)

PASS RECEIVING

RECEPTIONS
Most Receptions, Career
16   Lynn Swann, Pittsburgh, 4 games
15   Chuck Foreman, Minnesota, 3 games

Most Receptions, Game
11   Dan Ross, Cincinnati vs. San Francisco, 1982

YARDS GAINED

Most Yards Gained, Career
364 Lynn Swann, Pittsburgh, 4 games
268 John Stallworth, Pittsburgh, 4 games

Most Yards Gained, Game
161 Lynn Swann, Pittsburgh vs. Dallas, 1976

Longest Reception
80 Kenny King (from Plunkett), Oakland vs. Philadelphia, 1981 (TD)

INTERCEPTIONS BY

Most Interceptions By, Career
3 Chuck Howley, Dallas, 2 games
  Rod Martin, Oakland/L.A. Raiders, 2 games
2 Randy Beverly, N.Y. Jets, 1 game
  Jake Scott, Miami, 3 games
  Mike Wagner, Pittsburgh, 3 games
  Mel Blount, Pittsburgh, 4 games

Most Interceptions By, Game
3 Rod Martin, Oakland vs. Philadelphia, 1981

YARDS GAINED

Longest Return
75 Willie Brown, Oakland vs. Minnesota, 1977 (TD)

PUNTING

Most Punts, Career
17 Mike Elscheid, Oakland/Minnesota, 3 games

Most Punts, Game
9 Ron Widby, Dallas vs. Baltimore, 1971

Longest Punt
61 Jerrel Wilson, Kansas City vs. Green Bay, 1967

PUNT RETURNS

Most Punt Returns, Career
6 Willie Wood, Green Bay, 2 games
  Jake Scott, Miami, 3 games
  Theo Bell, Pittsburgh, 2 games
  Mike Nelms, Washington, 1 game

Most Punt Returns, Game
6 Mike Nelms, Washington vs. Miami, 1983

YARDS GAINED

Most Yards Gained, Career
52 Mike Nelms, Washington, 1 game
45 Jake Scott, Miami, 3 games

Most Yards Gained, Game
52 Mike Nelms, Washington vs. Miami, 1983

Longest Return
34   Darrell Green, Washington vs. L.A. Raiders, 1984

KICKOFF RETURNS

Most Kickoff Returns, Career
8   Larry Anderson, Pittsburgh, 2 games
7   Preston Pearson, Baltimore/Pittsburgh/Dallas, 5 games

Most Kickoff Returns, Game
5   Larry Anderson, Pittsburgh vs. Los Angeles, 1980
     Billy Campfield, Philadelphia vs. Oakland, 1981
     David Verser, Cincinnati vs. San Francisco, 1982

YARDS GAINED
Most Yards Gained Career
283   Fulton Walker, Miami, 2 games
207   Larry Anderson, Pittsburgh, 2 games

Most Yards Gained, Game
190   Fulton Walker, Miami vs. Washington, 1983

Longest Return
98   Fulton Walker, Miami vs. Washington, 1983 (TD)

COMBINED NET YARDS GAINED

ATTEMPTS
Most Attempts, Career
108   Franco Harris, Pittsburgh, 4 games
66   John Riggins, Washington, 2 games

Most Attempts, Game
39   John Riggins, Washington vs. Miami, 1983

YARDS GAINED
Most Yards Gained, Career
468   Franco Harris, Pittsburgh, 4 games
391   Lynn Swann, Pittsburgh, 4 games

Most Yards Gained, Game
209   Marcus Allen, L.A. Raiders vs. Washington, 1984

TEAM RECORDS

GAMES, VICTORIES, DEFEATS

Most Games
5   Dallas, 1971-72, 1976, 1978-79

Most Games Won
4   Pittsburgh, 1975-76, 1979-80

Most Games Lost
4   Minnesota, 1970, 1974-75, 1977

SCORING

Most Points, Game
38   L.A. Raiders vs. Washington, 1984
     San Francisco vs. Miami, 1985

Fewest Points, Game
3   Miami vs. Dallas, 1972

Most Points, Both Teams, Game
66   Pittsburgh (35) vs. Dallas (31), 1979

Fewest Points, Both Teams, Game
21   Washington (7) vs. Miami (14), 1973

TOUCHDOWNS
Most Touchdowns, Game
5   Green Bay vs. Kansas City, 1967
     Pittsburgh vs. Dallas, 1979
     L.A. Raiders vs. Washington, 1984
     San Francisco vs. Miami, 1985

Fewest Touchdowns, Game
0   Miami vs. Dallas, 1972

Most Touchdowns, Both Teams, Game
9   Pittsburgh (5) vs. Dallas (4), 1979

Fewest Touchdowns, Both Teams, Game
2   Baltimore (1) vs. N.Y. Jets (1), 1969

FIELD GOALS
Most Field Goals Attempted, Game
5   N.Y. Jets vs. Baltimore, 1969
     Dallas vs. Denver, 1978

Most Field Goals Attempted, Both Teams, Game
7   N.Y. Jets (5) vs. Baltimore (2), 1969

Fewest Field Goals Attempted, Both Teams, Game
1   Minnesota (0) vs. Miami (1), 1974

Most Field Goals, Game
4   Green Bay vs. Oakland, 1968
     San Francisco vs. Cincinnati, 1982

Most Field Goals, Both Teams, Game
4   Green Bay (4) vs. Oakland (0), 1968
     San Francisco (4) vs. Cincinnati (0), 1982
     Miami (3) vs. San Francisco (1), 1985

Fewest Field Goals, Both Teams, Game
0   Miami vs. Washington, 1973
     Pittsburgh vs. Minnesota, 1975

NET YARDS GAINED RUSHING AND PASSING

Most Yards Gained, Game
537 San Francisco vs. Miami, 1985

Fewest Yards Gained, Game
119 Minnesota vs. Pittsburgh, 1975

Most Yards Gained, Both Teams, Game
851   San Francisco (537) vs. Miami (314), 1985

Fewest Yards Gained, Both Teams, Game
452   Minnesota (119) vs. Pittsburgh (333), 1975

RUSHING

ATTEMPTS
Most Attempts, Game
57   Pittsburgh vs. Minnesota, 1975

Fewest Attempts, Game
9   Miami vs. San Francisco, 1985

Most Attempts, Both Teams, Game
81   Washington (52) vs. Miami (29), 1983

Fewest Attempts, Both Teams, Game
49   Miami (9) vs. San Francisco (40), 1985

YARDS GAINED
Most Yards Gained, Game
276   Washington vs. Miami, 1983

Fewest Yards Gained, Game
17   Minnesota vs. Pittsburgh, 1975

Most Yards Gained, Both Teams, Game
372   Washington (276) vs. Miami (96), 1983

Fewest Yards Gained, Both Teams, Game
171   Baltimore (69) vs. Dallas (102), 1971

PASSING

ATTEMPTS
Most Passes Attempted, Game
50   Miami vs. San Francisco, 1985

Fewest Passes Attempted, Game
7   Miami vs. Minnesota, 1974

Most Passes Attempted, Both Teams, Game
85   Miami (50) vs. San Francisco (35), 1985

Fewest Passes Attempted, Both Teams, Game
35   Miami (7) vs. Minnesota (28), 1974

COMPLETIONS
Most Passes Completed, Game
29   Miami vs. San Francisco, 1985

Fewest Passes Completed, Game
4   Miami vs. Washington, 1983

Most Passes Completed, Both Teams, Game
53   Miami (29) vs. San Francisco (24), 1985

Fewest Passes Completed, Both Teams, Game
19   Miami (4) vs. Washington (15), 1983

YARDS GAINED
Most Yards Gained, Game
326   San Francisco vs. Miami, 1985

Fewest Yards Gained, Game
35   Denver vs. Dallas, 1978

Most Yards Gained, Both Teams, Game
615   San Francisco (355) vs. Miami (294), 1985

Fewest Yards Gained, Both Teams, Game
156   Miami (69) vs. Washington (87), 1973

TIMES SACKED
Most Times Sacked, Game
7   Dallas vs. Pittsburgh, 1976

Fewest Times Sacked, Game
0   Baltimore vs. N.Y. Jets, 1969; vs. Dallas, 1971
    Minnesota vs. Pittsburgh, 1975
    Pittsburgh vs. Los Angeles, 1980
    Philadelphia vs. Oakland, 1981

Most Times Sacked, Both Teams, Game
9   Kansas City (6) vs. Green Bay (3), 1967
    Dallas (7) vs. Pittsburgh (2), 1976
    Dallas (5) vs. Denver (4), 1978
    Dallas (5) vs. Pittsburgh (4), 1979

Fewest Times Sacked, Both Teams, Game
1   Philadelphia (0) vs. Oakland (1), 1981

INTERCEPTIONS BY

Most Interceptions By, Game
4   N.Y. Jets vs. Baltimore, 1969
    Dallas vs. Denver, 1978

Most Interceptions By, Both Teams, Game
6   Baltimore (3) vs. Dallas (3), 1971

PUNTING

Most Punts, Game
9   Dallas vs. Baltimore, 1971

Fewest Punts, Game
2   Pittsburgh vs. Los Angeles, 1980

Most Punts, Both Teams, Game
15   Washington (8) vs. L.A. Raiders (7), 1984

Fewest Punts, Both Teams, Game
6   Oakland (3) vs. Philadelphia (3), 1981

PUNT RETURNS

Most Punt Returns, Game
6   Washington vs. Miami, 1983

Fewest Punt Returns, Game
0   Minnesota vs. Miami, 1974

Most Punt Returns, Both Teams, Game
9   Pittsburgh (5) vs. Minnesota (4), 1975

Fewest Punt Returns, Both Teams, Game
2   Dallas (1) vs. Miami (1), 1972

YARDS GAINED
Most Yards Gained, Game
52   Washington vs. Miami, 1983

Fewest Yards Gained, Game
-1   Dallas vs. Miami, 1972

Most Yards Gained, Both Teams, Game
74   Washington (52) vs. Miami (22), 1983

Fewest Yards Gained, Both Teams, Game
13   Miami (4) vs. Washington (9), 1973

KICKOFF RETURNS

Most Kickoff Returns, Game
7   Oakland vs. Green Bay, 1968
      Minnesota vs. Oakland, 1977
      Cincinnati vs. San Francisco, 1982
      Washington vs. L.A. Raiders, 1984
      Miami vs. San Francisco, 1985

Fewest Kickoff Returns, Game
1   N.Y. Jets vs. Baltimore, 1969
      L.A. Raiders vs. Washington, 1984

Most Kickoff Returns, Both Teams, Game
11   Los Angeles (6) vs. Pittsburgh (5), 1980
      Miami (7) vs. San Francisco (4), 1985

Fewest Kickoff Returns, Both Teams, Game
5   N.Y. Jets (1) vs. Baltimore (4), 1969
      Miami (2) vs. Washington (3), 1973

YARDS GAINED
Most Yards Gained, Game
222   Miami vs. Washington, 1983

Fewest Yards Gained, Game
17   L.A. Raiders vs. Washington, 1984

Most Yards Gained, Both Teams, Game
279   Miami (222) vs. Washington (57), 1983

Fewest Yards Gained, Both Teams, Game
78   Miami (33) vs. Washington (45), 1973

229

AFC - NFC Pro Bowl Results — NFC leads series 9-6

YEAR	DATE	WINNER	LOSER	SITE	ATTENDANCE
1985	Jan. 27	AFC 22	NFC 14	Honolulu	50,385
1984	Jan. 29	NFC 45	AFC 3	Honolulu	50,445
1983	Feb. 6	NFC 20	AFC 19	Honolulu	47,201
1982	Jan. 31	AFC 16	NFC 13	Honolulu	49,521
1981	Feb. 1	NFC 21	AFC 7	Honolulu	47,879
1980	Jan. 27	NFC 37	AFC 27	Honolulu	48,060
1979	Jan. 29	NFC 13	AFC 7	Los Angeles	46,281
1978	Jan. 23	NFC 14	AFC 13	Tampa	51,337
1977	Jan. 17	AFC 24	NFC 14	Seattle	64,151
1976	Jan. 26	NFC 23	AFC 20	New Orleans	30,546
1975	Jan. 20	NFC 17	AFC 10	Miami	26,484
1974	Jan. 20	AFC 15	NFC 13	Kansas City	66,918
1973	Jan. 21	AFC 33	NFC 28	Dallas	37,091
1972	Jan. 23	AFC 26	NFC 13	Los Angeles	53,647
1971	Jan. 24	NFC 27	AFC 6	Los Angeles	48,222

NUMBER-ONE DRAFT CHOICES

Season	Team	Player	Pos.	College
1985	Buffalo Bills	Bruce Smith	DE	Virginia Tech.
1984	New England	Irving Fryar	WR	Nebraska
1983	Baltimore	John Elway	QB	Stanford
1982	New England	Kenneth Sims	DT	Texas
1981	New Orleans	George Rogers	RB	South Carolina
1980	Detroit	Billy Sims	RB	Oklahoma
1979	Buffalo	Tom Cousineau	LB	Ohio State
1978	Houston	Earl Campbell	RB	Texas
1977	Tampa Bay	Ricky Bell	RB	So. California
1976	Tampa Bay	Lee Roy Selmon	DE	Oklahoma
1975	Atlanta	Steve Bartkowski	QB	California
1974	Dallas	Ed Jones	DE	Tennessee State
1973	Houston	John Matuszak	DE	Tampa
1972	Buffalo	Walt Patulski	DE	Notre Dame
1971	New England	Jim Plunkett	QB	Stanford
1970	Pittsburgh	Terry Bradshaw	QB	Louisiana Tech.
1969	Buffalo (AFL)	O.J. Simpson	RB	So. California
1968	Minnesota	Ron Yary	T	So. California
1967	Baltimore	Bubba Smith	DT	Michigan State
1966	Atlanta	Tommy Nobis	LB	Texas
	Miami (AFL)	Jim Grabowski	RB	Illinois
1965	N.Y. Giants	Tucker Frederickson	RB	Auburn
	Houston (AFL)	Lawrence Elkins	E	Baylor
1964	San Francisco	Dave Parks	E	Texas Tech.
	Boston (AFL)	Jack Concannon	QB	Boston College
1963	Los Angeles Rams	Terry Baker	QB	Oregon State
	Kansas City (AFL)	Buck Buchanan	DT	Grambling

Season	Team	Player	Pos.	College
1962	Washington	Ernie Davis	RB	Syracuse
	Oakland (AFL)	Roman Gabriel	QB	N. Carolina State
1961	Minnesota	Tommy Mason	RB	Tulane
	Buffalo (AFL)	Ken Rice	G	Auburn
1960	Los Angeles Rams	Billy Cannon	RB	LSU
	(AFL had no formal first pick)			
1959	Green Bay	Randy Duncan	QB	Iowa
1958	Chi. Cardinals	King Hill	QB	Rice
1957	Green Bay	Paul Hornung	HB	Notre Dame
1956	Pittsburgh	Gary Glick	DB	Colorado A&M
1955	Baltimore	George Shaw	QB	Oregon
1954	Cleveland	Bobby Garrett	QB	Stanford
1953	San Francisco	Harry Babcock	E	Georgia
1952	Los Angeles Rams	Bill Wade	QB	Vanderbilt
1951	N.Y. Giants	Kyle Rote	HB	SMU
1950	Detroit	Leon Hart	E	Notre Dame
1949	Philadelphia	Chuck Bednarik	C	Pennsylvania
1948	Washington	Harry Gilmer	QB	Alabama
1947	Chi. Bears	Bob Fenimore	HB	Oklahoma A&M
1946	Boston	Frank Dancewicz	QB	Notre Dame
1945	Chi. Cardinals	Charley Trippi	HB	Georgia
1944	Boston	Angelo Bertelli	QB	Notre Dame
1943	Detroit	Frank Sinkwich	HB	Georgia
1942	Pittsburgh	Bill Dudley	HB	Virginia
1941	Chi. Bears	Tom Harmon	HB	Michigan
1940	Chi. Cardinals	George Cafego	HB	Tennessee
1939	Chi. Cardinals	Ki Aldrich	C	TCU
1938	Cleveland	Corbett Davis	FB	Indiana
1937	Philadelphia	Sam Francis	FB	Nebraska
1936	Philadelphia	Jay Berwanger	HB	Chicago

1985 COLLEGIATE DRAFT

ROUND 1

No. Team	Name	Pos.	College
Start of Round: 8:02am			
1 BUFFALO	Smith, Bruce	DE	Virginia Tech
2 ATLANTA from Houston through Minnesota	Fralic, Bill	T	Pittsburgh
3 HOUSTON from Minnesota	Childress, Ray	DE	Texas A&M
4 MINNESOTA from Atlanta	Doleman, Chris	LB	Pittsburgh
5 INDIANAPOLIS	Bickett, Duane	LB	Southern California
6 DETROIT	Brown, Lomas	T	Florida
7 GREEN BAY from Cleveland through Buffalo	Ruettgers, Ken	T	Southern California
8 TAMPA BAY	Holmes, Ron	DE	Washington
9 PHILADELPHIA	Allen, Kevin	T	Indiana
10 NEW YORK JETS	Toon, Al	WR	Wisconsin
11 HOUSTON from New Orleans	Johnson, Richard	DB	Wisconsin
12 SAN DIEGO	Lachey, Jim	G	Ohio State
13 CINCINNATI	Brown, Eddie	WR	Miami
14 BUFFALO from Green Bay	Burroughs, Derrick	DB	Memphis State
15 KANSAS CITY	Horton, Ethan	RB	North Carolina
16 SAN FRANCISCO from New England	Rice, Jerry	WR	Mississippi Valley
17 DALLAS	Brooks, Kevin	DE	Michigan
18 ST. LOUIS	Nunn, Freddie Joe	LB	Mississippi
19 NEW YORK GIANTS	Adams, George	RB	Kentucky
20 PITTSBURGH	Sims, Darryl	DE	Wisconsin
21 LOS ANGELES RAMS	Gray, Jerry	DB	Texas
22 CHICAGO	Perry, William	DT	Clemson
23 LOS ANGELES RAIDERS	Hester, Jessie	WR	Florida State
24 NEW ORLEANS from Washington	Toles, Alvin	LB	Tennessee
25 CINCINNATI from Seattle	King, Emanuel	LB	Alabama
26 DENVER	Sewell, Steve	RB	Oklahoma
27 MIAMI	Hampton, Lorenzo	RB	Florida
28 NEW ENGLAND from San Francisco	Matich, Trevor	C	Brigham Young

End of Round: 11.38am Time of Round: 3 hrs, 36 mins Total Time: 3 hrs, 36 mins

ROUND 2

No. Team	Name	Pos.	College
Start of Round: 11.38am			
1 BUFFALO	Traynowicz, Mark	T	Nebraska
2 MINNESOTA	Holt, Issiac	DB	Alcorn State
3 DENVER from Houston	Johnson, Vance	WR	Arizona
4 INDIANAPOLIS	Anderson, Don	DB	Purdue
5 WASHINGTON from Atlanta	Nixon, Tory	DB	San Diego State
6 DETROIT	Glover, Kevin	C	Maryland
7 CLEVELAND	Allen, Greg	RB	Florida State
8 HOUSTON from Tampa Bay through Denver	Byrd, Richard	DE	So. Mississippi
9 PHILADELPHIA	Cunningham, Randall	QB	Nevada-Las Vegas
10 NEW ORLEANS	Gilbert, Daren	T	Cal State-Fullerton
11 SAN DIEGO	Davis, Wayne	DB	Indiana State
12 NEW YORK JETS	Lyles, Lester	DB	Virginia

No.	Team	Name	Pos.	College
13	KANSAS CITY	Hayes, Jonathan	TE	Iowa
14	BUFFALO from			
	Green Bay	Burkett, Chris	WR	Jackson State
15	KANSAS CITY	Horton, Ethan	RB	North Carolina
16	DALLAS	Penn, Jesse	LB	Virginia Tech
17	ATLANTA from			
	St. Louis	Gann, Mike	DE	Notre Dame
18	NEW YORK GIANTS	Robinson, Stacy	WR	North Dakota State
19	PITTSBURGH	Behning, Mark	T	Nebraska
20	NEW ENGLAND	Veris, Garin	DE	Stanford
21	CHICAGO	Phillips, Reggie	DB	Southern Methodist
22	LOS ANGELES RAMS	Scott, Chuck	WR	Vanderbilt
23	ST. LOUIS from			
	Washington through			
	Atlanta	Bergold, Scott	T	Wisconsin
24	NEW ENGLAND from			
	Los Angeles Raiders	Bowman, Jim	DB	Central Michigan
25	SEATTLE	Gill, Owen	RB	Iowa
26	DENVER	Fletcher, Simon	DE	Houston
27	SAN DIEGO from Miami	Dale, Jeffery	DB	Louisiana State
28	NEW ENGLAND from			
	San Francisco	Thomas, Ben	DE	Auburn

End of Round: 3.02pm Time of Round: 3 hrs, 24 mins Total Time: 7 hrs
Kansas City selected ahead of Buffalo which passed

ROUND 3

Start of Round: 3.02pm

No.	Team	Name	Pos.	College
1	BUFFALO	Reich, Frank	QB	Maryland
2	NEW YORK GIANTS			
	from Houston	Davis, Tyrone	DB	Clemson
3	MINNESOTA	Lowdermilk, Kirk	C	Ohio State
4	MINNESOTA from Atlanta	Meamber, Tim	LB	Washington
5	INDIANAPOLIS	Young, Anthony	DB	Temple
6	DETROIT	Johnson, James	LB	San Diego State
7	BUFFALO from Cleveland	Garner, Hal	LB	Utah State
8	TAMPA BAY	Randle, Ervin	LB	Baylor
9	MIAMI from Philadelphia	Little, George	DT	Iowa
10	MINNESOTA from			
	San Diego	Long, Tim	T	Memphis State
11	NEW YORK JETS	Elder, Donnie	DB	Memphis State
12	NEW ORLEANS	Del Rio, Jack	LB	Southern California
13	SAN DIEGO from			
	Kansas City	Hendy, John	DB	Cal State-Long Beach
14	CINCINNATI	Thomas, Sean	DB	Texas Christian
15	GREEN BAY	Moran, Rich	G	San Diego State
16	ST. LOUIS	Smith, Lance	T	Louisiana State
17	NEW YORK GIANTS	Johnston, Brian	C	North Carolina
18	PITTSBURGH	Hobley, Liffort	DB	Louisiana State
19	SAN FRANCISCO from			
	New England	Moore, Ricky	RB	Alabama
20	DALLAS	Ker, Crawford	G	Florida
21	LOS ANGELES RAMS	Hatcher, Dale	P	Clemson
22	CHICAGO	Maness, James	WR	Texas Christian
23	LOS ANGELES RAIDERS	Moffett, Tim	WR	Mississippi
24	LOS ANGELES RAIDERS			
	from Washington			
	through Houston	Adams, Stefon	DB	East Carolina
25	SEATTLE	Greene, Danny	WR	Washington
26	HOUSTON from Denver	Kelley, Mike	C	Notre Dame

No.	Team	Name	Pos.	College
27	MIAMI	Moyer, Alex	LB	Northwestern
28	NEW ENGLAND from			
	San Francisco	McMillian, Audrey	DB	Houston

End of Round: 4.17pm Time of Round: 1 hr, 15 mins Total Time: 8 hrs, 15 mins

ROUND 4

Start of Round: 4:17pm

No.	Team	Name	Pos.	College
1	MINNESOTA	Rhymes, Buster	WR	Oklahoma
2	BUFFALO	Reed, Andre	WR	Kutztown, Pa.
3	HOUSTON	Briehl, Tom	LB	Stanford
4	INDIANAPOLIS	Broughton, Willie	DE	Miami
5	ATLANTA	Harry, Emile	WR	Stanford
6	DETROIT	Hancock, Kevin	LB	Baylor
7	MIAMI from Cleveland	Smith, Mike	DB	Texas-El Paso
8	TAMPA BAY	Heaven, Mike	DB	Illinois
9	PHILADELPHIA	Naron, Greg	G	North Carolina
10	NEW YORK JETS	Allen, Doug	WR	Arizona State
11	NEW ORLEANS	Allen, Billy	DB	Florida State
12	SAN DIEGO	Mojsiejenko, Ralf	K	Michigan State
13	CINCINNATI	Tuggle, Anthony	DB	Nicholls State
14	GREEN BAY	Stanley, Walter	WR	Mesa, Colo.
15	KANSAS CITY	Olderman, Bob	G	Virginia
16	NEW YORK GIANTS	Bavaro, Mark	TE	Notre Dame
17	PITTSBURGH	Turk, Dan	C	Wisconsin
18	NEW ENGLAND	Toth, Tom	T	Western Michigan
19	DALLAS	Lavette, Robert	RB	Georgia Tech
20	ST. LOUIS	Wolfley, Ron	RB	West Virginia
21	CHICAGO	Butler, Kevin	K	Georgia
22	MINNESOTA from			
	Los Angeles Rams	Morrell, Kyle	DB	Brigham Young
23	LOS ANGELES RAIDERS			
	from Washington	Kimmel, Jamie	LB	Syracuse
24	NEW ENGLAND from			
	L.A. Raiders	Phelan, Gerard	WR	Boston College
25	SEATTLE	Davis, Tony	TE	Missouri
26	DENVER	McGregor, Keli	TE	Colorado State
27	MIAMI	Dellenbach, Jeff	T	Wisconsin
28	BUFFALO from			
	San Francisco	Hellestrae, Dale	T	Southern Methodist

End of Round: 5.32pm Time of Round 1 hr, 15 mins Total Time: 9 hrs, 30 mins

ROUND 5

Start of Round: 5:32pm

No.	Team	Name	Pos.	College
1	LOS ANGELES RAMS from			
	Buffalo	Greene, Kevin	LB	Auburn
2	DALLAS from Houston	Walker, Herschel	RB	Georgia
3	MINNESOTA	MacDonald, Mark	G	Boston College
4	ST. LOUIS from Atlanta	Dunn, K.D.	TE	Clemson
5	INDIANAPOLIS	Caron, Roger	T	Harvard
6	DETROIT	McIntosh, Joe	RB	North Carolina State
7	DALLAS from Cleveland			
	through Buffalo	Darwin, Matt	C	Texas A&M
8	NEW YORK JETS from			
	Tampa Bay	Benson, Troy	LB	Pittsburgh
9	PHILADELPHIA	Jiles, Dwayne	LB	Texas Tech
10	WASHINGTON from			
	New Orleans	Cherry, Raphel	RB	Hawaii

No.	Team	Name	Pos.	College
11	SEATTLE from San Diego	Napolitan, Mark	C	Michigan State
12	NEW YORK JETS	Luft, Brian	DT	Southern California
13	GREEN BAY	Noble, Brian	LB	Arizona State
14	KANSAS CITY	King, Bruce	RB	Purdue
15	CINCINNATI	Degrate, Tony	DT	Texas
16	SEATTLE from Pittsburgh	Brown, Arnold	DB	N. Carolina Central
17	CINCINNATI from New England	Davis, Lee	DB	Mississippi
18	BUFFALO from Dallas	Teal, Jimmy	WR	Texas A&M
19	ST. LOUIS	Wong, Louis	G	Brigham Young
20	NEW YORK GIANTS	Henderson, Tracy	WR	Iowa State
21	HOUSTON from L.A. Rams through Kansas City	Bush, Frank	LB	North Carolina State
22	NEW YORK JETS from Chicago	Smith, Tony	WR	San Jose State
23	LOS ANGELES RAIDERS	Reeder, Dan	RB	Delaware
24	PITTSBURGH from Washington	Jacobs, Cam	LB	Kentucky
25	SEATTLE	Jones, Johnnie	RB	Tennessee
26	HOUSTON from Denver	Johnson, Lee	K	Brigham Young
27	DENVER from Miami	Hinson, Billy	G	Florida
28	SAN FRANCISCO	Collie, Bruce	T	Texas-Arlington

End of Round: 6.40pm Time of Round: 1 hr, 8 mins Total Time: 10 hrs, 38 mins

ROUND 6

Start of Round: 6.40pm

No.	Team	Name	Pos.	College
1	BUFFALO	Hamby, Mike	DT	Utah State
2	MINNESOTA	Bono, Steve	QB	UCLA
3	LOS ANGELES RAIDERS from Houston	Hilger, Rusty	QB	Oklahoma State
4	DALLAS from Indianapolis	Ploeger, Kurt	DE	Gustavus Adolphus
5	MIAMI from Atlanta	Shorthose, George	WR	Missouri
6	DETROIT	Short, Stan	G	Penn State
7	CLEVELAND	Krerowicz, Mark	G	Ohio State
8	CINCINNATI from Tampa Bay	Stokes, Eric	T	Northeastern
9	KANSAS CITY from Philadelphia	Bostic, Jonathan	DB	Bethune-Cookman
10	SAN DIEGO	Lewis, Terry	DB	Michigan State
11	NEW YORK JETS	Deaton, Jeff	G	Stanford
12	ATLANTA from New Orleans	Pleasant, Reggie	DB	Clemson
13	HOUSTON from Kansas City	Krakoski, Joe	LB	Washington
14	CINCINNATI	Lester, Keith	TE	Murray State
15	GREEN BAY	Lewis, Mark	TE	Texas A&M
16	PHILADELPHIA from New England	Reeves, Ken	T	Texas A&M
17	DALLAS	Moran, Matt	G	Stanford
18	ST. LOUIS	Novacek, Jay	WR	Wyoming
19	NEW YORK GIANTS	Oliver, Jack	G	Memphis State
20	PITTSBURGH	Carr, Gregg	LB	Auburn
21	LOS ANGELES RAMS from Chicago	Young, Mike	WR	UCLA
22	LOS ANGELES RAMS	Johnson, Damone	TE	Cal Poly-Obispo
23	WASHINGTON	Lee, Danzell	TE	Lamar
24	MINNESOTA from Los Angeles Raiders	Newton, Tim	NT	Florida

No.	Team	Name	Pos.	College
25	NEW YORK GIANTS from			
	Seattle	Pembrook, Mark	DB	Cal State-Fullerton
26	NEW YORK JETS from			
	Denver	Miano, Rich	DB	Hawaii
27	MIAMI	Davenport, Ron	RB	Louisville
28	SAN FRANCISCO	Barry, Scott	QB	Cal-Davis

End of Round: 7.55pm Time of Round: 1 hr, 15 mins Total Time: 11 hrs, 53 mins

ROUND 7

Start of Round: 7.55pm

No.	Team	Name	Pos.	College
1	BUFFALO	Pitts, Ron	DB	UCLA
2	HOUSTON	Akiu, Mike	WR	Hawaii
3	GREEN BAY from			
	Minnesota	Wilson, Eric	LB	Maryland
4	CINCINNATI from Atlanta	Locklin, Kim	RB	New Mexico State
5	INDIANAPOLIS	Harbour, James	WR	Mississippi
6	DETROIT	Staten, Tony	DB	Angelo State
7	CLEVELAND	Langhorne, Reginald	WR	Elizabeth City State
8	TAMPA BAY	Prior, Mike	DB	Illinois State
9	WASHINGTON from			
	Philadelphia	Harris, Jamie	KR	Oklahoma State
10	DALLAS from N.Y. Jets			
	through Kansas City	Powe, Karl	WR	Alabama State
11	NEW ORLEANS	Martin, Eric	WR	Louisiana State
12	KANSAS CITY from			
	San Diego	Thomson, Vince	DE	Missouri Western
13	CINCINNATI	Walter, Joe	T	Texas Tech
14	GREEN BAY	Ellerson, Gary	RB	Wisconsin
15	KANSAS CITY	Heffernan, Dave	G	Miami
16	DALLAS	Herrmann, Jim	DE	Brigham Young
17	WASHINGTON from			
	St. Louis through			
	Kansas City	Vital, Lionel	RB	Nicholls State
18	LOS ANGELES RAIDERS			
	from N.Y. Giants	Belcher, Kevin	T	Wisconsin
19	PITTSBURGH	Andrews, Alan	TE	Rutgers
20	LOS ANGELES RAIDERS			
	from New England	Pattison, Mark	WR	Washington
21	LOS ANGELES RAMS	Bradley, Danny	RB	Oklahoma
22	CHICAGO	Bennett, Charles	DE	S.W. Louisiana
23	LOS ANGELES RAIDERS	Clark, Bret	DB	Nebraska
24	LOS ANGELES RAIDERS			
	from Washington			
	through New England	Haden, Nick	C	Penn State
25	SEATTLE	Mattes, Ron	T	Virginia
26	DENVER	Cameron, Dallas	NT	Miami
27	MIAMI	Reveiz, Fuad	K	Tennessee
28	SAN DIEGO from			
	San Francisco	Fellows, Mark	LB	Montana State

End of Round: 9.07pm Time of Round: 1 hr, 12 mins Total Time 13 hrs, 5 mins

ROUND 8

Start of Round: 9.07pm

No.	Team	Name	Pos.	College
1	BUFFALO	Robinson, Jacque	RB	Washington
2	MINNESOTA	Blair, Nikita	LB	Texas-El Paso
3	HOUSTON	Thomas, Chuck	C	Oklahoma
4	INDIANAPOLIS	Nichols, Ricky	WR	East Carolina

No.	Team	Name	Pos.	College
5	ATLANTA	Lee, Ashley	DB	Virginia Tech
6	DETROIT	Caldwell, Scotty	RB	Texas-Arlington
7	CLEVELAND	Banks, Fred	WR	Liberty Baptist
8	TAMPA BAY	Freeman, Phil	WR	Arizona
9	PHILADELPHIA	Polley, Tom	LB	Nevada-Las Vegas
10	NEW ORLEANS	Kohlbrand, Joe	DE	Miami
11	SAN DIEGO	Adams, Curtis	RB	Central Michigan
12	NEW YORK JETS	Monger, Matt	LB	Oklahoma State
13	GREEN BAY	Stills, Ken	DB	Wisconsin
14	KANSAS CITY	Hillary, Ira	WR	South Carolina
15	CINCINNATI	Strobel, Dave	LB	Iowa
16	ST. LOUIS	Monaco, Rob	G	Vanderbilt
17	NEW YORK GIANTS	Rouson, Lee	RB	Colorado
18	PITTSBURGH	Newsome, Harry	P	Wake Forest
19	ATLANTA from			
	New England	Washington, Ronnie	LB	N.E. Louisiana
20	DALLAS	Gonzales, Leon	WR	Bethune-Cookman
21	CHICAGO	Buxton, Steve	T	Indiana State
22	LOS ANGELES RAMS	McIntyre, Marlon	RB	Pittsburgh
23	WASHINGTON	Wilburn, Barry	DB	Mississippi
24	LOS ANGELES RAIDERS	Wingate, Leonard	DT	South Carolina State
25	SEATTLE	Lewis, Judious	WR	Arkansas State
26	DENVER	Riley, Eric	DB	Florida State
27	MIAMI	Sharp, Dan	TE	Texas Christian
28	NEW ENGLAND from			
	San Francisco	Hodge, Milford	DT	Washington State

End of Round: 10.23pm Time of Round: 1 hr, 16 mins Total Time: 14 hrs, 21 mins

ROUND 9
Start of Round: 10.23pm

No.	Team	Name	Pos.	College
1	BUFFALO	Jones, Glenn	DB	Norfolk State
2	HOUSTON	Tasker, Steve	KR	Northwestern
3	MINNESOTA	Covington, Jaime	RB	Syracuse
4	ATLANTA	Moon, Micah	LB	North Carolina
5	INDIANAPOLIS	Boyer, Mark	TE	Southern California
6	DETROIT	James, June	LB	Texas
7	PHILADELPHIA from			
	Cleveland	Toub, Dave	C	Texas-El Paso
8	TAMPA BAY	Calabria, Steve	QB	Colgate
9	PHILADELPHIA	Drake, Joe	DT	Arizona
10	SAN DIEGO	Berner, Paul	QB	Pacific
11	NEW YORK JETS	Waters, Mike	RB	San Diego State
12	NEW ORLEANS	Johnson, Earl	DB	South Carolina
13	KANSAS CITY	Armentrout, Mike	DB	S.W. Missouri
14	CINCINNATI	Cruise, Keith	DE	Northwestern
15	GREEN BAY	Johnson, Morris	G	Alabama A&M
16	NEW YORK GIANTS	Wright, Frank	NT	South Carolina
17	PITTSBURGH	Small, Fred	LB	Washington
18	PITTSBURGH from			
	New England	Harris, Andre	DB	Minnesota
19	DALLAS	Strasburger, Scott	LB	Nebraska
20	ST. LOUIS	Williams, Scott	TE	Georgia
21	LOS ANGELES RAMS	Swanson, Gary	LB	Cal Poly-Obispo
22	LOS ANGELES RAIDERS	Sydnor, Chris	DB	Penn State
23	WASHINGTON	Geier, Mitch	G	Troy State
24	SEATTLE	Otto, Bob	DE	Idaho State

No.	Team	Name	Pos.	College
25	DENVER	Smith, Daryl	DB	North Alabama
26	CHICAGO	Sanders, Thomas	RB	Texas A&M
27	MIAMI	Hinds, Adam	DB	Oklahoma State
28	SAN DIEGO from			
	San Francisco	Remsberg, Dan	T	Abilene Christian

End of Round: 11.30pm Time of Round 1 hr, 7 mins Total Time: 15 hrs 28 mins
Los Angeles Raiders, Washington, Seattle and Denver selected ahead of Chicago which passed

ROUND 10
Start of Round: 11.30pm

1	BUFFALO	Babyar, Chris	G	Illinois
2	MINNESOTA	Johnson, Juan	WR	Langston, Okla.
3	HOUSTON	Golic, Mike	DE	Notre Dame
4	INDIANAPOLIS	Pinesett, Andre	DT	Cal State-Fullerton
5	ATLANTA	Martin, Brent	C	Stanford
6	DETROIT	Beauford, Clayton	WR	Auburn
7	CLEVELAND	Williams, Larry	G	Notre Dame
8	TAMPA BAY	Igwebuike, Donald	K	Clemson
9	PHILADELPHIA	Kelso, Mark	DB	William & Mary
10	NEW YORK JETS	Glenn, Kerry	DB	Minnesota
11	WASHINGTON from			
	New Orleans	Orr, Terry	RB	Texas
12	SAN DIEGO	King, David	DB	Auburn
13	CINCINNATI	King, Bernard	LB	Syracuse
14	GREEN BAY	Burgess, Ronnie	DB	Wake Forest
15	KANSAS CITY	Smith, Jeff	RB	Nebraska
16	PITTSBURGH	White, Oliver	TE	Kentucky
17	DENVER from			
	New England	Funck, Buddy	QB	New Mexico
18	DALLAS	Jones, Joe	TE	Virginia Tech
19	ST. LOUIS	Williams, Dennis	RB	Furman
20	NEW YORK GIANTS	Dubroc, Gregg	LB	Louisiana State
21	CHICAGO	Coryatt, Pat	DT	Baylor
22	LOS ANGELES RAMS	Love, Duval	G	UCLA
23	LOS ANGELES RAIDERS			
	from Washington	McKenzie, Reggie	LB	Tennessee
24	LOS ANGELES RAIDERS	Myres, Albert	DB	Tulsa
25	SEATTLE	Conner, John	QB	Arizona
26	DENVER	Anderson, Ron	LB	Southern Methodist
27	MIAMI	Pendleton, Mike	DB	Indiana
28	SEATTLE from			
	San Francisco	Bowers, James	DB	Memphis State

End of Round: 12.37am Time of Round: 1 hr, 7 mins, Total Time: 16 hrs, 35 mins

ROUND 11
Start of Round: 12.37am

1	HOUSTON	Drewrey, Willie	KR	West Virginia
2	BUFFALO	Seawright, James	LB	South Carolina
3	MINNESOTA	Williams, Tim	DB	North Carolina A&T
4	ATLANTA	Ayres, John	DB	Illinois
5	LOS ANGELES RAMS from			
	INDIANAPOLIS	Flutie, Doug	QB	Boston College
6	DETROIT	Harris, Kevin	DB	Georgia
7	CLEVELAND	Tucker, Travis	TE	Southern Connecticut
8	TAMPA BAY	Williams, James	RB	Memphis State
9	PHILADELPHIA	Hunter, Herman	RB	Tehnessee State

No.	Team	Name	Pos.	College
10	WASHINGTON from			
	New Orleans	McKenzie, Raleigh	G	Tennessee
11	SAN DIEGO	Smith, Jeff	NT	Kentucky
12	NEW YORK JETS	White, Brad	DE	Texas Tech
13	KANSAS CITY	Jackson, Chris	C	Southern Methodist
14	GREEN BAY	Shield, Joe	QB	Trinity, Conn.
15	NEW ENGLAND	Lewis, Paul	RB	Boston U.
16	CINCINNATI	Stanfield, Harold	TE	Mississippi College
17	DALLAS	Dellocono, Neal	LB	UCLA
18	ST. LOUIS	Anderson, Ricky	K	Vanderbilt
19	NEW YORK GIANTS	Young, Allen	DB	Virginia Tech
20	PITTSBURGH	Matichak, Terry	DB	Missouri
21	LOS ANGELES RAMS	Brown, Kevin	DB	Northwestern
22	CHICAGO	Morrissey, James	LB	Michigan State
23	LOS ANGELES RAIDERS	Strachan, Steve	RB	Boston College
24	WASHINGTON	Kimble, Garry	DB	Sam Houston State
25	SEATTLE	Cooper, Louis	LB	Western Carolina
26	DENVER	Rolle, Gary	WR	Florida
27	MIAMI	Jones, Mike	RB	Tulane
28	SAN FRANCISCO	Wood, David	DE	Arizona

End of Round: 1.38am Time of Round: 1 hr, 1 min Total Time 17 hrs, 36 mins
Houston selected ahead of Buffalo which passed.
Kansas City selected ahead of Green Bay which passed.
New England selected ahead of Cincinnati which passed.

ROUND 12
Start of Round: 1.38am

No.	Team	Name	Pos.	College
1	WASHINGTON from			
	Buffalo	Hamel, Dean	DT	Tulsa
2	MINNESOTA	Jones, Byron	NT	Tulsa
3	HOUSTON	Vonder Haar, Mark	DT	Minnesota
4	INDIANAPOLIS	Burnette, Dave	T	Central Arkansas
5	ATLANTA	Whisenhunt, Ken	TE	Georgia Tech
6	DETROIT	Weaver, Mike	G	Georgia
7	CLEVELAND	Swanson, Shane	WR	Nebraska
8	TAMPA BAY	Rockford, Jim	DB	Oklahoma
9	PHILADELPHIA	Russell, Todd	DB	Boston College
10	SAN DIEGO	Simmons, Tony	DE	Tennessee
11	NEW YORK JETS	Wallace, Bill	WR	Pittsburgh
12	NEW ORLEANS	Songy, Treg	DB	Tulane
13	KANSAS CITY	Le Bel, Harper	C	Colorado State
14	CINCINNATI	Garza, Louis	T	New Mexico State
15	GREEN BAY	Meyer, Jim	P	Arizona State
16	DALLAS	Jordan, Karl	LB	Vanderbilt
17	ST. LOUIS	Young, Lonnie	DB	Michigan State
18	NEW YORK GIANTS	Welch, Herb	DB	UCLA
19	PITTSBURGH	Sanchez, Jeff	DB	Georgia
20	NEW ENGLAND	Mumford, Tony	RB	Penn State
21	SAN DIEGO from Chicago	Pearson, Bret	TE	Wisconsin
22	TAMPA BAY from			
	L.A. Rams	Melka, Jim	LB	Wisconsin
23	WASHINGTON	Winn, Bryant	LB	Houston
24	LOS ANGELES RAIDERS	Polk, Raymond	DB	Oklahoma State
25	BUFFALO from Seattle	Woodside, Paul	K	West Virginia
26	DENVER	Lynch, Dan	G	Washington State
27	MIAMI	Noble, Ray	DB	California
28	SAN FRANCISCO	Chumley, Donald	DT	Georgia

End of Round: 2.29am Time of Round 51mins Total Time: 18 hrs, 27 mins

NCAA FOOTBALL STATISTICS

Passing

	Att.	Comp.	Pct.	Yds.	TDs.	Int.	Avg. Yds.	Rtg
Doug Flutie (Boston College)	386	233	60.4	3454	27	11	8.95	101.4
Randall Cunningham (Nevada-Las Vegas)	332	208	62.7	2628	24	9	7.92	100.1
Bob DeMarco (Central Michigan)	173	98	56.6	1427	12	4	8.25	97.0
Frank Reich (Maryland)	169	108	63.9	1446	9	5	8.56	96.2
Bernie Kosar (Miami, Florida)	416	262	63.0	3642	25	16	8.75	95.2
Damon Allen (Cal State-Fullerton)	330	178	53.9	2469	20	3	7.48	94.8
Chuck Long (Iowa)	283	187	66.1	2410	16	13	8.52	92.5
Rusty Hilger (Oklahoma State)	240	141	58.8	1843	7	5	7.68	84.0
Mark Stevens (Utah)	216	117	54.2	1889	11	9	8.75	83.2
Mike Tomczak (Ohio State)	207	121	58.5	1662	9	8	8.03	82.4

Rushing

	Games	Att.	Yds.	Avg.	TDs.	Yds/Game
Curtis Adams (Cent. Michigan)	10	222	1204	5.4	13	120.4
Johnnie Jones (Tennessee)	11	229	1290	5.6	10	117.3
Ethan Horton (North Carolina)	11	238	1247	5.2	6	113.4
Robert Lavette (Georgia Tech)	11	260	1189	4.6	14	108.1
Greg Allen (Florida State)	9	133	971	7.3	8	107.9
Steve Morgan (Toledo)	11	305	1137	3.7	10	103.4
George Adams (Kentucky)	11	253	1085	4.3	13	98.6
Jeff Smith (Nebraska)	10	177	935	5.3	7	93.5

Receiving

	Games	No.	Yds.	Avg.	TDs.	Receptions per game
Larry Willis (Fresno State)	12	79	1251	15.8	8	6.6
Gerard Phelan (Boston College)	11	64	971	15.2	3	5.8
Keith Edwards (Vanderbilt)	11	60	576	9.6	2	5.5
David Mills (Brigham Young)	12	60	1023	17.1	7	5.0
Mark Dowdell (Bowling Green)	11	55	596	10.8	4	5.0
Alan Andrews (Rutgers)	8	40	511	12.8	2	5.0
Eddie Brown (Miami, Fla.)	12	59	1114	18.9	9	4.9
Chuck Scott (Vanderbilt)	11	54	975	18.1	8	4.9
Kevin Bowman (San Jose State)	11	54	652	12.1	4	4.9
Greg Hill (Maryland)	11	51	820	16.1	4	4.6

All-Purpose Ground Gainers

	Games	Yds. Rush	Yds. Rec.	Yds. P. Ret.	Yds. K. Ret.	Total Yds.	Yds/ Game
George Adams (Kentucky)	11	1085	330	0	274	1689	153.5
Curtis Adams (Cent. Michigan)	10	1204	55	0	168	1427	142.7
Ethan Horton (North Carolina)	11	1247	254	0	0	1501	136.5
Kevin Lowe (Wyoming)	12	857	104	0	642	1603	133.6
Steve Morgan (Toledo)	11	1137	268	0	0	1405	127.7
Jeff Smith (Nebraska)	10	935	81	225	36	1277	127.7
Johnnie Jones (Tennessee)	11	1290	86	0	0	1376	125.1
Mike Waters (San Diego State)	11	704	234	0	339	1337	121.5
Robert Lavette (Georgia Tech)	11	1189	146	0	0	1335	121.4
Willie Drewrey (West Virginia)	11	0	442	343	546	1331	121.0

Scoring

	Games	TDs.	EP/Att	FG/Att	Pts.	Points/ Game
Bobby Raymond (Florida)	11	0	34/35	23/26	103	9.4
Kevin Butler (Georgia)	11	0	23/23	23/28	92	8.4
Mike Prindle (W. Michigan)	11	0	18/20	24/30	90	8.2
Fuad Reveiz (Tennessee)	11	0	29/30	20/23	89	8.1
Donald Igwebuike (Clemson)	11	0	41/41	16/17	89	8.1
Jess Atkinson (Maryland)	11	0	37/38	17/20	88	8.0
Curtis Adams (Cent. Michigan)	10	13	0	0	78	7.8
Richard Spelman (Hawaii)	11	0	22/22	21/29	85	7.7
Tom Angstadt (Rutgers)	10	0	20/20	19/28	77	7.7

Total Offense

	Game	Yds. Rushing	Yds. Passing	Total* TDs.	Total Yards	Yds/ Play	Yds/ Game
Doug Flutie (Boston College)	11	149	3454	30	3603	8.0	327.5
Bernie Kosar (Miami, Fla.)	12	-230	3642	29	3412	7.3	284.3
Bob Frasco (San Jose State)	11	118	2688	24	2806	5.8	255.1
Damon Allen (Cal St.-Fullerton)	12	220	2469	25	2689	6.2	224.1
R. Cunningham (Nevada-Las Vegas)	12	10	2628	26	2638	6.1	219.8
Kurt Page (Vanderbilt)	11	- 64	2405	17	2341	6.0	212.8
Paul Berner (Pacific)	10	- 71	2107	14	2036	5.9	203.6
Mark Stevens (Utah)	12	440	1889	24	2329	6.2	194.1
Chuck Long (Iowa)	12	-174	2410	20	2236	6.1	186.3

*Touchdowns passed for plus rushing touchdowns

Field Goals

	Games	FGAtt	FG	Pct.	FG/ Game
Mike Prindle (Western Michigan)	11	30	24	.800	2.18
Bobby Raymond (Florida)	11	26	23	.885	2.09
Kevin Butler (Georgia)	11	28	23	.821	2.09
Richard Spelman (Hawaii)	11	29	21	.724	1.91
Tom Angstadt (Rutgers)	10	28	19	.679	1.90
Fuad Reveiz (Tennessee)	11	23	20	.870	1.82
Mike Clendenen (Houston)	11	22	18	.818	1.64
Jess Atkinson (Maryland)	11	20	17	.850	1.55
Ricky Gann (Texas Tech)	11	26	17	.654	1.55

Punting

	Games	No.	Yds.	Avg.
Ricky Anderson (Vanderbilt)	11	58	2793	48.2
Randall Cunningham (Nevada-Las Vegas)	11	59	2803	47.5
Rick Donnelly (Wyoming)	12	63	2990	47.5
Lee Johnson (Brigham Young)	12	57	2593	45.5
Chip Andrews (Georgia)	11	63	2858	45.4
Buzzy Sawyer (Baylor)	11	72	3227	44.8
Paul Calhoun (Kentucky)	11	60	2667	44.5
Harry Newsome (Wake Forest)	11	57	2512	44.1
Ralf Mojsiejenko (Michigan State)	11	72	3171	44.0
Chuck Razmic (Indiana)	11	57	2505	43.9

COLLEGE BOWL RESULTS

Regular season records are indicated in brackets.

December 15
California Bowl at Fresno, California
Nevada-Las Vegas, (10-2) 30, vs. Toledo, (8-2-1) 13.

Independence Bowl at Shreveport, Louisiana
Air Force, (7-4) 23, vs. Virginia Tech, (8-3) 7.

December 21
Holiday Bowl at San Diego, California
Brigham Young, (12-0) 24, vs. Michigan, (6-5) 17.

December 22
Florida Citrus Bowl at Orlando, Florida
Georgia, (7-4) 17, vs. Florida State, (7-3-1) 17.

Sun Bowl at El Paso, Texas
Maryland, (8-3) 28, vs. Tennessee, (7-3-1) 27.

Cherry Bowl at Detroit, Michigan
Army, (7-3-1) 10, vs. Michigan State, (6-5) 6.

December 26
Freedom Bowl at Anaheim, California
Iowa, (7-4-1) 55, vs. Texas, (7-3-1) 17.

December 27
Liberty Bowl at Memphis, Tennessee
Auburn, (8-4) 21, vs. Arkansas, (7-3-1) 15.

December 28
Gator Bowl at Jacksonville, Florida
Oklahoma State, (9-2) 21, vs. South Carolina, (10-1) 14.

December 29
Aloha Bowl at Honolulu
Southern Methodist, (9-2) 27, vs. Notre Dame, (7-4) 20.

Hall of Fame Bowl at Birmingham, Alabama
Kentucky, (8-3) 20, vs. Wisconsin, (7-3-1) 19.

December 31
Peach Bowl at Atlanta, Georgia
Virginia, (7-2-2) 27, vs. Purdue, (7-4) 24.

Bluebonnet Bowl at Houston, Texas
West Virginia, (7-4) 31, vs. Texas Christian, (8-3) 14.

January 1
Cotton Bowl at Dallas, Texas
Boston College, (9-2) 45, vs. Houston (7-4) 28.

Fiesta Bowl at Tempe, Arizona
UCLA, (8-3) 39, vs. Miami, Fla., (8-4) 37.

Rose Bowl at Pasadena, California
Southern California, (8-3) 20, vs. Ohio State, (9-2) 17.

Sugar Bowl at New Orleans, Louisiana
Nebraska, (9-2) 28, vs. Louisiana State, (8-2-1) 10.

Orange Bowl at Miami, Florida
Washington, (10-1) 28, vs. Oklahoma, (9-1-1) 17.

HEISMAN TROPHY WINNERS

1984 — Doug Flutie, Boston, QB
1983 — Mike Rozier, Nebraska, TB
1982 — Herschel Walker, Georgia, TB
1981 — Marcus Allen, Southern California, TB
1980 — George Rogers, South Carolina, HB
1979 — Charles White, Southern California, TB
1978 — Billy Sims, Oklahoma, HB
1977 — Earl Campbell, Texas, FB
1976 — Tony Dorsett, Pittsburgh, HB
1975 — Archie Griffin, Ohio State, HB
1974 — Archie Griffin, Ohio State, HB
1973 — John Cappelletti, Penn State, HB
1972 — Johnny Rogers, Nebraska, FL
1971 — Pat Sullivan, Auburn, QB
1970 — Jim Plunkett, Stanford, QB
1969 — Steve Owens, Oklahoma, HB
1968 — O.J. Simpson, Southern California, TB
1967 — Gary Beban, UCLA, QB
1966 — Steve Spurrier, Florida, QB
1965 — Mike Garrett, Southern California, TB
1964 — John Huarte, Notre Dame, QB
1963 — Roger Staubach, Navy, QB
1962 — Terry Baker, Oregon State, QB
1961 — Ernie Davis, Syracuse, HB
1960 — Joe Bellino, Navy, HB
1959 — Billy Cannon, LSU, HB
1958 — Pete Dawkins, Army, HB
1957 — John David Crow, Texas A&M, HB
1956 — Paul Hornung, Notre Dame, QB
1955 — Howard Cassady, Ohio State, HB
1954 — Alan Ameche, Wisconsin, FB
1953 — John Lattner, Notre Dame, HB
1952 — Billy Vessels, Oklahoma, HB
1951 — Dick Kazmaier, Princeton, HB
1950 — Vic Janowicz, Ohio State, HB
1949 — Leon Hart, Notre Dame, HB
1948 — Doak Walker, SMU, HB
1947 — John Lujack, Notre Dame, QB
1946 — Glenn Davis, Army, HB
1945 — Doc Blanchard, Army, HB
1944 — Les Horvath, Ohio State, HB
1943 — Angelo Bertelli, Notre Dame, QB
1942 — Frank Sinkwich, Georgia, HB
1941 — Bruce Smith, Minnesota, HB
1940 — Tom Harmon, Michigan, HB
1939 — Nile Kinnick, Iowa, HB
1938 — Davey O'Brien, TCU, QB
1937 — Clint Frank, Yale, HB
1936 — Larry Kelley, Yale, E
1935 — Jay Berwanger, Chicago, HB

1984 SEASON RESULTS

WEEK 1

SUNDAY, SEPTEMBER 2

Atlanta Falcons at New Orleans Saints	36—28
Cincinnati Bengals at Denver Broncos	17—20
Kansas City Chiefs at Pittsburgh Steelers	37—27
Los Angeles Raiders at Houston Oilers	24—14
Miami Dolphins at Washington Redskins	35—17
New England Patriots at Buffalo Bills	21—17
New York Jets at Indianapolis Colts	23—14
Philadelphia Eagles at New York Giants	27—28
St. Louis Cardinals at Green Bay Packers	23—24
San Diego Chargers at Minnesota Vikings	42—13
San Francisco 49ers at Detroit Lions	30—27
Tampa Bay Buccaneers at Chicago Bears	14—34

MONDAY, SEPTEMBER 3

Cleveland Browns at Seattle Seahawks	0—33
Dallas Cowboys at Los Angeles Rams	20—13

WEEK 2

THURSDAY, SEPTEMBER 6

Pittsburgh Steelers at New York Jets	23—17

SUNDAY, SEPTEMBER 9

Buffalo Bills at St. Louis Cardinals	7—37
Cleveland Browns at Los Angeles Rams	17—20
Dallas Cowboys at New York Giants	7—28
Denver Broncos at Chicago Bears	0—27
Detroit Lions at Atlanta Falcons	27—24
Green Bay Packers at Los Angeles Raiders	7—28
Indianapolis Colts at Houston Oilers	35—21
Kansas City Chiefs at Cincinnati Bengals	27—22
Minnesota Vikings at Philadelphia Eagles	17—19
New England Patriots at Miami Dolphins	7—28
San Diego Chargers at Seattle Seahawks	17—31
Tampa Bay Buccaneers at New Orleans Saints	13—17

MONDAY, SEPTEMBER 10

Washington Redskins at San Francisco 49ers	31—37

WEEK 3

SUNDAY, SEPTEMBER 16

Atlanta Falcons at Minnesota Vikings	20—27
Chicago Bears at Green Bay Packers	9—7
Cincinnati Bengals at New York Jets	23—43
Denver Broncos at Cleveland Browns	24—14
Detroit Lions at Tampa Bay Buccaneers	17—21
Houston Oilers at San Diego Chargers	14—31
Los Angeles Raiders at Kansas City Chiefs	22—20
Los Angeles Rams at Pittsburgh Steelers	14—24
New Orleans Saints at San Francisco 49ers	20—30
New York Giants at Washington Redskins	14—30
Philadelphia Eagles at Dallas Cowboys	17—23
St. Louis Cardinals at Indianapolis Colts	34—33
Seattle Seahawks at New England Patriots	23—38

MONDAY, SEPTEMBER 17

Miami Dolphins at Buffalo Bills	21—17

WEEK 4

SUNDAY, SEPTEMBER 23

Chicago Bears at Seattle Seahawks .... 9—38
Green Bay Packers at Dallas Cowboys .... 6—20
Houston Oilers at Atlanta Falcons .... 10—42
Indianapolis Colts at Miami Dolphins .... 7—44
Kansas City Chiefs at Denver Broncos .... 0—21
Los Angeles Rams at Cincinnati Bengals .... 24—14
Minnesota Vikings at Detroit Lions .... 29—28
New York Jets at Buffalo Bills .... 28—26
Pittsburgh Steelers at Cleveland Browns .... 10—20
St. Louis Cardinals at New Orleans Saints .... 24—34
San Francisco 49ers at Philadelphia Eagles .... 21— 9
Tampa Bay Buccaneers at New York Giants .... 14—17
Washington Redskins at New England Patriots .... 26—10

MONDAY, SEPTEMBER 24

San Diego Chargers at Los Angeles Raiders .... 30—33·

WEEK 5

SUNDAY, SEPTEMBER 30

Atlanta Falcons at San Francisco 49ers .... 5—14
Buffalo Bills at Indianapolis Colts .... 17—31
Cleveland Browns at Kansas City Chiefs .... 6—10
Dallas Cowboys at Chicago Bears .... 23—14
Detroit Lions at San Diego Chargers .... 24—27
Green Bay Packers at Tampa Bay Buccaneers .... 27—30
Los Angeles Raiders at Denver Broncos .... 13—16
Miami Dolphins at St. Louis Cardinals .... 36—28
New England Patriots at New York Jets .... 28—21
New Orleans Saints at Houston Oilers .... 27—10
New York Giants at Los Angeles Rams .... 12—33
Philadelphia Eagles at Washington Redskins .... 10—20
Seattle Seahawks at Minnesota Vikings .... 20—12

MONDAY, OCTOBER 1

Cincinnati Bengals at Pittsburgh Steelers .... 17—38

WEEK 6

SUNDAY, OCTOBER 7

Atlanta Falcons at Los Angeles Rams .... 30—28
Denver Broncos at Detroit Lions .... 28— 7
Houston Oilers at Cincinnati Bengals .... 3—13
Miami Dolphins at Pittsburgh Steelers .... 31— 7
Minnesota Vikings at Tampa Bay Buccaneers .... 31—35
New England Patriots at Cleveland Browns .... 17—16
New Orleans Saints at Chicago Bears .... 7—20
New York Jets at Kansas City Chiefs .... 17—16
Philadelphia Eagles at Buffalo Bills .... 27—17
St. Louis Cardinals at Dallas Cowboys .... 31—20
San Diego Chargers at Green Bay Packers .... 34—28
Seattle Seahawks at Los Angeles Raiders .... 14—28
Washington Redskins at Indianapolis Colts .... 35— 7

MONDAY, OCTOBER 8

San Francisco 49ers at New York Giants .... 31—10

WEEK 7

SUNDAY, OCTOBER 14
Buffalo Bills at Seattle Seahawks ....28—31
Chicago Bears at St. Louis Cardinals ....21—38
Cincinnati Bengals at New England Patriots............................14—20
Dallas Cowboys at Washington Redskins..................................14—34
Houston Oilers at Miami Dolphins...10—28
Indianapolis Colts at Philadelphia Eagles .... 7—16
Los Angeles Rams at New Orleans Saints................................28—10
Minnesota Vikings at Los Angeles Raiders ....20—23
New York Giants at Atlanta Falcons ....19— 7
New York Jets at Cleveland Browns...24—20
Pittsburgh Steelers at San Francisco 49ers ....20—17
San Diego Chargers at Kansas City Chiefs...............................13—31
Tampa Bay Buccaneers at Detroit Lions.................................... 7—13
MONDAY, OCTOBER 15
Green Bay Packers at Denver Broncos......................................14—17

WEEK 8

SUNDAY, OCTOBER 21
Chicago Bears at Tampa Bay Buccaneers.................................44— 9
Cleveland Browns at Cincinnati Bengals..................................... 9—12
Denver Broncos at Buffalo Bills ....37— 7
Detroit Lions at Minnesota Vikings...16—14
Kansas City Chiefs at New York Jets .... 7—28
Los Angeles Raiders at San Diego Chargers.............................44—37
Miami Dolphins at New England Patriots..................................44—24
New Orleans Saints at Dallas Cowboys....................................27—30
New York Giants at Philadelphia Eagles...................................10—24
Pittsburgh Steelers at Indianapolis Colts ....16—17
San Francisco 49ers at Houston Oilers.....................................34—21
Seattle Seahawks vs. Green Bay Packers at Milwaukee ....24—30
Washington Redskins at St. Louis Cardinals..............................24—26
MONDAY, OCTOBER 22
Los Angeles Rams at Atlanta Falcons ....24—10

WEEK 9

SUNDAY, OCTOBER 28
Atlanta Falcons at Pittsburgh Steelers ....10—35
Buffalo Bills at Miami Dolphins .... 7—38
Cincinnati Bengals at Houston Oilers..21—13
Denver Broncos at Los Angeles Raiders...................................22—19
Detroit Lions at Green Bay Packers... 9—41
Indianapolis Colts at Dallas Cowboys .... 3—22
Minnesota Vikings at Chicago Bears .... 7—16
New Orleans Saints at Cleveland Browns..................................16—14
New York Jets at New England Patriots.....................................20—30
St. Louis Cardinals at Philadelphia Eagles ....34—14
San Francisco 49ers at Los Angeles Rams ....33— 0
Tampa Bay Buccaneers at Kansas City Chiefs..........................20—24
Washington Redskins at New York Giants..................................13—37
MONDAY, OCTOBER 29
Seattle Seahawks at San Diego Chargers ....24— 0

WEEK 10

SUNDAY, NOVEMBER 4
Cincinnati Bengals at San Francisco 49ers..............................17—23
Cleveland Browns at Buffalo Bills ....13—10
Green Bay Packers at New Orleans Saints..............................23—13
Houston Oilers at Pittsburgh Steelers .... 7—35
Kansas City Chiefs at Seattle Seahawks .... 0—45
Los Angeles Raiders at Chicago Bears.................................. 6—17
Los Angeles Rams at St. Louis Cardinals...............................16—13
Miami Dolphins at New York Jets ....31—17
New England Patriots at Denver Broncos ....19—26
New York Giants at Dallas Cowboys.....................................19— 7
Philadelphia Eagles at Detroit Lions ....23—23
San Diego Chargers at Indianapolis Colts ....38—10
Tampa Bay Buccaneers at Minnesota Vikings ....24—27
MONDAY, NOVEMBER 5
Atlanta Falcons at Washington Redskins................................14—27

WEEK 11

SUNDAY, NOVEMBER 11
Buffalo Bills at New England Patriots ....10—38
Chicago Bears at Los Angeles Rams ....13—29
Dallas Cowboys at St. Louis Cardinals.................................24—17
Denver Broncos at San Diego Chargers ....16—13
Detroit Lions at Washington Redskins ....14—28
Houston Oilers at Kansas City Chiefs ....17—16
Indianapolis Colts at New York Jets .... 9— 5
Minnesota Vikings vs. Green Bay Packers at Milwaukee ....17—45
New Orleans Saints at Atlanta Falcons ....17—13
New York Giants at Tampa Bay Buccaneers ....17—20
Philadelphia Eagles at Miami Dolphins ....23—24
Pittsburgh Steelers at Cincinnati Bengals ....20—22
San Francisco 49ers at Cleveland Browns...............................41— 7
MONDAY, NOVEMBER 12
Los Angeles Raiders at Seattle Seahawks...............................14—17

WEEK 12

SUNDAY, NOVEMBER 18
Cleveland Browns at Atlanta Falcons...................................23— 7
Dallas Cowboys at Buffalo Bills .... 3—14
Detroit Lions at Chicago Bears ....14—16
Kansas City Chiefs at Los Angeles Raiders .... 7—17
Los Angeles Rams vs. Green Bay Packers at Milwaukee .... 6—31
Miami Dolphins at San Diego Chargers ....28—34
Minnesota Vikings at Denver Broncos ....21—42
New England Patriots at Indianapolis Colts ....50—17
New York Jets at Houston Oilers ....20—31
St. Louis Cardinals at New York Giants ....10—16
Seattle Seahawks at Cincinnati Bengals................................26— 6
Tampa Bay Buccaneers at San Francisco 49ers ....17—24
Washington Redskins at Philadelphia Eagles ....10—16
MONDAY, NOVEMBER 19
Pittsburgh Steelers at New Orleans Saints ....24—27

WEEK 13

THURSDAY, NOVEMBER 22
Green Bay Packers at Detroit Lions..28—31
New England Patriots at Dallas Cowboys ....17—20
SUNDAY, NOVEMBER 25
Atlanta Falcons at Cincinnati Bengals..14—35
Buffalo Bills at Washington Redskins..14—41
Chicago Bears at Minnesota Vikings ....34— 3
Indianapolis Colts at Los Angeles Raiders .... 7—21
Houston Oilers at Cleveland Browns...10—27
Kansas City Chiefs at New York Giants...27—28
Los Angeles Rams at Tampa Bay Buccaneers ....34—33
Philadelphia Eagles at St. Louis Cardinals ....16—17
San Diego Chargers at Pittsburgh Steelers ....24—52
San Francisco 49ers at New Orleans Saints...................................35— 3
Seattle Seahawks at Denver Broncos ....27—24
MONDAY, NOVEMBER 26
New York Jets at Miami Dolphins..17—28

WEEK 14

THURSDAY, NOVEMBER 29
Washington Redskins at Minnesota Vikings.....................................31—17
SUNDAY, DECEMBER 2
Cincinnati Bengals at Cleveland Browns..20—17
Dallas Cowboys at Philadelphia Eagles...26—10
Denver Broncos at Kansas City Chiefs ....13—16
Detroit Lions at Seattle Seahawks ....17—38
Indianapolis Colts at Buffalo Bills..15—21
Los Angeles Raiders at Miami Dolphins ....45—34
New Orleans Saints at Los Angeles Rams.......................................21—34
New York Giants at New York Jets...20—10
Pittsburgh Steelers at Houston Oilers ....20—23
St. Louis Cardinals at New England Patriots ....33—10
San Francisco 49ers at Atlanta Falcons ....35—17
Tampa Bay Buccaneers at Green Bay Packers ....14—27
MONDAY, DECEMBER 3
Chicago Bears at San Diego Chargers .... 7—20

WEEK 15

SATURDAY, DECEMBER 8
Buffalo Bills at New York Jets ....17—21
Minnesota Vikings at San Francisco 49ers .... 7—51
SUNDAY, DECEMBER 9
Atlanta Falcons at Tampa Bay Buccaneers .... 6—23
Cincinnati Bengals at New Orleans Saints.......................................24—21
Cleveland Browns at Pittsburgh Steelers ....20—23
Green Bay Packers at Chicago Bears ....20—14
Houston Oilers at Los Angeles Rams ....16—27
Miami Dolphins at Indianapolis Colts ....35—17
New England Patriots at Philadelphia Eagles ....17—27
New York Giants at St. Louis Cardinals..21—31
San Diego Chargers at Denver Broncos ....13—16
Seattle Seahawks at Kansas City Chiefs .... 7—34
Washington Redskins at Dallas Cowboys ....30—28

WEEK 16

FRIDAY, DECEMBER 14
Los Angeles Rams at San Francisco 49ers ....16—19
SATURDAY, DECEMBER 15
Denver Broncos at Seattle Seahawks ....31—14
New Orleans Saints at New York Giants ....10— 3
SUNDAY, DECEMBER 16
Buffalo Bills at Cincinnati Bengals ....21—52
Chicago Bears at Detroit Lions ....30—13
Cleveland Browns at Houston Oilers ....27—20
Green Bay Packers at Minnesota Vikings ....38—14
Indianapolis Colts at New England Patriots ....10—16
Kansas City Chiefs at San Diego Chargers ....42—21
New York Jets at Tampa Bay Buccaneers ....21—41
Philadelphia Eagles at Atlanta Falcons ....10—26
Pittsburgh Steelers at Los Angeles Raiders ....13— 7
St. Louis Cardinals at Washington Redskins ....27—29
MONDAY, DECEMBER 17
Dallas Cowboys at Miami Dolphins ....21—28

FIRST ROUND PLAYOFF GAMES

SUNDAY, DECEMBER 23

American Football Conference
Los Angeles Raiders at Seattle Seahawks .... 7—13

National Football Conference
New York Giants at Los Angeles Rams ....16—13

DIVISIONAL PLAYOFF GAMES

SATURDAY, DECEMBER 29

American Football Conference
Seattle Seahawks at Miami Dolphins ....10—31

National Football Conference
New York Giants at San Francisco 49ers ....10—21
SUNDAY, DECEMBER 30

American Football Conference
Pittsburgh Steelers at Denver Broncos ....24—17

National Football Conference
Chicago Bears at Washington Redskins ....23—19

CONFERENCE CHAMPIONSHIP GAMES, SUPER BOWL XIX, AND AFC-NFC PRO BOWL

SUNDAY, JANUARY 6

American Football Conference Championship Game
Pittsburgh Steelers at Miami Dolphins ....28—45

National Football Conference Championship Game
Chicago Bears at San Francisco 49ers .... 0—23
SUNDAY, JANUARY 20
Super Bowl XIX Miami Dolphins vs San Francisco 49ers ....16—38
SUNDAY, JANUARY 27
AFC-NFC Pro Bowl at Honolulu, Hawaii ....22—14

1984 FINAL STANDINGS

AMERICAN FOOTBALL CONFERENCE (AFC)

EASTERN DIVISION

	W	L	T	PF	PA
Miami Dolphins	14	2	0	513	298
New England Patriots	9	7	0	362	352
New York Jets	7	9	0	332	364
Indianapolis Colts	4	12	0	239	414
Buffalo Bills	2	14	0	250	454

CENTRAL DIVISION

Pittsburgh Steelers	9	7	0	387	310
Cincinnati Bengals	8	8	0	339	339
Cleveland Browns	5	11	0	250	297
Houston Oilers	3	13	0	240	437

WESTERN DIVISION

Denver Broncos	13	3	0	353	241
Seattle Seahawks	12	4	0	418	282
Los Angeles Raiders	11	5	0	368	278
Kansas City Chiefs	8	8	0	314	324
San Diego Chargers	7	9	0	394	413

NATIONAL FOOTBALL CONFERENCE (NFC)

EASTERN DIVISION

	W	L	T	PF	PA
Washington Redskins	11	5	0	426	310
New York Giants	9	7	0	299	301
St. Louis Cardinals	9	7	0	423	345
Dallas Cowboys	9	7	0	308	308
Philadelphia Eagles	6	9	1	278	320

CENTRAL DIVISION

Chicago Bears	10	6	0	325	248
Green Bay Packers	8	8	0	390	309
Tampa Bay Buccaneers	6	10	0	335	380
Detroit Lions	4	11	1	283	408
Minnesota Vikings	3	13	0	276	484

WESTERN DIVISION

San Francisco 49ers	15	1	0	475	227
Los Angeles Rams	10	6	0	346	316
New Orleans Saints	7	9	0	298	361
Atlanta Falcons	4	12	0	281	382

PAXDIRT (handwritten)

1985 SEASON SCHEDULE

WEEK 1   Result
Sunday, September 8
Denver Broncos at Los Angeles Rams .... ~~I + 4~~   **16 – 13**   I
Detroit Lions at Atlanta Falcons .... G + 0   17 – 21   G
Green Bay Packers at New England Patriots ...... I + 6   5 – 6   G
Indianapolis Colts at Pittsburgh Steelers ...... G – 16   20 – 38   G
Kansas City Chiefs at New Orleans Saints .... I + 15   38 – 16   I
Miami Dolphins at Houston Oilers .... I + 4   31 – 21   I
New York Jets at Los Angeles Raiders .... 23 – 14   G
Philadelphia Eagles at New York Giants .... G + 3   24 – 23   I
St. Louis Cardinals at Cleveland Browns .... I + 125   17 – 49   G
San Diego Chargers at Buffalo Bills .... I + 21   7 – 21   I
San Francisco 49ers at Minnesota Vikings .... I – 35   49 – 7   I
Seattle Seahawks at Cincinnati Bengals .... I + 2   32 – 34 or I
Tampa Bay Buccaneers at Chicago Bears .... G – 26   0 – 36   G
Monday, September 9
Washington Redskins at Dallas Cowboys .... I + 10   24 – 14   I

WEEK 2   I + 71
Thursday, September 12
Los Angeles Raiders at Kansas City Chiefs ...... G + 19   38 – 14   G
Sunday, September 15
Atlanta Falcons at San Francisco 49ers .... I + 5   17 – 31   I
Buffalo Bills at New York Jets .... I + 16   13 – 10   I
Cincinnati Bengals at St. Louis Cardinals ...... I + 4   23 – 24   I
Dallas Cowboys at Detroit Lions .... I – 13   24 – 29   I
Houston Oilers at Washington Redskins .... I + 25   21 – 6   I
Indianapolis Colts at Miami Dolphins .... I + 5.4   61 – 17   I
Los Angeles Rams at Philadelphia Eagles .... I + 9   28 – 14   I
Minnesota Vikings at Tampa Bay Buccaneers ...... I + 26   30 – 42   I
New England Patriots at Chicago Bears .... I + 2   22 – 23   G
New Orleans Saints at Denver Broncos .... I + 1   17 – 28   I
New York Giants at Green Bay Packers .... I + 55   7 – 56   I
Seattle Seahawks at San Diego Chargers .... I + 11   41 – 28   I
Monday, September 16
Pittsburgh Steelers at Cleveland Browns .... G + 11   28 – 17   G

WEEK 3   I + 272
Thursday, September 19
Chicago Bears at Minnesota Vikings .... ___ – ___
Sunday, September 22
Cleveland Browns at Dallas Cowboys .... ___ – ___
Denver Broncos at Atlanta Falcons .... ___ – ___
Detroit Lions at Indianapolis Colts .... ___ – ___
Houston Oilers at Pittsburgh Steelers .... ___ – ___
Kansas City Chiefs at Miami Dolphins .... ___ – ___
New England Patriots at Buffalo Bills .... ___ – ___
New York Jets vs. Green Bay Packers at Milwaukee ... ___ – ___
Philadelphia Eagles at Washington Redskins ..... ___ – ___
St. Louis Cardinals at New York Giants .... ___ – ___
San Diego Chargers at Cincinnati Bengals .... ___ – ___
San Francisco 49ers at Los Angeles Raiders ..... ___ – ___
Tampa Bay Buccaneers at New Orleans Saints ..... ___ – ___
Monday, September 23
Los Angeles Rams at Seattle Seahawks .... ___ – ___

WEEK 4   **Result**
Sunday, September 29
Atlanta Falcons at Los Angeles Rams ....____—____
Cleveland Browns at San Diego Chargers.........................____—____
Dallas Cowboys at Houston Oilers.....................................____—____
Green Bay Packers at St. Louis Cardinals ....____—____
Indianapolis Colts at New York Jets ....____—____
Los Angeles Raiders at New England Patriots ....____—____
Miami Dolphins at Denver Broncos....................................____—____
Minnesota Vikings at Buffalo Bills.....................................____—____
New Orleans Saints at San Francisco 49ers ....____—____
New York Giants at Philadelphia Eagles ....____—____
Seattle Seahawks at Kansas City Chiefs ....____—____
Tampa Bay Buccaneers at Detroit Lions ....____—____
Washington Redskins at Chicago Bears ....____—____
Monday, September 30
Cincinnati Bengals at Pittsburgh Steelers.........................____—____

WEEK 5
Sunday, October 6
Buffalo Bills at Indianapolis Colts ....____—____
Chicago Bears at Tampa Bay Buccaneers ....____—____
Dallas Cowboys at New York Giants ....____—____
Detroit Lions at Green Bay Packers ....____—____
Houston Oilers at Denver Broncos ....____—____
Kansas City Chiefs at Los Angeles Raiders ....____—____
Minnesota Vikings at Los Angeles Rams...........................____—____
New England Patriots at Cleveland Browns ....____—____
New York Jets at Cincinnati Bengals ....____—____
Philadelphia Eagles at New Orleans Saints ....____—____
Pittsburgh Steelers at Miami Dolphins ....____—____
San Diego Chargers at Seattle Seahawks ....____—____
San Francisco 49ers at Atlanta Falcons ....____—____
Monday, October 7
St. Louis Cardinals at Washington Redskins ....____—____

WEEK 6
Sunday, October 13
Atlanta Falcons at Seattle Seahawks.................................____—____
Buffalo Bills at New England Patriots ....____—____
Chicago Bears at San Francisco 49ers...............................____—____
Cleveland Browns at Houston Oilers ....____—____
Denver Broncos at Indianapolis Colts ....____—____
Detroit Lions at Washington Redskins ....____—____
Kansas City Chiefs at San Diego Chargers ....____—____
Los Angeles Rams at Tampa Bay Buccaneers ....____—____
Minnesota Vikings vs. Green Bay Packers at Milwaukee .....____—____
New Orleans Saints at Los Angeles Raiders ....____—____
New York Giants at Cincinnati Bengals ....____—____
Philadelphia Eagles at St. Louis Cardinals ....____—____
Pittsburgh Steelers at Dallas Cowboys ....____—____
Monday, October 14
Miami Dolphins at New York Jets.......................................____—____

Sunday, October 20
Cincinnati Bengals at Houston Oilers .... —
Dallas Cowboys at Philadelphia Eagles .... —
Indianapolis Colts at Buffalo Bills .... —
Los Angeles Raiders at Cleveland Browns .... —
Los Angeles Rams at Kansas City Chiefs............................. —
New Orleans Saints at Atlanta Falcons .... —
New York Jets at New England Patriots .... —
St. Louis Cardinals at Pittsburgh Steelers .... —
San Diego Chargers at Minnesota Vikings .... —
San Francisco 49ers at Detroit Lions.................................... —
Seattle Seahawks at Denver Broncos .... —
Tampa Bay Buccaneers at Miami Dolphins .... —
Washington Redskins at New York Giants .... —
Monday, October 21
Green Bay Packers at Chicago Bears .... —

WEEK 8
Sunday, October 27
Atlanta Falcons at Dallas Cowboys...................................... —
Buffalo Bills at Philadelphia Eagles .... —
Denver Broncos at Kansas City Chiefs................................. —
Green Bay Packers at Indianapolis Colts.............................. —
Houston Oilers at St. Louis Cardinals................................... —
Miami Dolphins at Detroit Lions.. —
Minnesota Vikings at Chicago Bears .... —
New England Patriots at Tampa Bay Buccaneers................. —
New York Giants at New Orleans Saints................................ —
Pittsburgh Steelers at Cincinnati Bengals............................ —
San Francisco 49ers at Los Angeles Rams .... —
Seattle Seahawks at New York Jets...................................... —
Washington Redskins at Cleveland Browns .... —
Monday, October 28
San Diego Chargers at Los Angeles Raiders .... —

WEEK 9
Sunday, November 3
Chicago Bears at Green Bay Packers .... —
Cincinnati Bengals at Buffalo Bills .... —
Cleveland Browns at Pittsburgh Steelers .... —
Denver Broncos at San Diego Chargers .... —
Detroit Lions at Minnesota Vikings .... —
Kansas City Chiefs at Houston Oilers................................... —
Los Angeles Raiders at Seattle Seahawks .... —
Miami Dolphins at New England Patriots............................... —
New Orleans Saints at Los Angeles Rams .... —
New York Jets at Indianapolis Colts .... —
Philadelphia Eagles at San Francisco 49ers........................ —
Tampa Bay Buccaneers at New York Giants......................... —
Washington Redskins at Atlanta Falcons............................... —
Monday, November 4
Dallas Cowboys at St. Louis Cardinals................................. —

WEEK 10   **Result**
Sunday, November 10
Atlanta Falcons at Philadelphia Eagles.................................____—____
Cleveland Browns at Cincinnati Bengals ....____—____
Dallas Cowboys at Washington Redskins ....____—____
Detroit Lions at Chicago Bears...____—____
Green Bay Packers at Minnesota Vikings...........................____—____
Houston Oilers at Buffalo Bills..____—____
Indianapolis Colts at New England Patriots ....____—____
Los Angeles Raiders at San Diego Chargers ....____—____
Los Angeles Rams at New York Giants...............................____—____
New York Jets at Miami Dolphins..____—____
Pittsburgh Steelers at Kansas City Chiefs ....____—____
St. Louis Cardinals at Tampa Bay Buccaneers...................____—____
Seattle Seahawks at New Orleans Saints...........................____—____
Monday, November 11
San Francisco 49ers at Denver Broncos ....____—____

WEEK 11
Sunday, November 17
Buffalo Bills at Cleveland Browns.......................................____—____
Chicago Bears at Dallas Cowboys......................................____—____
Cincinnati Bengals at Los Angeles Raiders ....____—____
Kansas City Chiefs at San Francisco 49ers ....____—____
Los Angeles Rams at Atlanta Falcons ....____—____
Miami Dolphins at Indianapolis Colts ....____—____
Minnesota Vikings at Detroit Lions ....____—____
New England Patriots at Seattle Seahawks ....____—____
New Orleans Saints vs. Green Bay Packers at Milwaukee..____—____
Pittsburgh Steelers at Houston Oilers.................................____—____
St. Louis Cardinals at Philadelphia Eagles ....____—____
San Diego Chargers at Denver Broncos..............................____—____
Tampa Bay Buccaneers at New York Jets ....____—____
Monday, November 18
New York Giants at Washington Redskins ....____—____

WEEK 12
Sunday, November 24
Atlanta Falcons at Chicago Bears.......................................____—____
Cincinnati Bengals at Cleveland Browns ....____—____
Denver Broncos at Los Angeles Raiders ....____—____
Detroit Lions at Tampa Bay Buccaneers ....____—____
Green Bay Packers at Los Angeles Rams...........................____—____
Indianapolis Colts at Kansas City Chiefs ....____—____
Miami Dolphins at Buffalo Bills...____—____
New England Patriots at New York Jets...............................____—____
New Orleans Saints at Minnesota Vikings ....____—____
New York Giants at St. Louis Cardinals ....____—____
Philadelphia Eagles at Dallas Cowboys ....____—____
San Diego Chargers at Houston Oilers................................____—____
Washington Redskins at Pittsburgh Steelers ....____—____
Monday, November 25
Seattle Seahawks at San Francisco 49ers..........................____—____

WEEK 13   **Result**
Thursday, November 28
New York Jets at Detroit Lions .... ___—___
St. Louis Cardinals at Dallas Cowboys .... ___—___
Sunday, December 1
Buffalo Bills at San Diego Chargers .... ___—___
Cleveland Browns at New York Giants .... ___—___
Denver Broncos at Pittsburgh Steelers .... ___—___
Houston Oilers at Cincinnati Bengals .... ___—___
Kansas City Chiefs at Seattle Seahawks .... ___—___
Los Angeles Raiders at Atlanta Falcons .... ___—___
Los Angeles Rams at New Orleans Saints .... ___—___
Minnesota Vikings at Philadelphia Eagles .... ___—___
New England Patriots at Indianapolis Colts .... ___—___
San Francisco 49ers at Washington Redskins .... ___—___
Tampa Bay Buccaneers at Green Bay Packers .... ___—___
Monday December 2
Chicago Bears at Miami Dolphins .... ___—___

WEEK 14
Sunday, December 8
Atlanta Falcons at Kansas City Chiefs .... ___—___
Cleveland Browns at Seattle Seahawks .... ___—___
Dallas Cowboys at Cincinnati Bengals .... ___—___
Detroit Lions at New England Patriots .... ___—___
Indianapolis Colts at Chicago Bears .... ___—___
Los Angeles Raiders at Denver Broncos .... ___—___
Miami Dolphins at Green Bay Packers .... ___—___
New Orleans Saints at St. Louis Cardinals .... ___—___
New York Giants at Houston Oilers .... ___—___
New York Jets at Buffalo Bills .... ___—___
Pittsburgh Steelers at San Diego Chargers .... ___—___
Tampa Bay Buccaneers at Minnesota Vikings .... ___—___
Washington Redskins at Philadelphia Eagles .... ___—___
Monday, December 9
Los Angeles Rams at San Francisco 49ers .... ___—___

WEEK 15
Saturday, December 14
Chicago Bears at New York Jets .... ___—___
Kansas City Chiefs at Denver Broncos .... ___—___
Sunday, December 15
Buffalo Bills at Pittsburgh Steelers .... ___—___
Cincinnati Bengals at Washington Redskins .... ___—___
Green Bay Packers at Detroit Lions .... ___—___
Houston Oilers at Cleveland Browns .... ___—___
Indianapolis Colts at Tampa Bay Buccaneers .... ___—___
Minnesota Vikings at Atlanta Falcons .... ___—___
New York Giants at Dallas Cowboys .... ___—___
Philadelphia Eagles at San Diego Chargers .... ___—___
St. Louis Cardinals at Los Angeles Rams .... ___—___
San Francisco 49ers at New Orleans Saints .... ___—___
Seattle Seahawks at Los Angeles Raiders .... ___—___
Monday, December 16
New England Patriots at Miami Dolphins .... ___—___

WEEK 16   Result

Friday, December 20
Denver Broncos at Seattle Seahawks.............................____—____
Saturday, December 21
Pittsburgh Steelers at New York Giants ....____—____
Washington Redskins at St. Louis Cardinals ....____—____
Sunday, December 22
Atlanta Falcons at New Orleans Saints ....____—____
Buffalo Bills at Miami Dolphins......................................____—____
Chicago Bears at Detroit Lions......................................____—____
Cincinnati Bengals at New England Patriots..................____—____
Cleveland Browns at New York Jets...............................____—____
Dallas Cowboys at San Francisco 49ers........................____—____
Green Bay Packers at Tampa Bay Buccaneers..............____—____
Houston Oilers at Indianapolis Colts..............................____—____
Philadelphia Eagles at Minnesota Vikings.....................____—____
San Diego Chargers at Kansas City Chiefs ....____—____
Monday, December 23
Los Angeles Raiders at Los Angeles Rams....................____—____

FIRST ROUND PLAYOFF GAMES
Sunday, December 29, 1985
American Football Conference

_Patriots_____ 12 at _Jets_____ 3____

National Football Conference

_Giants_____ 26 at _49ers_____ 14___

DIVISIONAL PLAYOFF GAMES
Saturday, January 4, 1986
American Football Conference

_Browns_____ 21 at _Dolphins_____ 24___

National Football Conference

_Cowboys____ 0 at _Rams_____ 20___

Sunday, January 5, 1986
American Football Conference

_____at_____

National Football Conference

_____at_____

**CONFERENCE CHAMPIONSHIP GAMES, SUPER BOWL XX, AND
AFC-NFC PRO BOWL**
Sunday, January 12, 1986
American Football Conference Championship Game

_____at_____
National Football Conference Championship Game

_____at_____
Sunday, January 26, 1986
Super Bowl XX at Louisiana Superdome, New Orleans

_____vs_____
Sunday, February 2, 1986
AFC-NFC Pro Bowl at Honolulu, Hawaii

AFC _____vs.NFC _____